Nelson

GRAMMAR

TEACHER'S BOOK

WENDY WREN

Nelson

Design: Clive Sutherland
Editorial: Liz Harman
In-house design: Lorraine Inglis

Thomas Nelson & Sons Ltd
Nelson House
Mayfield Road
Walton-on-Thames
Surrey KT12 5PL
United Kingdom

I(T)P® Thomas Nelson is an International Thomson Company
I(T)P® is used under licence

First published by Thomas Nelson & Sons Ltd 1998

ISBN 0-17-424717-6
9 8 7 6 5 4 3 2
02 01 00 99 98

Printed by Zrinski Printing & Publishing House, Čakovec,
Croatia

Contents

1 *Nelson Grammar* at a glance

5–7 years NC level 2; English Language 5–14 level A–B

Page	Workbook 1	Workbook 2
2	the alphabet	the alphabet
3	the alphabet	the alphabet
4	common nouns	common nouns
5	common nouns	common nouns
6	adjectives	adjectives
7	adjectives	adjectives
8	verbs	verbs
9	verbs	verbs
10	the alphabet	the alphabet
11	the alphabet	the alphabet
12	nouns	nouns
13	nouns and adjectives	nouns and adjectives
14	verbs	verbs
15	verbs	verbs
16	*Check-up*	*Check-up*

Page/Unit		Book A
4/5	Unit 1	small and capital letters
6/7	Unit 2	common nouns
8/9	Unit 3	adjectives
10/11	Unit 4	nouns and adjectives
12/13	Unit 5	verbs
14/15	Unit 6	alphabetical order
16/17	Unit 7	present-tense verbs
18/19		*Check-up 1*
20/21	Unit 8	plurals – adding 's'
22/23	Unit 9	proper nouns – names
24/25	Unit 10	sentences – statements
26/27	Unit 11	present-tense verbs
28/29	Unit 12	adjectives
30/31	Unit 13	sentences – statements
32/33		*Check-up 2*
34/35	Unit 14	questions
36/37	Unit 15	common nouns
38/39	Unit 16	present-tense verbs
40/41	Unit 17	proper nouns – names
42/43	Unit 18	sentences – statements and questions
44/45	Unit 19	adjectives
46/48		*Check-up 3*

7–11/12 years NC level 2/3–5; English Language 5–14 level B–D

Page/Unit	Book 1	Book 2
4/5 Unit 1	common concrete nouns	proper nouns – place names
6/7 Unit 2	adjectives – in front of nouns	comparing two adjectives
8/9 Unit 3	singular and plural – adding 's'	confusing words – to/too/two
10/11 Unit 4	prepositions – on, up, over, etc.	conjunctions – so, because
12/13 Unit 5	proper nouns – people	simple present-tense verbs
14/15 Unit 6	pronouns – he, she, it, they	present tense of the verb 'to be'
16/17 Unit 7	confusing words – to/two	proper nouns – days, months, special days
18/19	*Check-up 1*	*Check-up 1*
20/21 Unit 8	common and proper nouns	present tense of the verb 'to be'
22/23 Unit 9	adjectives and names	comparison of three or more adjectives
24/25 Unit 10	sentences – statements	contractions – verb 'to be'
26/27 Unit 11	verbs – recognition	adverbs – how, when, where
28/29 Unit 12	sentences – questions	prepositions – from, near, etc.
30/31 Unit 13	verbs – recognition	indefinite articles – 'a' and 'an'
32/33	*Check-up 2*	*Check-up 2*
34/35 Unit 14	adjectives – colours	simple past-tense verbs
36/37 Unit 15	conjunctions – and	confusing words – where/were/we're, there/their
38/39 Unit 16	verb families	singular and plural – adding 'es'
40/41 Unit 17	pronouns – I, he, she, it, they, we	adverbs – pairs
42/43 Unit 18	adjectives – numbers	irregular past-tense verbs
44/45 Unit 19	conjunctions – but	sentences – importance of verbs
46/48	*Check-up 3*	*Check-up 3*

7–11/12 years NC level 2/3–5; English Language 5–14 level B–D

2 Level and content correlations

5–6 years NC level 2; English Language 5–14 level A

Workbook 1: introduces alphabetical order, nouns, verbs and adjectives. The activities give children the opportunity to practise ordering the letters of the alphabet, and to identify and trace words which fall into the categories: noun, adjective and verb.

Workbook 2: continues work on the alphabet, nouns, adjectives and verbs. The activities reinforce children's understanding of alphabetical order and give them the opportunity to identify and write nouns, adjectives and verbs, both as single words and in the context of completing sentences.

6–7 years NC level 2; English Language 5–14 level A–B

Book A
small letters and capital letters
common nouns
proper nouns – names of people and animals
adjectives
simple present-tense verbs
singular and plural – adding 's'
simple sentences – statements and questions

7–8 years NC level 2; English Language 5–14 level B

Book 1
common nouns
proper nouns – names of people
adjectives – colours and numbers
simple present-tense verbs and verb families
singular and plural – adding 's'
simple sentences – statements and questions
prepositions (e.g. on, up, over, under, in)
pronouns (e.g. he, she, it, they)
conjunctions – and, but

8–9 years NC level 3; English Language 5–14 level B–C

Book 2
proper nouns – places, days, months, special days
adjectives – comparison of two; comparison of three or more
verbs – simple present-tense verbs; the verb 'to be'; 'to be' plus 'ing'; simple past-tense verbs; irregular past-tense verbs
singular and plural – adding 'es'
sentences – the importance of the verb
prepositions
conjunctions – so, because
contractions of the present tense of the verb 'to be'
how, when and where pairs of adverbs
indefinite articles

9–10 years NC level 4; English Language 5–14 level C

Book 3
nouns – collective; possessive; irregular plurals; proper nouns (titles)
adjectives – number order; regular and irregular; comparative and superlative
verbs – past participles; future; irregular present-tense
singular and plural – words ending in 'ies', 'f', 'fe', 'v', 'o'
sentences – subject and object; subject and verb agreement; subject and predicate
prepositions
pronouns (e.g. myself, yourself, himself, herself)
conjunctions – who, which
contractions
adverbs – regular comparison; irregular forms
direct and reported speech

9–10 years NC level 5; English Language 5–14 level D

Book 4
nouns – abstract; compound; plural possessive nouns; nouns formed from verbs
adjectives – position; possessive; adjectives formed from nouns and verbs
verbs – auxiliary; active; passive
sentences – simple; compound; complex; improving sentences; use of commas; double negatives
pronouns – possessive and relative
phrases
clauses
paragraphs
prefixes

3 How *Nelson Grammar* works

Nelson Grammar comprises:
* 6 levels – 2 Workbooks and 5 Pupil Books
* Books A, 1 and 2 have 19 units, each comprising and introduction followed by Focus and Practice tasks
* Books 3 and 4 have 26 units, each comprising an introduction followed by Focus, Practice and Extension tasks
* Book A has a Focus and a Practice Copymaster for each unit
* Books 1–4 have an Extension Copymaster for each unit
* Book A has 7 Extension Copymasters
* Books 1 and 2 share 7 Improve Your Writing Copymasters
* Books 3 and 4 share 9 Improve Your Writing Copymasters

The teaching of English has always suffered from 'fashionable trends' and to teach, or not to teach, grammar is an area that has suffered more than most. The debate should not centre on if grammar should be taught, but why and how.

The reasons for teaching grammar are self-evident. An awareness of the structure of a language facilitates the manipulating of that language. Pupils are required to know the 'purpose' for which they write and the 'audience' they address. These requirements demand an awareness of style which embodies deliberate choices, such as tense, comparative language, connectives, contractions, etc. How can pupils choose if they do not know the choices?

An awareness of how the language works is also essential to inform a pupil's critical judgement. Proofreading and editing their work in draft form requires the ability to recognise incorrect grammatical structures and non-agreement of nouns and verbs, and to be able to improve and vary sentence structure to produce the right style and tone, etc. How can pupils correct their work if they do not know what is wrong with it?

'How' grammar is taught has long been viewed as frozen somewhere in the mid nineteenth century as a series of dry exercises which have no other end but the exercises themselves. The author makes no apology for the fact that exercises, structured and carefully graded, are the basis of *Nelson Grammar*, but the aim of these exercises is to give pupils the opportunity to improve their writing by using the grammar they have learnt to inform the style and accuracy of their work.

The unit titles in the Pupil Books have been kept simple. Children are not faced with a multitude of seemingly unconnected titles. The work falls into broad categories, such as 'Nouns', 'Sentences', 'Verbs', etc so the titles of the units become familiar and give the children confidence that they are dealing with an area they already know something about.

Nelson Grammar offers teachers a range of classroom management options:

1 The whole class work on the same unit, with some children being restricted to the Focus activities. In Book A, some children can progress to the Practice section. Focus and Practice Copymasters are provided as, at this early stage, it is recognised that most children will need more than just the exercises in the Pupil Book. In Books 1–4 some children can progress to the Extension exercise and for children who complete all three sections, there is an Extension Copymaster. When *Nelson Grammar* is used in this way, it is possible to allocate a regular timetabled slot to the teaching of grammar.

2 If the abilities of the class become more varied, it may be sensible to group the children, with each group working on a particular unit. This is more likely to be effective if the amount of time allocated to 'formal' grammar teaching varies according to different children's needs. It is feasible to work this way, given the constant structure of the Pupil Books in the scheme.

3 Some teachers may prefer their pupils to use the Pupil Books individually. This approach will be most appropriate if the teacher decides to let each child work at his or her own pace, or if the teacher uses the course as a resource to which all children are referred to support individualised problems as they occur.

PUPIL BOOKS

Each Pupil Book unit comprises:

Introduction (all Pupil Books)
The grammatical concept is explained and examples are given. If related previous work has been introduced earlier, that is revised so that the new work can be seen as a continuation.

Focus (all Pupil Books)
An initial activity which usually requires the children to *recognise* the particular grammatical point.

Practice (all Pupil Books)
An activity which requires the children, with support, to *use* the grammatical concept.

Extension (Pupil Books 3 and 4)
Usually more than one activity in which children can build on previous knowledge and use the grammatical concept in their own writing.

COPYMASTERS

The Copymasters provide a variety of activities to extend children's ability to use the grammatical concept.

TEACHER'S BOOK

A facsimile of each unit from the Pupil Books is reproduced in the Teacher's Book and the corresponding answers are provided. The 'Previous work' section for each unit charts all previous work on that topic, making it easy to allow individual children to revisit work if reinforcement is needed.

4 Glossary

Within each section of the glossary, the items come in the order in which they are to be found in the Pupil Books.

A simple explanation is followed by examples and, where appropriate, exceptions to the given rule.

ADJECTIVES

Adjectives are also known as describing words. They describe nouns and pronouns.

An adjective can describe:

what kind	a *big* box
	an *unhappy* man
what position	the *next* day
	the *last* bus

Colour adjectives

Colour words are adjectives, for example:

the *red* flag
a *blue* boat

A few colour words can be nouns, for example:

an *orange* (fruit)
a *green* (grassed area)
a *violet* (flower)

Number adjectives

Number words are adjectives, for example:

ten rabbits
eighty-two minutes

Number words are known as cardinal numbers.

Number-order adjectives

Words which describe numerical order are adjectives, for example:

He was *second* in the race.
It was the *fourth* time she'd missed the bus.

Number-order words are known as ordinal numbers.

Comparative adjectives

Comparative adjectives compare two nouns or pronouns.

Short, regular comparative adjectives are usually formed by adding 'er', for example:

| dark | *darker* |
| kind | *kinder* |

Sometimes, forming comparative adjectives requires an adjustment to the spelling of the root word, for example:

| heavy | *heavier* |
| big | *bigger* |

Long adjectives form their comparative with 'more', for example:

| important | *more important* |
| frightening | *more frightening* |

Superlative adjectives

Superlative adjectives compare three or more nouns or pronouns.

Short, regular superlative adjectives are usually formed by adding 'est', for example:

| dark | darker | *darkest* |
| kind | kinder | *kindest* |

Sometimes, forming superlative adjectives requires an adjustment to the spelling of the root word, for example:

| heavy | heavier | *heaviest* |
| big | bigger | *biggest* |

Long adjectives tend to form their superlative with 'most', for example:

| important | more important | *most important* |
| frightening | more frightening | *most frightening* |

Irregular comparative and superlative adjectives

A few adjectives change completely in their comparative and superlative forms, for example:

bad	*worse*	*worst*
good	*better*	*best*
little	*less*	*least*
much	*more*	*most*
many	*more*	*most*
some	*more*	*most*

Adjective phrases

An adjective phrase is a group of words without a proper verb, used to describe a noun or pronoun, for example:

The *angry, frightened old* man got off the bus.
The sea, *smooth and calm*, looked like a mirror.
The trees were *tall and stately*.
The cat *with the long tail* is called Tom.

Possessive adjectives

Possessive adjectives show who or what possesses (owns) a noun, for example:

my hat
your book
his stick
her jumper
its tail
our house
their pets

Adjective clauses

An adjective clause contains a proper verb and describes a noun or pronoun.

Adjective clauses begin with the words 'who', 'which' or 'that', for example:

I work for the man *who runs the garden centre*.
They bought the horse *which looked calm and gentle*.
I want to find the key *that fits this lock*.

Forming adjectives

Adjectives can be formed from:

nouns	peril	a *perilous* journey
	distance	the *distant* mountain
verbs	to grow	the *grown* man
	hide	the *hidden* treasure

Some nouns and verbs are used as adjectives, for example:

nouns	a *city* dweller	
	a *library* book	
verbs	to run	the *running* track
	to manage	the *managing* director

ADVERBS

Adverbs are words which give us extra information about verbs.

Adverbs tell us how, when or where something happens or is done, for example:

how	He ran *quickly*.
when	She arrived *late*.
where	The car stopped *here*.

Adverb pairs

Adverbs can be used in pairs to add further detail to the action, for example:

how	He ran *very quickly*.
when	She arrived *extremely late*.
where	The car stopped *near here*.

Comparative adverbs

Comparative adverbs are used to compare the actions of two people or things.

Adverbs ending in 'ly' usually form their comparative with 'more', for example:

soundly	*more* soundly
beautifully	*more* beautifully

Adverbs which do not end in 'ly' usually form their comparative with 'er', for example:

fast	*faster*
low	*lower*

Superlative adverbs

Superlative adverbs are used to compare the actions of three or more people or things.

Adverbs ending in 'ly' usually form their comparative with 'most', for example:

soundly	more soundly	*most soundly*
beautifully	more beautifully	*most beautifully*

Adverbs which do not end in 'ly' usually form their superlative with 'est', for example:

fast	faster	*fastest*
low	lower	*lowest*

Irregular comparative and superlative adverbs

A few adverbs change completely in their comparative and superlative forms, for example:

well	*better*	*best*
badly	*worse*	*worst*

Adverb phrases

An adverb phrase is a group of words without a proper verb, used to describe how, when or where actions take place, for example:

how	The horse galloped *like the wind*.
when	*Before the sun set*, we had pitched camp.
where	The cottage stood *at the edge of the wood*.

Adverb clauses

An adverb clause contains a proper verb and describes how, when or where actions take place.

Adverb clauses begin with conjunctions, for example:

how	The boy fell *because the branch broke*.
when	I will go out *after I have washed my hair*.
where	She went to that shop *because it was just around the corner*.

ALPHABET

The alphabet contains 26 letters, from which all English words are formed.

Five of the letters are vowels – a, e, i, o, u – the rest are consonants.

The letter 'y' can sometimes act as a vowel, for example:

sk*y*
cr*y*

The letters can be written in lower case (small letters) e.g. a, b, c, d, e . . . or in upper case (capital letters) e.g. A, B, C, D, E . . .

Alphabetical order

To put letters or words in alphabetical order is to arrange them so that the first letter of each word is in the order in which it appears in the alphabet, for example:

<u>a</u>nt	<u>b</u>aby	<u>c</u>ot	<u>d</u>esk

Words beginning with the same letter are arranged by their second letter and so on, for example:

a<u>i</u>r	a<u>n</u>t	a<u>p</u>ple	a<u>t</u>tack

ARTICLES

The indefinite article is 'a' or 'an', for example:

a car	*a* box
an orange	*an* ice cream

The definite article is 'the', for example:

the flower	*the* rug

CONFUSING WORDS

Pairs or groups of words can be confusing if they sound the same but are spelled and used differently.

to, two, too

'To' can be used as part of the verb family name (infinitive) e.g. to go, to look, for example:

I need *to* make a cake.

'To' can also be used to denote movement towards, for example:

We went *to* the shops.

'Two' is used to denote a quantity, for example:

I need *two* eggs for this cake.

'Too' can be used to denote 'as well as', for example:

I need some flour, *too*.

'Too' can also be used to denote 'more or different from what is expected':

The oven was *too* hot.

there/their

'There' is used to denote place (notice the word 'here' is in 'there'), for example:

> We have to go over *there*.

'Their' is used to denote ownership, for example:
> *Their* holiday was a great success.

where/were/we're

'Where' is used to denote place (notice the word 'here' in 'where'), for example:

> I don't know *where* I put it.

'Were' is part of the past tense of the verb 'to be', for example:

> We *were* at the hospital yesterday.

'We're' is a contraction of 'we are', for example:

> *We're* not going out just yet.

CONJUNCTIONS

Conjunctions are sometimes known as connectives. They are words used to join sentences, for example:

> The boy kicked the ball. He scored a goal.
> The boy kicked the ball *and* he scored a goal.

> I have found the key *but* I can't open the door.
> She needed some eggs *so* she went to the shop.
> Fred was late getting home *because* he missed the bus.
> I am going swimming *although* I don't feel well.

Some conjunctions can come at the beginning of a sentence, for example:

> *Although* we were scared, we entered the cave.

CONTRACTIONS

A contraction is a shortened form of a word, with an apostrophe to show where a letter or letters have been missed out. Contractions are often used when writing direct speech.

The apostrophe, when used in this way, is known as the apostrophe of omission, for example:

I am	I'm
must not	mustn't
we will	we'll
should not	shouldn't

There are some words which have other changes in their shortened form, for example:

will not	*won't*

NOUNS

Nouns are also known as naming words.

Common nouns

Most nouns are common nouns, for example:

> bat
> ship
> piano
> horse

Proper nouns

Proper nouns begin with a capital letter and are the names of specific things, for example:

people	Sarah
	Christopher
	Mrs Patel
	Dr Leigh
places	Australia
	Indian Ocean
	Mount Everest
	River Nile
days of the week	Monday
	Tuesday
	Wednesday
months of the year	January
	February
	March
special days and festivals	New Year's Eve
	St Andrew's Day
	Ramadan
book, film and play titles	Wuthering Heights
	Gone with the Wind
	The Merchant of Venice

Usually, only the important words in the title begin with capital letters.

Collective nouns

Collective nouns are words used to denote a group or collection of things, for example:

> a *flock* of sheep
> a *herd* of elephants
> an *army* of soldiers
> a *bunch* of flowers

Singular possessive nouns

Singular possessive nouns use the apostrophe of possession ('s) to show ownership.

The apostrophe comes after the singular owner, for example:

> the *dog's* lead
> the *book's* cover
> *Tom's* car

Plural possessive nouns

Plural possessive nouns use the apostrophe of possession (') to show ownership.

The apostrophe comes after the plural owners, for example:

> the *dogs'* leads
> the *books'* covers
> the *drivers'* cars

If a noun makes its plural without a final 's', then 's is added, for example:

> the *children's* coats
> the *geese's* pond

Abstract nouns

Abstract nouns denote qualities, feelings and times, for example:

qualities   He was known for his *heroism*.
            His *stupidity* was unbelievable.
feelings   Her *happiness* knew no bounds.
            The old woman's *gratitude* was touching.
times   The *morning* was cool and damp.
            The *celebration* was a great success.

Nouns formed from verbs

Nouns can be formed from verbs, usually by adding a suffix like 'ing', 'er' or 'ment', for example:

to build   a build*ing*
              a build*er*
to arrange   an arrange*ment*
to write   the writ*er*
              the writ*ing*

PREFIXES

A prefix is a group of letters added to the front of a word to modify its meaning.

Some prefixes form opposites, for example:

suitable   *un*suitable
valid   *in*valid
prudent   *im*prudent
agree   *dis*agree
logical   *il*logical
climax   *anti*climax

Some prefixes have special meanings, for example:

uni   (one)   *uni*form
bi   (two)   *bi*ped
tri   (three)   *tri*angle
super   (over/beyond)   *super*sonic
pre   (before)   *pre*viously
post   (after)   *post*humous

PREPOSITIONS

A preposition is a word that shows the relationship of a noun or pronoun to other words in a sentences.

Relationship in position

Some prepositions show where an object or person is positioned in relation to something else, for example:

The boots were *in* the cupboard.
The garage was built *behind* the house.
The road ran *alongside* the stream.

Relationship in time

Some prepositions show the relationship of events in time, for example:

It was very quiet *after* the storm.
He needed to practise *for* ten minutes.

PRONOUNS

Pronouns stand in place of nouns, for example:

Mary ate an apple.   *She* ate an apple.
Gary flew a kite.   *He* flew a kite.
The people shouted.   *They* shouted.

Possessive pronouns

Possessive pronouns show ownership or possession, for example:

That scarf is *his*.
This book is *mine*.
Those clothes are *theirs*.

The possessive pronouns are:

mine	yours	his	hers	its	ours	theirs

Relative pronouns

Relative pronouns have two functions:
1 to take the place of nouns;
2 to act as conjunctions related to the noun that comes before them in the sentence, for example:

Here is the ball *which* I found in the garden.
Do you know the lady *who* has moved in next door?

The relative pronouns are:

who	whom	whose	which	that

SENTENCES

A sentence begins with a capital letter, ends with a full stop, a question mark or an exclamation mark and makes sense, for example:

Harry is riding his bicycle.
Is Harry riding his bicycle?
It is dangerous for Harry to ride his bicycle!

Subject and object

Simple sentences contain a subject and an object.
    Subjects and objects are nouns and pronouns.
    The subject tells who or what the sentence is about.
    The object tells who or what is having something done to it.

    The cat drinks the milk.

subject = 'The cat'
object = 'the milk'

Direct speech

Some sentences show the actual words that someone has said. These sentences need special punctuation.
    Inverted commas go around the actual words spoken.

    "I need to see the headteacher."

If the spoken words are followed by details of the speaker, for example, 'said Fred', then a comma is placed before the closing inverted commas.

    "I need to see the headteacher," said Jane.

If the spoken words are a question, a question mark is placed before the closing inverted commas.

    "Do you need to see the headteacher?" asked Paul.

If the spoken words signal the end of the sentence, a full stop, an exclamation mark or a question mark is placed before the closing inverted commas.

    Jane said, "I need to see the headteacher."
    Paul asked, "Do you need to see the headteacher?"

Sometimes, direct speech is split by unspoken words, for example, 'said Jane'.

    "I need to see the headteacher," said Jane, "and I

need to see her now!"
"Please tell me why you need to see her," said Paul. "I will go and see if she is free."

Subject and predicate

The subject is the thing or person the sentence is about. The predicate is the rest of the sentence, for example:

The man cleaned the car.

'The man' = subject
'cleaned the car' = predicate

The predicate of a sentence always contains the verb.

Subjects are not always one word and predicates can be much more interesting, for example:

The young man cleaned the muddy car.

'The young man' = subject
'cleaned the muddy car' = predicate.

Double negatives

Contractions which end in 'n't' and the words 'no', 'not', 'nothing', 'never' and 'nowhere' are negative words.

If there are two negative words in one sentence, they usually make the meaning positive, for example:

I *don't* want *no* pudding.

This means 'I do want some pudding.'

The correct sentence should be:

I don't want any pudding.

Indirect speech

Indirect or reported speech is when we write about what someone has said but do not use the actual spoken words, for example:

| direct speech | "My tyre had a puncture," said Rita. |
| reported speech | Rita said that her tyre had a puncture. |

Main clauses

A main clause carries the core meaning of the sentence and it must contain a proper verb and can be a sentence on its own, or part of a longer sentence, for example:

| sentence | The dog growled angrily. |
| main clause | *The dog growled angrily* and ran off. |

A main clause does not have to come first in the sentence, for example:

Even though it was dark, *the boys played in the snow*.

main clause = 'the boys played in the snow'

Commas in sentences

Commas are used in sentences in the several ways.

1 to separate actual spoken words from the rest of the sentence, for example:

"I will ring you tomorrow," said the manager.

2 to separate items in a list, for example:

We need paint, brushes, wallpaper, paste and a ladder.

3 to separate parts of a sentence to help the reader make sense of it, for example:

My dog, which rarely strays, has been missing for two days.
You want your tea before you go out, don't you?

Compound sentences

A compound sentence is made up of two or more simple, single-clause sentences joined by 'and', 'but' or 'or', for example:

| simple sentences | The tractor was stuck in the mud. The farmer couldn't move it. |
| compound sentence | The tractor was stuck in the mud and the farmer couldn't move it. |

Both parts of a compound sentence are sentences in their own right.

Complex sentences

A complex sentence has two or more clauses which are not of equal importance.

The main clause could stand as a sentence by itself but the other clauses couldn't, for example:

The road was covered with broken eggs which fell from the lorry.

'The road was covered with broken eggs' = main clause; 'which fell from the lorry' = adverb clause, which needs the main clause in order to make sense.

Paragraphs

Paragraphs are groups of sentences within a longer piece of writing, which have a common theme or topic.

The beginning of a paragraph is often indicated by indenting 20 mm from the left-hand margin.

SINGULAR AND PLURAL

Nouns form their plurals in a variety of ways.
The most common way is to add an 's', for example:

bat	bat*s*
leg	leg*s*
panda	panda*s*

For nouns ending in 's', 'ch', 'sh' and 'x', add 'es', for example:

grass	grass*es*
match	match*es*
bush	bush*es*
fox	fox*es*

For nouns ending in 'y', take off the 'y' and add 'ies', for example:

pony	pon*ies*
fly	fl*ies*
lorry	lorr*ies*

If the letter before the 'y' is a vowel, just add 's', for example:

| tray | tray*s* |
| bay | bay*s* |

For nouns ending in 'f' or 'fe', change the 'f' or 'fe' to 'v' and add 'es', for example:

knife	kni*ves*
scarf	scar*ves*
loaf	loa*ves*

There are some exceptions:

chiefs	cliffs	dwarfs	gulfs	sheriffs
waifs	oafs	reefs	roofs	muffs
handkerchiefs				

'Wharf' can be 'wharfs' or 'wharves'.
'Hoof' can be 'hoofs' or 'hooves'.

For most nouns ending in 'o', add 'es', for example:

tomato	tomato*es*
potato	potato*es*

If the noun is related to music, such as the name of a musical instrument or type of voice, just add 's', for example:

piano	piano*s*
piccolo	piccolo*s*

Some nouns have irregular plurals which follow none of the above rules, for example:

child	children
sheep	sheep
person	people
goose	geese
foot	feet
tooth	teeth

SUFFIXES

Suffixes are groups of letters added to the end of a word to modify the meaning of a root word.

Suffixes can change the tense of a verb, for example:

jump	jump*ing*	jump*ed*
cry	cry*ing*	cried

Suffixes can be added to adjectives and adverbs to form comparatives and superlatives, for example:

high	high*er*	high*est*
soft	soft*er*	soft*est*

Suffixes can change a root word from one part of speech to another, for example:

fame = abstract noun	fam*ous* = adjective
manage = verb	manage*ment* = abstract noun

VERBS

Verbs are also known as action or doing words.

Verb tenses

The tense of a verb tells you when the action was done, for example:

simple present tense	I walk
continuous present tense	I am walking
simple past tense	I walked
continuous past tense	I was walking
imperfect past tense	I have walked
pluperfect tense	I had walked
future tense	I shall walk

Some verbs have an irregular past tense, for example:

I *eat* my breakfast.   I *ate* my breakfast.
I *have eaten* my breakfast.

I *write* a letter.   I *wrote* a letter.
I *have written* a letter.

Verb family name

The verb family name is the infinitive and begins with 'to', for example:

to walk	to breathe	to sing	to catch

Verb 'to be'

The verb 'to be' is often used as an auxiliary verb to form tenses, for example:

present continuous tense	I *am* walking.
continuous past tense	I *was* walking.

These are the important tenses of the verb 'to be':

Present	Past	Future
I am	I was	I shall be
you are	you were	you will be
he is	he was	he will be
she is	she was	she will be
it is	it was	it will be
we are	we were	we shall be
you are	you were	you will be
they are	they were	they will be

Auxiliary verbs

Auxiliary verbs are known as 'helper verbs' and are used to show tense, for example:

to be	we *were* going
to have	we *have* gone

'Can' and 'may' are also auxiliary verbs, for example:

I can walk. = I am able to walk.
I may walk. = I have permission to walk.

Subject and verb agreement

A singular subject must have a singular verb and a plural subject must have a plural verb, for example:

The *girl sings* in the choir.
The *girls sing* in the choir.

I am bored.
We are bored.

Active and passive

When the subject of a sentence does the action, the verb is active, for example:

John *weeded* the garden.
Mum *did* the shopping.

When the subject of a sentence has the action done to it, the verb is passive, for example:

The garden *was weeded* by John.
The shopping *was done* by Mum.

Workbook 1 and 2 answers

Workbook 1

Page 2
The alphabet – letter recognition
Children should colour the pictures as directed.

Page 3
The alphabet – letter recognition, ordering letters
Children should join the dots in the correct order to make the picture.

Page 4
Naming words – recognition of names for simple objects
Children should write the words and match them with the correct pictures.

Page 5
Naming words – recognition of names for simple objects
Children should write the words.

Page 6
Describing words – recognising what objects are like
Children should write the words and match the objects into pairs.

Page 7
Describing words – recognising what objects are like
Children should write the words and draw the pictures.

Page 8
Doing words – recognising actions
Children should write the words and draw the pictures.

Page 9
Doing words – recognising actions
Children should underline the correct verbs (sleeping, fishing, flying, falling) and write the words.

Page 10
The alphabet – alphabetical order of small letters
a **b** c d e f **g h** i j k **l** m n o p q r s t u **v** w x **y z**

Page 11
The alphabet – alphabetical order of small letters
a **b** c d e f **g h** i j k **l** m n o p q r s t u **v** w x **y z**

Page 12
Naming words – recognising simple names
Children should underline the correct nouns (mop, king, drum, tree) and write the words.

Page 13
Naming words and describing words – recognising objects and their descriptions
Children should underline the correct descriptions (old man, hot sun, small ant) and write the words.

Page 14
Doing words – recognising simple actions
Children should write the words and match them with the correct pictures.

Page 15
Doing words – recognising simple actions
Children should colour the pictures correctly and write the words.

Page 16 *Check-up*

bed	ball
happy	tall/thin/big

The frog is **jumping**.
The cat is **sleeping**.

Workbook 1

Page 2
The alphabet – capital letters
A **B** C **D** E F **G H** I **J** K **L** M N O
P **Q** R S T U V **W** X **Y Z**

Page 3
The alphabet – capital letters
A **B** C **D** E F **G H** I **J** K **L** M N O
P **Q** R S T U V **W** X **Y Z**

Page 4
Naming words – rhyming words

mat	**pan**	**hen**	**tin**
rat	man	pen	pin
cat	van	ten	bin

Page 5
Naming words – beginning with the same letter

car	dog	book
cat	duck	bear
cap	dish	bed
		(also ball, boot)

Page 6
Describing words

hot	cold
big	small
young	old
long	short

Page 7
Describing words – colours
This is a <u>red</u> flower.
This is a <u>yellow</u> balloon.
This is a <u>blue</u> book.
This is a <u>green</u> hat.
This is a <u>brown</u> dog.
This is a <u>black</u> cat.

Page 8
Doing words

digging	pecking	swinging
winking	splashing	cooking

Page 9
Doing words
He is **hitting** the ball.
She is **locking** the door.
She is **cutting** the paper.
He is **mopping** the floor.

Page 10
The alphabet – alphabetical order
Children should join the dots in the correct order to make the pictures.

Page 11
The alphabet – alphabetical order

ant	doll	gate
bin	egg	hill
cat	fan	ink

Page 12
Naming words – simple sentences
The **cat** is in the **tree**.
The **man** is in the **car**.
The **box** is on the **bed**.
The **hen** is on the **log**.

Page 13
Naming words and describing words – recognising objects and their descriptions

a **wet dog**	a **long dress**
a **broken cup**	a **round ball**

Page 14
Doing words – simple present tense
I **eat** food.
I **sleep** in a bed.
I **wash** with water.
I **ride** to school.
I **play** with a ball.
I **read** my book.

Page 15
Doing words – simple present tense
The cat <u>sleeps</u> on the wall.
The hen <u>pecks</u> at her food.
The rabbit <u>hops</u> on the grass.
The duck <u>swims</u> on the pond.
The boys <u>run</u> down the street.
The girl <u>rings</u> the bell.

Page 16 *Check-up*

tent	box
long/sharp pencil	**long** road
cutting	sweeping

15

Book A – Contents/Scope and Sequence

Page/Unit		Focus	Practice
4/5	Unit 1	the alphabet	alphabetical order, small and capital letters
6/7	Unit 2	naming words – adding letters to make naming words	recognising naming words in picture stimuli
8/9	Unit 3	describing words – adding letters	choosing appropriate describing words
10/11	Unit 4	naming words and describing words – matching	recognising naming words and describing words
12/13	Unit 5	doing words – choosing appropriate words	matching doing words to pictures
14/15	Unit 6	alphabetical order – letters	alphabetical order – simple words
16/17	Unit 7	doing words – matching doing words to pictures	choosing appropriate doing words
18/19		*Check-up 1*	*Check-up 1*
20/21	Unit 8	plurals – adding 's'	writing plural words, recognising plural words
22/23	Unit 9	special naming words – recognition	writing special naming words
24/25	Unit 10	writing sentences – capital letters and full stops	ordering words to make sentences
26/27	Unit 11	doing words – recognition	writing action sentences from picture clues
28/29	Unit 12	describing words – recognition	adding describing words to sentences
30/31	Unit 13	writing sentences – capital letters and full stops	writing sentences from picture clues in sequence
32/33		*Check-up 2*	*Check-up 2*
34/35	Unit 14	questions – recognition	telling sentences and asking sentences, writing questions
36/37	Unit 15	naming words – writing from picture clues and initial letters	completing sentences with naming words
38/39	Unit 16	doing words – choosing appropriate doing words	answering questions with doing words
40/41	Unit 17	special naming words – recognition	answering questions with special naming words
42/43	Unit 18	writing sentences – using full stops and question marks	writing telling sentences and questions
44/45	Unit 19	describing words – adding describing words	improving sentences with describing words
46/48		*Check-up 3*	*Check-up 3*

Focus copymaster	Practice copymaster	Page/Unit	
small and capital letters	alphabetical order	4/5	Unit 1
word and picture matching	writing naming words, word and picture matching	6/7	Unit 2
word and picture matching	writing colour words	8/9	Unit 3
identifying naming words and describing words	writing naming words and describing words	10/11	Unit 4
word and picture matching	writing doing words, word and picture matching	12/13	Unit 5
letters in alphabetical order	words in alphabetical order	14/15	Unit 6
word and picture matching	writing doing words, word and picture matching	16/17	Unit 7
Check-up 1	*Check-up 1*	18/19	
making plurals with 's'	completing and writing sentences	20/21	Unit 8
identifying special naming words	writing special naming words	22/23	Unit 9
capital letters and full stops	writing sentences from picture clues	24/25	Unit 10
identifying doing words	writing sentences from picture clues	26/27	Unit 11
identifying describing words	writing describing words/sentences	28/29	Unit 12
completing sentences	ordering sentences	30/31	Unit 13
Check-up 2	*Check-up 2*	32/33	
identifying questions, using question marks	writing questions	34/35	Unit 14
identifying naming words	writing sentences	36/37	Unit 15
word and picture matching	writing doing words/sentences	38/39	Unit 16
identifying special naming words	writing titles	40/41	Unit 17
identifying questions and answers	writing questions and answers	42/43	Unit 18
writing describing words	writing sentences	44/45	Unit 19
Check-up 3	*Check-up 3*	46/48	

Extension copymasters	
1	naming words – wordsearch
2	naming words – crossword
3	describing words – wordsearch
4	describing words – crossword
5	doing words – wordsearch
6	doing words – crossword
7	identifying naming, describing and doing words

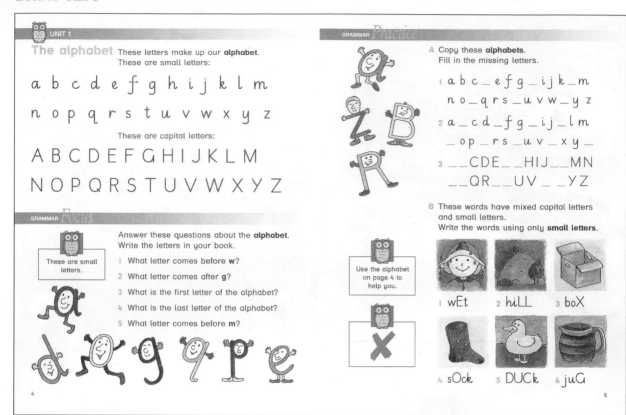

see Glossary, page 9 – Alphabet

Previous work

Workbook 1
page 2
page 3
page 10
page 11

Workbook 2
page 2
page 3
page 10
page 11

Pupil Book answers

Focus

1 v
2 h
3 a
4 z
5 l

Practice

A

1 a b c **d** e f g **h** i j k **l** m n o **p** q r s
   t u v w **x** y z

2 a b c **d** e f g **h** i j k **l** m n o p q **r**
   s t u v w **x** y **z**

3 **A** B C D E F **G** H I J **K L** M N
   O P Q R **S T** U V W **X** Y Z

B

1 wet   2 hill   3 box
4 sock   5 duck   6 jug

Copymaster answers

Focus

Children should copy the lower- and upper-case writing.

Practice

A
a b c d e f g h i j k l m n o p q r s t
u v w x y z

B

| f | y | v |
| c | n | h |

C

| H | S | X |
| G | R | P |

D

SAND	POT
HOUSE	FISH
SUN	CLAP

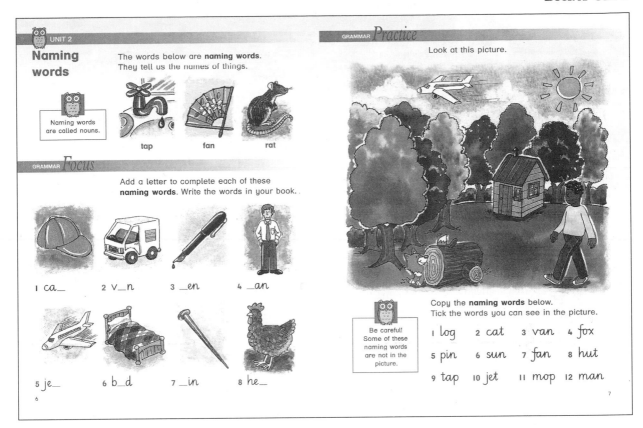

see Glossary, page 11 – Nouns

Previous work

Workbook 1
page 4
page 5
page 12
page 13

Workbook 2
page 4
page 5
page 12
page 13

Pupil Book answers

Focus

1 cap	2 van
3 pen	4 **m**an
5 jet	6 bed
7 **p**in	8 hen

Practice

1 log ✓	2 cat
3 van	4 fox ✓
5 pin	6 sun ✓
7 fan	8 hut ✓
9 tap	10 jet ✓
11 mop	12 man ✓

Copymaster answers

Focus

Children should draw lines to connect the nouns to the correct parts of the picture.

Practice

Children should correctly label the seven objects in the picture.

Book A Unit 3

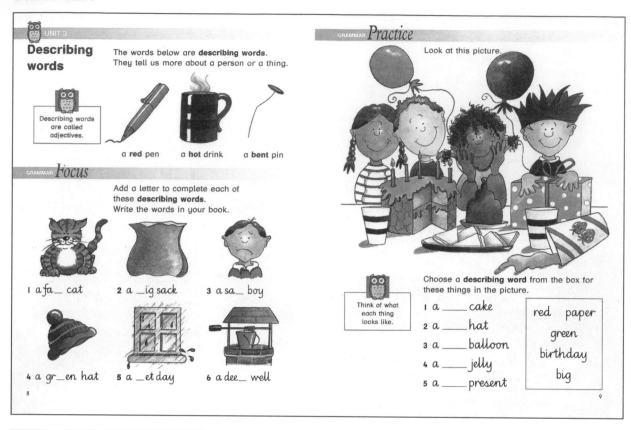

see Glossary, page 9 – Adjectives

Previous work

Workbook 1
page 6
page 7
page 13

Workbook 2
page 6
page 7
page 13

Pupil Book answers

Focus

1 a **fa**t cat
2 a **bi**g sack
3 a sa**d** boy
4 a gr**ee**n hat
5 a **w**et day
6 a dee**p** well

Practice

1 a **birthday/big** cake
2 a **paper** hat
3 a **red** balloon
4 a **green** jelly
5 a **birthday/big** present

Copymaster answers

Focus

Children should draw lines to connect the adjectives to the correct parts of the picture.

Practice

Answers will be individual to the children.

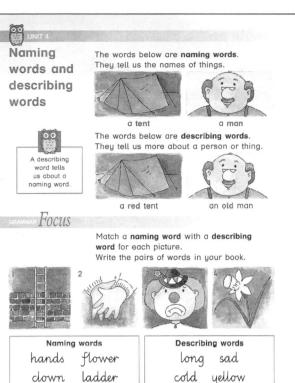

see Glossary, page 11 – Nouns and
page 9 – Adjectives

Previous work

Workbook 1
page 4
page 5
page 6
page 7
page 12
page 13

Workbook 2
page 4
page 5
page 6
page 7
page 12
page 13

Book A
pages 6/7
pages 8/9

Pupil Book answers

Focus

| 1 long ladder | 2 cold hands |
| 3 sad clown | 4 yellow flower |

Practice

A

| 1 bag | 2 bird | 3 duck |
| 4 hat | 5 man | |

B

1 hot, ready	2 long
3 black, lost	4 wet
5 large	

Copymaster answers

Focus

Naming words: duck
tent
pen
bell
fox
sock

Describing words: flat
long
wet
small
big
tall

Practice

A

*Answers will be individual to the
children, for example:*

1 *The **box/case** is very heavy.*
2 *I would like a **bike/book** for my
birthday.*
3 *Look at that **man/tree/ship**.*
4 *There is a **bird/kite/cat** in the tree.*

B

*Answers will be individual to the
children, for example:*

1 *The **big box** is very heavy.*
2 *I would like a **red bike** for my
birthday.*
3 *Look at that **tall tree**.*
4 *There is a **frightened cat** in the
tree.*

see Glossary, page 14 – Verbs

Previous work

Workbook 1
page 8
page 9
page 14
page 15

Workbook 2
page 8
page 9
page 14
page 15

Pupil Book answers

Focus

1 yelling	2 waving
3 sucking	4 kicking

Practice

1 eating	2 reading
3 singing	4 sleeping
5 winking	6 running

Copymaster answers

Focus

Children should draw lines to connect the verbs to the correct parts of the picture.

Practice

Children should correctly label the actions in the picture.

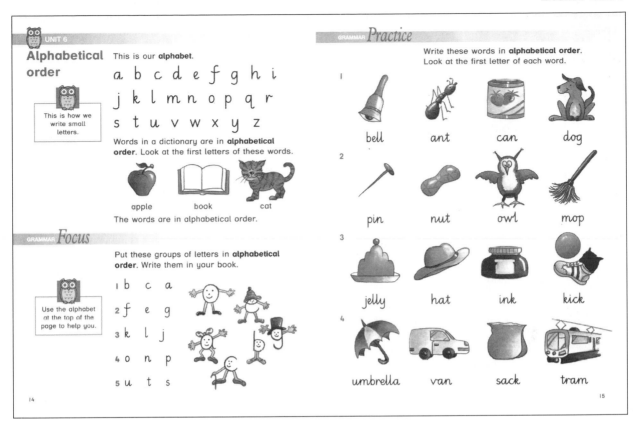

see Glossary, page 10 – Alphabet

Previous work

Workbook 1
page 2
page 3
page 10
page 11

Workbook 2
page 2
page 3
page 10
page 11

Book A
pages 4/5

Pupil Book answers

Focus

1	a	b	c
2	e	f	g
3	j	k	l
4	n	o	p
5	s	t	u

Practice

1	ant	bell	can	dog
2	mop	nut	owl	pin
3	hat	ink	jelly	kick
4	sack	tram	umbrella	van

Copymaster answers

Focus

A

a b **c d** e f g **h i j k** l m n
o p **q r** s t **u** v w x y **z**

B

1	n	o	p	
2	d	e	f	
3	j	k	l	
4	u	v	w	x
5	r	s	t	u

Practice

1	ant	2	bee
3	cat	4	dog
5	elephant	6	frog
7	goat	8	horse

Children may use different nouns such as: kitten, wasp, puppy, pony, sheep. If so, they should correctly order the answers alphabetically.

see Glossary, page 14 – Verbs

Previous work

Workbook 1
page 8
page 9
page 14
page 15
Workbook 2
page 8
page 9
page 14
page 15
Book A
pages 12/13

Pupil Book answers

Focus

1 hopping   2 scratching
3 growling   4 playing

Practice

1 fly   sing
2 swim   grow
3 eat   hunt
4 jump   sleep

Copymaster answers

Focus

Children should draw lines to connect the verbs to the correct parts of the picture.

Practice

Children should correctly label the actions in the picture.

Check-up I

The alphabet

Copy this **alphabet** into your book.
Fill in the missing letters.

_ _ c d _ f _ _ _ j _ l m

n _ _ q _ s _ _ v w _ y _

Alphabetical order

Put each of these groups of words into **alphabetical order**.

1	sell	queen	rock	trick
2	log	jump	kick	men
3	owl	mop	pen	not
4	van	well	ten	up

Naming words

Copy the **naming words** from each list.

1	is	pin	sock	bus
2	jug	cup	his	at
3	not	pen	bed	bat
4	bad	man	an	leg
5	fed	wet	peg	hill

Describing words

Copy the **describing words** from each list.

1	peg	red	tidy	bed
2	old	cot	sad	long
3	pet	ten	green	fog
4	hot	dog	box	cold
5	thin	mug	happy	bun

Doing words

A What are these people **doing**?

1 _____ 2 _____ 3 _____ 4 _____

B Copy the **doing word** from each sentence.

1 The seal swims in the sea.
2 The fox drinks the water.
3 The snake hisses at the man.
4 The mouse nibbles the cheese.
5 The spider spins the web.

18   19

The alphabet

a b c d e f g h i j k l m n o p q r s t
u v w x y z

Alphabetical order

1	queen	rock	sell	trick
2	jump	kick	log	men
3	mop	not	owl	pen
4	ten	up	van	well

Naming words

1	pin	sock	bus
2	jug	cup	
3	pen	bed	bat
4	man	leg	
5	peg	hill	

Describing words

1	red	tidy	
2	old	sad	long
3	ten	green	
4	hot	cold	
5	thin	happy	

Doing words

1 swims
2 drinks
3 hisses
4 nibbles
5 spins

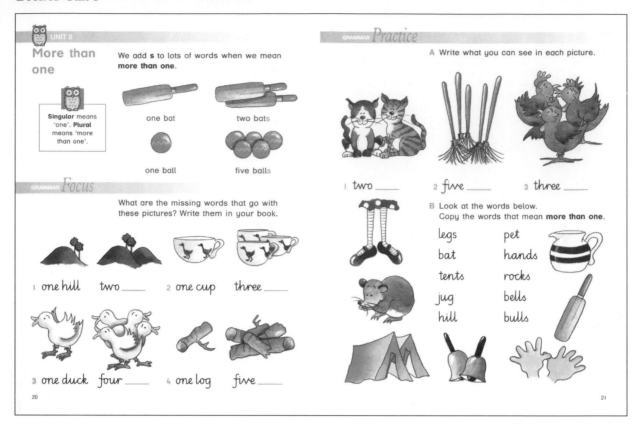

see Glossary, page 13 – Singular
and plural

Previous work

None

Pupil Book answers

Focus

1 two **hills**
3 four **ducks**
2 three **cups**
4 five **logs**

Practice

A
1 two **cats**
3 three **hens**
2 five **mops**

B
legs
tents
hands
rocks
bells
bulls

Copymaster answers

Focus

A
frogs   ducks
trucks   drums

B
1 two **crabs**
3 four **shells**
2 three **nests**
4 five **cups**

Practice

A
1 Two little **dogs** were playing in
   the park.
2 There are three **pens** on my desk.
3 How many **birds** can you see?

B
*Answers will be individual to the
children.*

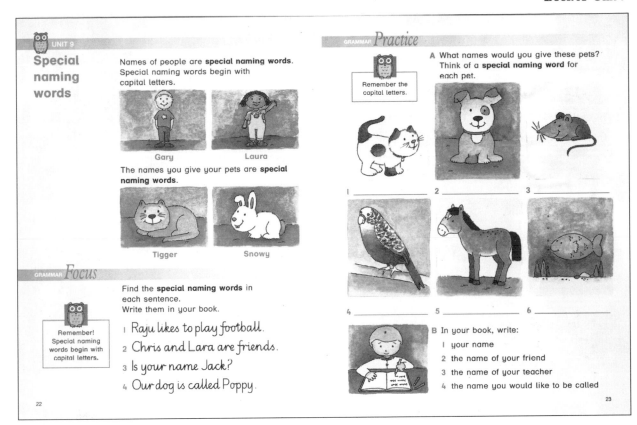

see Glossary, page 11 – Nouns

Previous work

Workbook 1
page 4
page 5
page 12
page 13

Workbook 2
page 4
page 5
page 12
page 13

Book A
pages 6/7
pages 10/11

Pupil Book answers

Focus

1 Raju
2 Chris, Lara
3 Jack
4 Poppy

Practice

A
Answers will be individual to the children. Each must start with a capital letter.

B
Answers will be individual to the children.

Copymaster answers

Focus

A
1–6 Dean, Sam, Toby, Kim, Jane, Pam

B
1 My brother is called <u>Garth</u>.
2 <u>Luke</u> lives on a farm.
3 Do you know a girl called <u>Jill</u>?
4 <u>Sue</u> and <u>Paul</u> are late.
5 My name is <u>Mary Kate Green</u>.

Practice

A
1 Neil
2 Hilda
3 Jenny
4 Mick

B and **C**
Answers will be individual to the children.

UNIT 10

Writing sentences

A **sentence** starts with a **capital letter**.
A sentence usually ends with a **full stop**.
These are sentences:

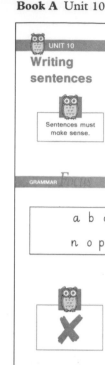

Sentences must make sense.

The bell is ringing.   This sack is torn.

GRAMMAR Focus

A Here is the alphabet in small letters.

a b c d e f g h i j k l m
n o p q r s t u v w x y z

In your book, write the alphabet in **capital letters**.

B Copy these **sentences**.
Put in the missing **capital letters** and **full stops**.

1 sita has hurt her leg
2 we are going fishing today
3 the boys got on the bus
4 tom wrote a letter to his friend

24

GRAMMAR Practice

Look for the capital letters and full stops.

Make **sentences** by putting the words in the right order.
The pictures will help you.

1 are a The snowman. children making

2 playing park. The in twins are the

3 will My start. car not

4 read book. have I this

25

---

see Glossary, page 12 – Sentences

Previous work

None

Pupil Book answers

Focus

A

A B C D E F G H I J K L M N O P Q R S T U V W X Y Z

B

1 **S**ita has hurt her leg.
2 **W**e are going fishing today.
3 **T**he boys got on the bus.
4 **T**om wrote a letter to his friend.

Practice

1 The children are making a snowman.
2 The twins are playing in the park.
3 My car will not start.
4 I have read this book.

Copymaster answers

Focus

A

A B C D E F G H I J K L M N O P Q R S T U V W X Y Z

B

1 **W**e play football at school.
2 **M**y cat is fat.
3 **T**he bell rings at playtime.
4 **F**rogs live in ponds.

Practice

Answers will be individual to the children, for example:

The boy kicks the ball and it lands in the pond.
The boy kneels down to reach the ball. He falls into the pond with the ball and is cross and wet.

see Glossary, page 14 – Verbs

Previous work

Workbook 1
page 8
page 9
page 14
page 15

Workbook 2
page 8
page 9
page 14
page 15

Book A
pages 12/13
pages 16/17

Pupil Book answers

Focus

1 chases
2 bangs
3 climbs

Practice

Answers will be individual to the children, for example:

1 *The bird pecks at the ground.*
 The bird catches a worm.
2 *The children build a snowman.*
 The bird sits on his hat.
3 *The fish swims.*
 The fish jumps.
4 *The man gets into his car.*
 The man drives his car.

Copymaster answers

Focus

A

1 feeding	2 dusting
3 fishing	4 dripping

B

1 Lara **brushes** her hair.
2 Mum **mashes** the potatoes.
3 The elephant **lifts** his trunk.
4 The sheep **run** in the field.
5 The cow **sleeps** in the barn.

Practice

Answers will be individual to the children.

Describing words

Describing words tell us more about a person or thing.

Describing words are called adjectives.

The **long** snake is hiding in the **green** grass.

GRAMMAR *Focus*

Write the **describing words** in your book.

Number 3 has two describing words.

1 The red flag is flying today. 2 The small boy is crying.

3 The dirty coat and muddy boots are on the floor.

28

GRAMMAR *Practice*

Describing words make sentences more interesting.

Copy the sentences below.
Add **describing words** of your own to finish them.

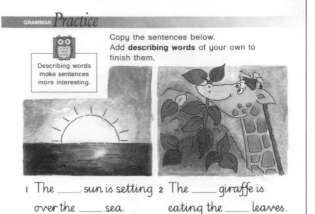

1 The ____ sun is setting over the ____ sea. 2 The ____ giraffe is eating the ____ leaves.

3 The ____ clouds are covering the ____ moon. 4 The ____ rabbit is hiding behind the ____ tree.

29

---

see Glossary, page 9 – Adjectives

Previous work

Workbook 1
page 6
page 7
page 13

Workbook 2
page 6
page 7
page 13

Book A
pages 8/9
pages 10/11

Pupil Book answers

Focus

1 red
2 small
3 dirty, muddy

Practice

Answers will be individual to the children, for example:

1 *The **yellow/shining/bright** sun is setting over the **blue/calm** sea.*
2 *The **tall/happy** giraffe is eating the **green/tasty** leaves.*
3 *The **grey/stormy** clouds are covering the **yellow/bright** moon.*
4 *The **little/grey/scared** rabbit is hiding behind the **tall/large/big** tree.*

Copymaster answers

Focus

A

1–6 thin, short, pretty, small, pink, old

B

1 I have a <u>blue</u> coat.
2 The <u>hot</u> drink is on the table.
3 There is a <u>big</u> hole in my sock.
4 That <u>red</u> flower is a poppy.
5 We have found the <u>lost</u> dog.

Practice

A

Answers will be individual to the children, for example:

1 *fierce*   *frightening*
2 *sad*   *funny*
3 *thin*   *long*
4 *fizzy*   *cold*

B

Answers will be individual to the children, for example:

1 *I am feeling very **happy** today.*
2 *The pencil is very **sharp**.*
3 *He was a **clever** boy.*

Writing sentences

Sentences must make sense.

A **sentence** starts with a **capital letter** and usually ends with a **full stop**.

Tracy is waiting for the bus.

It is raining.

She is very wet.

Focus

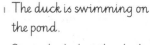

Copy these **sentences** into your book. Put rings around the **capital letters** and **full stops**.

1 The duck is swimming on the pond.

2 Simon looked at the clock.

3 My pen has run out of ink.

4 Please post this letter for me.

5 The tin is on the top shelf.

30

Practice

Look at the pictures. Write a **sentence** about each picture.

31

---

see Glossary, page 12 – Sentences

Previous work

Book A
pages 24/25

Pupil Book answers

Focus

1 **T**he duck is swimming on the pond**.**
2 **S**imon looked at the clock**.**
3 **M**y pen has run out of ink**.**
4 **P**lease post this letter for me**.**
5 **T**he tin is on the top shelf**.**

Practice

Answers will be individual to the children, for example:

1 *The man is driving his car.*
2 *He hears a bang.*
3 *His tyre is flat.*
4 *He gets another tyre from the boot.*
5 *He waves to a lorry driver for help.*
6 *The lorry splashes him.*

Copymaster answers

Focus

Answers will be individual to the children, for example:

1 *My sister is two years older than me.*
2 *In the morning I am going to the zoo.*
3 *When it was raining I used my new umbrella.*
4 *After school I go shopping with Mum.*
5 *The old man has a little white dog.*

Practice

1 Tim opened the door.
2 Tim put the cat out.
3 The door banged shut.

Answers to part 4 will be individual to the children, for example:

4 *Tim climbed in through the window.*

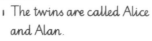

Check-up 2

More than one

Look at the words below.
Copy the words that mean **more than one**.

rings	cots	click
snails	king	bells
mill	cups	neck
locks	hats	door

Special naming words

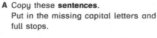

Copy the **special naming word** from each sentence.

1 The twins are called Alice and Alan.

2 My pet snake is called Sam.

3 Sara likes to swim.

4 Beauty is a black horse.

Writing sentences

A Copy these **sentences**.
Put in the missing capital letters and full stops.

1 the house is very old

2 it has no door

3 some windows are broken

32

B Make **sentences** by putting the words in the right order

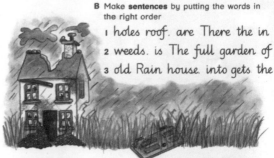

1 holes roof. are There the in

2 weeds. is The full garden of

3 old Rain house. into gets the

Doing words

Use these **doing words** in sentences of your own.

1 sing   2 jump

3 run   4 kick

5 peck   6 play

7 clap   8 eat

Describing words

Add a **describing word** to each sentence to make it more interesting.

1 The clock is in the hall.

2 I found this shell on the beach.

3 I can see the moon.

4 There are sheep in the field.

33

More than one

rings	cots
snails	bells
cups	locks

Special naming words

1 Alice, Alan
2 Sam
3 Sara
4 Beauty

Writing sentences

A
1 **T**he house is very old**.**
2 **I**t has no door**.**
3 **S**ome windows are broken**.**

B
1 There are holes in the roof.
2 The garden is full of weeds.
3 Rain gets into the old house.

Doing words

Answers will be individual to the children.

Describing words

Answers will be individual to the children, for example:

1 *The **old** clock is in the hall.*
2 *I found this **pretty** shell on the beach.*
3 *I can see the **full** moon.*
4 *There are sheep in the **big** field.*

see Glossary, page 12 – Sentences

Previous work

Book A
pages 24/25
pages 30/31

Pupil Book answers

Focus

1 Where are you going?
3 What are you going to buy?
5 Will you get some oranges too?

Practice

A
1 Do you like cheese?
2 I like to drink milk.
3 Will you stay for tea?
4 Is it ready now?
5 Can I help you?

B

Answers will be individual to the children, for example:
1 *Where are **you going?***
2 *Why does **that dog keep barking?***
3 *When can **I come to tea?***
4 *What is **in that box?***
5 *Who will **ring the bell?***

Copymaster answers

Focus

A

The following should be ticked:
1 Are you feeling well?
3 Do you know the way?
4 What time is it?

B
1 What is in the box?
2 Shall we have a look?
3 There are some pens in the box.
4 Are there any pencils?
5 I can't see any.
6 Will you shut the box?

Practice

A

Answers will be individual to the children, for example:
1 Why is the man hiding behind the tree?
2 What is the girl smiling about?
3 Why is she cross?
4 What is in the box?

B

Answers will be individual to the children, for example:
1 *How **old are you?***
2 *What **is your sister called?***
3 *Where **do you live?***

see Glossary, page 11 – Nouns

Previous work

Workbook 1
page 4
page 5
page 12
page 13

Workbook 2
page 4
page 5
page 12
page 13

Book A
pages 6/7
pages 10/11
pages 22/23

Pupil Book answers

Focus

1 bee 2 boot 3 nest
4 shed 5 flag 6 king

Practice

1 The dog is digging in the **sand**.
2 Andrew is making a **castle**.
3 Dad is eating a **cake**.
4 The baby is asleep in the **chair**.
5 There is a boat on the **sea**.

Copymaster answers

Focus

A

1–6 dress, shed, shelf, brush, jug, nut

B

1 The sun is shining.
2 There are three birds flying.
3 Can you see the ship?
4 The waves are very big.
5 I like swimming in the sea.

Practice

Answers will be individual to the children, for example:

The **bird** *has a broken* **wing**.
The **girl** *is carrying a* **bag**.
A **page** *in this* **book** *is torn.*
The **monkey** *is climbing the* **tree**.
The **spaceship** *has landed on the* **moon**.

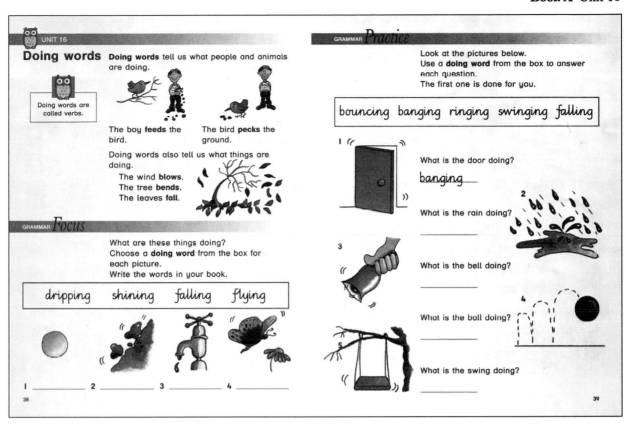

see Glossary, page 14 – Verbs

Previous work

Workbook 1
page 8
page 9
page 14
page 15

Workbook 2
page 8
page 9
page 14
page 15

Book A
pages 12/13
pages 16/17
pages 26/27

Pupil Book answers

Focus

1 shining	2 falling
3 dripping	4 flying

Practice

1 banging
2 falling
3 ringing
4 bouncing
5 swinging

Copymaster answers

Focus

Children should draw lines to connect the verbs to the correct parts of the picture.

Practice

A

Answers will be individual to the children, for example:

1 *digging*	*smiling*
2 *diving*	*splashing*
3 *bending*	*blowing*
4 *flying*	*raining*

B

Answers will be individual to the children, for example:

Flags were flying at the fair.
I saw flowers growing by the road.
The ships were sailing on the sea.

UNIT 17
Special naming words

Special naming words are called proper nouns.

Special naming words begin with a capital letter.
Names of people are special naming words.
Names of pets are special naming words.

Mrs Brown has two cats.
They are called Sandy and Mandy.

GRAMMAR *Focus*

Find the **special naming words** in each sentence.
Write them in your book.

1 My pony is called Lucky.
2 Mr Clark and Mr Kasim are friends.
3 Sue has a hamster called Bunty.
4 We have called our stick insects Twig and Mig.

40

GRAMMAR *Practice*

A Use **special naming words** to answer these questions.
  1 What is your first name?
  2 What is your last name?
  3 What is your middle name?

B Look at this picture.

Rose Jessica Sanjay Rory

Remember the capital letters.

Use **special naming words** to answer each question.
  1 Who lives at number 3?
  2 Who lives at number 2?
  3 Who lives at number 1?
  4 Who lives at number 4?
  5 Who has a dog?
  6 Who has a cat?

41

---

see Glossary, page 11 – Nouns

Previous work

Workbook 1
page 4
page 5
page 12
page 13

Workbook 2
page 4
page 5
page 12
page 13

Book A
pages 6/7
pages 10/11
pages 22/23
pages 36/37

Pupil Book answers

Focus

1 Lucky
2 Mr Clark, Mr Kasim
3 Sue, Bunty
4 Twig, Mig

Practice

A
Answers will be individual to the children.

B
1 Sanjay   2 Jessica
3 Rose   4 Rory
5 Rose   6 Sanjay

Copymaster answers

Focus

A
1 **Mr White** has an odd pet.
2 It is a snake called **Bing**.
3 **Mr White** and **Bing** go out for walks.
4 **Miss Davis** does not like **Bing**.
5 **Miss Davis** has a pet goldfish called **Drip**.

B
1 Anita   Barry   Cathy
2 Deepak   Eddy   Frank
3 Greg   Hugh   Imran

C
Answers will be individual to the children.

Practice

A
1 Captain Smythe   2 Mr Hall
3 Doctor Dhiri   4 Mrs Jenkins

B
1 Tom   2 Tina
3 Sarah   4 John
5 Ali   6 Ben

C
Answers will be individual to the children.

see Glossary, page 12 – Sentences

Previous work

Book A
pages 24/25
pages 30/31
pages 34/35

Pupil Book answers

Focus

1 What time is it?
2 I am late for school.
3 Did you eat your breakfast?
4 What did you have?
5 I had tea and toast.

Practice

Answers will be individual to the children, for example:

1
A man is reading a newspaper.
A lady is getting on the train.
The guard has a green flag.

2
What is the boy putting on the train?
Where is the train going?
How many cases are on the trolley?

Copymaster answers

Focus

A
Are you hungry?
Where did you find it?

B
No, I had a fat worm for tea.
I found it under a leaf.

Practice

Answers will be individual to the children.

Describing words

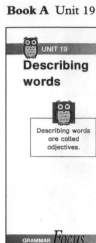

Describing words are called adjectives.

Describing words tell us more about a person or a thing.
Describing words make sentences more interesting.

We can write about the picture like this:
    The waves tossed the ship.
This is a more interesting sentence, using describing words:
    The **huge** waves tossed the **battered** ship.

GRAMMAR *Focus*

old   muddy

wooden

Choose a **describing word** from the box to make each sentence more interesting.
Write the sentences in your book.

1 The fire is burning the house.
2 The book is torn.
3 The man climbs out of the ditch.

44

GRAMMAR *Practice*

Use **describing words** of your own to make these sentences more interesting.

1 The balloon is in the sky.
2 The tiger lives in the jungle.

3 The old man has a stick.
4 The boy is making a tree house.

45

---

see Glossary, page 9 – Adjectives

Previous work

Workbook 1
page 6
page 7
page 13

Workbook 2
page 6
page 7
page 13

Book A
pages 8/9
pages 10/11
pages 28/29

Pupil Book answers

Focus

1 The fire is burning the **wooden** house.
2 The **old** book is torn.
3 The man climbs out of the **muddy** ditch.

Practice

Answers will be individual to the children, for example:

1 The **colourful** balloon is in the **blue** sky.
2 The **fierce** tiger lives in the **dark** jungle.
3 The **old** man has a **walking** stick.
4 The **young** boy is making a **wooden** tree house.

Copymaster answers

Focus

A

Answers will be individual to the children, for example:

1 a **hissing/long** snake
2 a **yellow/beautiful** flower

3 the **wooden/old** house
4 the **heavy/torn** sacks
5 a **small/big** tent
6 the **sharp/dangerous** rocks

B

Answers will be individual to the children, for example:

1 open, square
2 floppy, tall
3 playful, little
4 hot, burning
5 fierce, frightening

Practice

A

Answers will be individual to the children, for example:

1 bouncy, blue
2 cuddly, cute

B

Answers will be individual to the children, for example:

We crept into the **spooky** castle.
The **damp** air made us shiver.
Wild flowers were growing in the meadow.

Check-up 3

The alphabet

Fill in the missing letters.

1 a b _ _ e f _ h i

2 j _ l _ n _ p _ _

3 S T _ V _ X _ _

Alphabetical order

Put the words in **alphabetical order**.

1 nut   man   owl

2 dig   bat   car

3 Lee   Hannah   Caroline

4 Ryan   Bob   Sita

Naming words

A Write the **naming words** from each of these sentences.

1 Put the cup on the table.

2 I have my book and pen.

3 Can you find the shoes?

B Write a sentence using each of these **naming words**.

1 snake   2 game   3 cart

4 tree   5 street   6 stamp

46

Describing words

A Write the **describing words** from these sentences.

1 This is a steep hill.

2 These are hard sums.

3 It is a dark night.

B Write a sentence using each of these **describing words**.

1 small   2 tall   3 fresh

4 best   5 dusty   6 flat

Doing words

A Write the **doing words** from these sentences.

1 Tony swims every day.

2 The girls ride their bicycles.

3 My cat sleeps in my bedroom.

B Write a sentence using each of these **doing words**.

1 walk   2 hunts   3 eat

4 shouts   5 write   6 runs

More than one

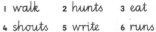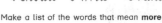

Make a list of the words that mean **more than one**.

plums   tank   tricks   frogs

crab   bees   weeds   room

47

The alphabet

1 a b **c** d e f **g** h i
2 j **k** l **m** n o p **q r**
3 S T U V W X Y Z

Alphabetical order

1 man   nut   owl
2 bat   car   dig
3 Caroline   Hannah   Lee
4 Bob   Ryan   Sita

Naming words

A
1 cup   table
2 book   pen
3 shoes

B
Answers will be individual to the children.

Describing words

A
1 steep
2 hard
3 dark

B
Answers will be individual to the children.

Doing words

A
1 swims
2 ride
3 sleeps

B
Answers will be individual to the children.

More than one

plums
tricks
frogs
bees
weeds

Special naming words

Write the **special naming words** with capital letters.

wave	greg	barn	george
card	mr little	peggy	bert
star	mrs pope	andy	farm

Sentences

A Copy these **sentences**.
Add the **capital letters** and **full stops**.

1 he will go to a cricket match

2 there is no post today

3 here is the book you wanted

B Make **sentences** by putting the words in the right order.

1 has bicycle A wheels. two

2 book. reading am I good a

3 gone Dad shops. to has the

Questions

Which of these are **questions**?
Write the questions with question marks.

1 Is it raining

2 The weather is fine

3 Will I need an umbrella

48

Special naming words

Greg	George	
Mr Little	Peggy	Bert
Mrs Pope	Andy	

Sentences

A
1 **H**e will go to the cricket match.
2 **T**here is no post today.
3 **H**ere is the book you wanted.

B
1 A bicycle has two wheels.
2 I am reading a good book.
3 Dad has gone to the shops.

Questions
1 Is it raining?
3 Will I need an umbrella?

Extension copymaster 1

Children should locate the nouns on the wordsearch.

Extension copymaster 2

Across	Down
3 mop	1 pen
4 nest	2 tap
	3 man

Extension copymaster 3

Children should locate the nouns on the wordsearch.

Extension copymaster 4

Across	Down
2 happy	1 tall
5 sad	4 old
	5 sharp

Extension copymaster 5

Children should locate the nouns on the wordsearch.

Extension copymaster 6

Across	Down
4 eating	1 flying
5 jumping	3 skipping
6 hopping	

Extension copymaster 7

When coloured correctly, the picture will show a cat on a wall.

Book 1 – Contents/Scope and Sequence

Page/Unit		Focus	Practice
4/5	Unit 1	nouns – choosing nouns from picture clues	making lists of connected nouns
6/7	Unit 2	adjectives – choosing appropriate adjectives	cloze – adding appropriate adjectives
8/9	Unit 3	singular and plural – writing plural words with 's'	listing singular and plural nouns, recognising plurals
10/11	Unit 4	prepositions – cloze to add appropriate prepositions	pairing prepositions which are opposites
12/13	Unit 5	proper nouns – identifying	writing proper nouns with capital letters
14/15	Unit 6	pronouns – identifying	substituting pronouns for nouns in sentences
16/17	Unit 7	confusing words – completing sentences with 'two' or 'to'	phrases with 'two' or 'to', writing sentences
18/19		*Check-up 1*	*Check-up 1*
20/21	Unit 8	nouns – identifying common nouns and proper nouns	identifying proper nouns within sentences and writing them with capital letters
22/23	Unit 9	adjectives – writing adjectives	writing adjectives to describe a picture
24/25	Unit 10	simple sentences – adding capital letters and full stops	completing sentences
26/27	Unit 11	verbs – choosing appropriate verbs	completing verb webs
28/29	Unit 12	questions – identifying questions	ending sentences with full stops and question marks
30/31	Unit 13	verbs – identifying verbs in sentences	choosing appropriate verbs to complete sentences
32/33		*Check-up 2*	*Check-up 2*
34/35	Unit 14	adjectives – matching colour adjectives to nouns	cloze – appropriate colour adjectives
36/37	Unit 15	conjunctions – using 'and' to join sentences	changing nouns into pronouns, joining sentences with 'and'
38/39	Unit 16	verbs – classifying verbs into families	choosing the correct form of verbs to complete sentences
40/41	Unit 17	pronouns – choosing pronouns for picture clues	substituting pronouns for nouns and proper nouns
42/43	Unit 18	adjectives – writing number adjectives	identifying number and colour adjectives
44/45	Unit 19	conjunctions – using 'but'	changing nouns and proper nouns into pronouns, joining with 'but'
46/48		*Check-up 3*	*Check-up 3*

Extension	Copymaster	Page/Unit	
identifying nouns in a short story	identifying and writing nouns	4/5	Unit 1
identifying adjectives in a short story	identifying and writing adjectives	6/7	Unit 2
choosing singular or plural words to complete sentences	adding 's'	8/9	Unit 3
identifying prepositions in a short story	identifying and writing prepositions	10/11	Unit 4
completing sentences with nouns	names of people	12/13	Unit 5
writing sentences using pronouns	identifying and writing pronouns	14/15	Unit 6
choosing 'two' or 'to' to complete sentences	correct usage of 'two' and 'to'	16/17	Unit 7
Check-up 1	*Check-up 1*	18/19	
completing a story using common and proper nouns	common and proper nouns	20/21	Unit 8
adding adjectives to improve a story	writing sentences with adjectives	22/23	Unit 9
ordering words to make sentences	ordering simple sentences	24/25	Unit 10
cloze – completing sentences with appropriate verbs	identifying and writing present-tense verbs	26/27	Unit 11
writing questions to go with given answers	writing questions, question words	28/29	Unit 12
writing sentences for picture clues and identifying the verbs	writing sentences for given verbs	30/31	Unit 13
Check-up 2	*Check-up 2*	32/33	
writing sentences using colour adjectives	writing sentences with colour adjectives	34/35	Unit 14
writing short sentences, joining with 'and'	using 'and'	36/37	Unit 15
classifying verbs, writing verb family names	verb family names	38/39	Unit 16
completing sentences using pronouns	identifying pronouns, using pronouns instead of nouns	40/41	Unit 17
writing sentences using colour and number adjectives	number adjectives	42/43	Unit 18
using 'and' or 'but' to join sentences	using 'and' or 'but'	44/45	Unit 19
Check-up 3	*Check-up 3*	46/48	

The upper boxed illustration contains the following pupil book content:

Nouns

Nouns are naming words.
They tell us the names of things.

cat   **ball**   **fish**   jug

Naming words are called **nouns**.

Focus

Look at these pictures.
For each picture, choose the correct **noun** from the box. Write the nouns in your book.

hat
dog
peg
mug
man
bag

1 _____   2 _____   3 _____
4 _____   5 _____   6 _____

Practice

A Look around the room.
Write the names of ten **nouns** you can see.

B Write the names of ten **nouns** you can see in this picture.

Extension

Read this story.
Write the **nouns** in your book.

The girl was playing with her dog in the garden. The dog was running after a ball. The ball went under a bush. The dog went under the bush to find the ball.

---

see Glossary, page 11 – Nouns

Previous work

Workbook 1
page 4
page 5
page 12
page 13

Workbook 2
page 4
page 5
page 12
page 13

Book A
pages 6/7
pages 10/11
pages 22/23
pages 36/37
pages 40/41

Pupil Book answers

Focus

1 peg
2 mug
3 man
4 dog
5 bag
6 hat

Practice

A
Answers will be individual to the children.

B
Possible answers include:

rock	sea	water
bird	seagull	hat
girl	sunglasses	hair
mat	bottle	starfish
shell	book	sand
sand castle	flag	boy
umbrella	rug	spade
flask	rubber ring	man

Extension

girl   dog   garden   ball   bush

Copymaster answers

A

cage	grass	house
lamp	desk	telephone
fence	box	chair

B
Answers will be individual to the children, for example:

shelf	tin	trolley
people	fruit	freezers

C
Answers will be individual to the children, for example:

tree	grass	bird
flowers	spade	swing

D
Answers will be individual to the children, for example:
*The bird pecked at the **ground**. It was looking for **food**. It found a **worm** and caught it in its **beak**. The bird flew to the top of a **tree** to eat its **dinner**.*

The following is a reproduction of the pupil book pages:

UNIT 2

Adjectives

Adjectives are describing words. They tell us more about a person or thing.

All these words describe the pictures.

small   dirty   happy   white   old   big

GRAMMAR *Focus*

Choose an **adjective** from the box for each animal. Write the words in your book.

little
fluffy
brown
big
long
fat

1 ____   2 ____   3 ____
4 ____   5 ____   6 ____

6

GRAMMAR *Practice*

Look at the picture.
Copy these sentences and fill in the missing **adjectives**.
You can use words from the box or adjectives of your own.

old   large   small   red

1 The lady in the ____ coat is at the bus stop.
2 The ____ boy is crying.
3 The ____ man has an umbrella.
4 On the roof there is a ____ cat.

GRAMMAR *Extension*

Read this story.
Write the **adjectives** in your book.

It was Ben's birthday. He wanted a blue bicycle with red handles. He had seen it in the new shop in town. He got some lovely cards and a big book of ghost stories. Mum and Dad had hidden the shiny bicycle in the shed. Ben was very happy when he saw the bicycle.

7

---

see Glossary, page 9 – Adjectives

Previous work

Workbook 1
page 6
page 7
page 13

Workbook 2
page 6
page 7
page 13

Book A
pages 8/9
pages 10/11
pages 28/29
pages 44/45

Pupil Book answers

1 brown
2 fat
3 fluffy
4 big
5 little
6 long

Practice

1 The lady in the **red** coat is at the bus stop.
2 The **small** boy is crying.
3 The **old** man has an umbrella.
4 On the roof there is a **large** cat.

Extension

blue, red, new, lovely, big, ghost, shiny, happy

Copymaster answers

A

| happy | wicked | miserable |
| beautiful | old | cold |

B

Answers will be individual to the children, for example:
1 *tall, flowering, (colour), beautiful*
2 *fierce, large, (colour), ugly*

C

Answers will be individual to the children.

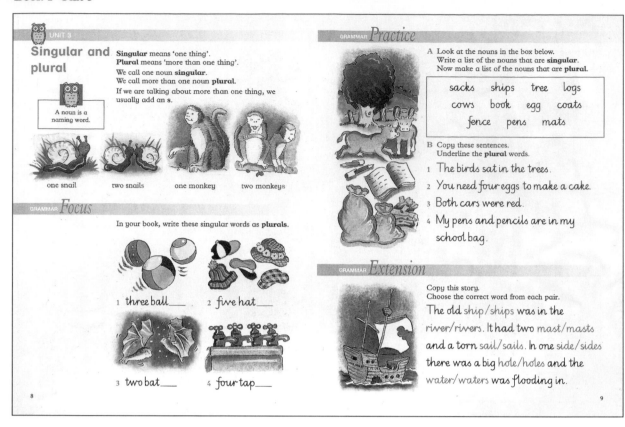

see Glossary, page 13 – Singular and plural

Previous work

Book A
pages 20/21

Pupil Book answers

Focus

1 three balls   2 five hats
3 two bats   4 four taps

Practice

A

SINGULAR	PLURAL
tree	sacks
book	ships
egg	logs
fence	cows
	coats
	pens
	mats

B

1 The <u>birds</u> sat in the <u>trees</u>.
2 You need four <u>eggs</u> to make a cake.
3 Both <u>cars</u> were red.
4 My <u>pens</u> and <u>pencils</u> are in my school bag.

Extension

The old **ship** was in the **river**.
It had two **masts** and a torn **sail**.
In one **side** there was a big **hole**
and the **water** was flooding in.

Copymaster answers

A

1 I took my **dogs** to the park.
2 If you drop the **jugs** they will break.
3 The **birds** made a nest in the tree.
4 The **doors** are painted red.
5 Please fetch some **pegs**.

B

<u>cars</u>	book	tiger
<u>elephants</u>	<u>buns</u>	
cup	<u>trees</u>	ball
<u>desks</u>	<u>windows</u>	

C

1 wall
2 pea
3 plant
4 tractor

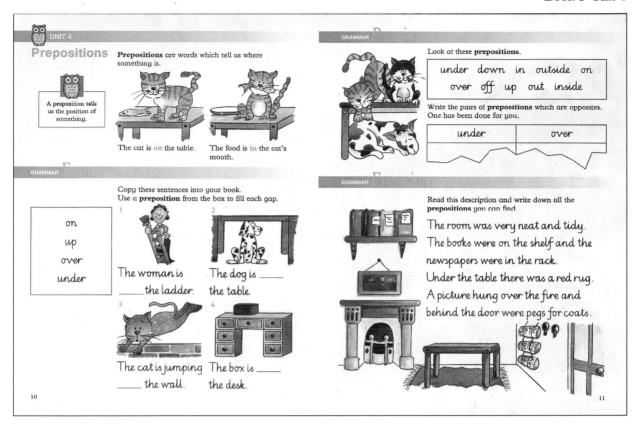

see Glossary, page 12 – Prepositions

Previous work

None

Pupil Book answers

Focus

1 The woman is **up** the ladder.
2 The dog is **under** the table.
3 The cat is jumping **over** the wall.
4 The box is **on** the desk.

Practice

under	over
down	up
in	out
outside	inside
on	off

Extension

on, in, under, over, behind

Copymaster answers

A

bottle	over	hand	inside
jumps	laughing	in	
down	pencil	it	on
under	cap		
outside	knock	up	light
off	out	sign	

B

1 The dog buried his bone **under/behind** a bush.
2 It is very windy **outside**.
3 Look **in/inside/on** the cupboard for your shoes.
4 I go **down/up** the stairs in the morning.
5 Get **off/on** the bus when you reach the shops.

C

Answers will be individual to the children, for example:
The man is walking **on** *the tightrope.*
The boat is **going** *under the bridge.*

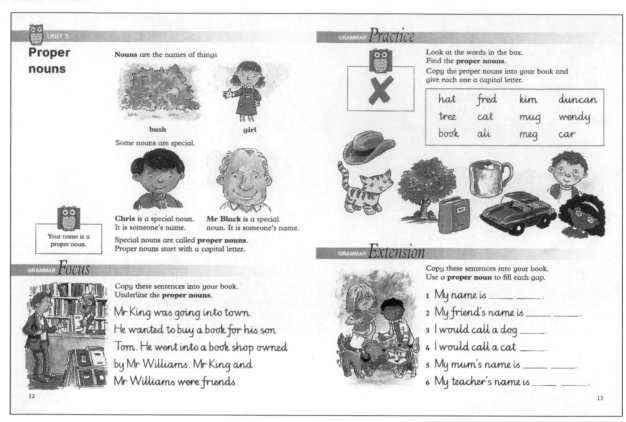

see Glossary, page 11 – Nouns

Previous work

Workbook 1
page 4
page 5
page 12
page 13

Workbook 2
page 4
page 5
page 12
page 13

Book A
pages 6/7
pages 10/11
pages 22/23
pages 36/37
pages 40/41

Book 1
pages 4/5

Pupil Book answers

Focus

Mr King was going into town.
He wanted to buy a book for his son
Tom. He went into a book shop
owned by Mr Williams. Mr King
and Mr Williams were friends.

Practice

Fred   Kim   Duncan
Wendy   Ali   Meg

Extension

Answers will be individual to the children.

Copymaster answers

A

1	Paul Smith	2	Carlton Barret
3	Victor Grant	4	Daisy Harris
5	Aftab Raja	6	Maria Garcia
7	Sarah Brown	8	Tom Finch

B

Answers will be individual to the children, for example:

Jason	Robert	Peter
Susan	Beth	Cathy
William	Lynn	Mike
Dominic	Nathan	Tim

C

Answers will be individual to the children.

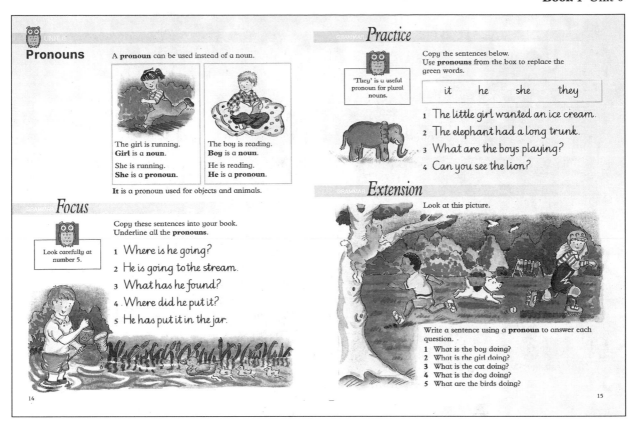

see Glossary, page 12 – Pronouns

Previous work

None

Pupil Book answers

Focus

1 Where is <u>he</u> going?
2 <u>He</u> is going to the stream.
3 What has <u>he</u> found?
4 Where did <u>he</u> put <u>it</u>?
5 <u>He</u> has put <u>it</u> in the jar.

Practice

1 **She** wanted an ice cream.
2 **It** had a long trunk.
3 What are **they** playing?
4 Can you see **it**?

Extension

1 **He** is running.
2 **She** is roller skating.
3 **It** is climbing the tree.
4 **It** is chasing the ball.
5 **They** are flying (in the sky).

Copymaster answers

A

<u>she</u>   boy   <u>it</u>   woman
<u>they</u>   elephant   <u>he</u>   girl

B

1 **He** is sleeping.
2 **She** is cycling.
3 **It** is washing.
4 **They** are painting.

C

1 **They** were late for school.
2 **She** walked quickly down the street.
3 **They** flew south for the winter.

see Glossary, page 10 – Confusing words

Previous work

None

Pupil Book answers

Focus

1 There were **two** cakes left.
2 The stone sank **to** the bottom of the pond.
3 It is five minutes **to** six.
4 The **two** cups were broken.
5 We have playtime at **two** o'clock.

Practice

1 I went **to** bed.
2 sixty-**two**
3 **two** pence
4 Jill ran **to** the park.
5 It is four days **to** Christmas.

Extension

Sally was going **to** the shops. She wanted **to** buy some bread and **two** tins of soup. On the way home she saw **two** of her friends. Sally waved **to** her friends and took the **two** tins of soup home.

Copymaster answers

A

1 **Two** shopping days before Christmas
2 **To** the zoo
3 Tickets **two** pounds
4 Next ferry at **two** o'clock
5 **Two**-way traffic

B

1 I am going **to** write a letter.
2 Please buy **two** pounds of apples.
3 In **two** minutes the bell will ring.
4 Can we go **to** the swimming pool?
5 This path leads **to** the village.

C and D

Answers will be individual to the children.

Check-up 1

Nouns and adjectives

A In your book, write a list of the **nouns** you can see in this picture.

B Write an **adjective** to go with each noun in your list.

Plurals

A These words are singular. Write the **plurals**.

1 car	2 stamp	3 hat
4 book	5 pen	6 pig
7 mat	8 road	9 shoe

B Use three of the **plurals** in sentences of your own.

Prepositions

Copy these sentences.
Fill each gap, using a **preposition** from the box.

over	up
out	on

1 Sam is climbing _____ the stairs.
2 Rupa found the book _____ the shelf.
3 The cat jumped _____ the fence.
4 Raj took the dog _____ for a walk.

18

Proper nouns Find the **proper nouns** in this box. Write them with capital letters.

tim	lamb	mrs desai	frog
paul	dan	cap	mr letts

Pronouns

Copy these sentences.
Fill each gap with a **pronoun**.

1 Ian felt sick because _____ had eaten too much.
2 If Tina wanted, _____ could go to the match.
3 Aunt Mary was cross with the dog because _____ had chewed the rug.

Confusing words

Copy these sentences.
Fill each gap with two or to.

1 The sign pointed _____ the shops.
2 There were _____ socks on the washing line.
3 Which way do we go _____ get home.
4 The _____ bats were broken.
5 I have _____ leave in ten minutes.

19

Nouns and adjectives

A
Answers will be individual to the children. Possible answers include:
tree   cat   bird   nest
bush   flower   dog   grass
fence

B
Answers will be individual to the children.

Plurals

A
1 cars
2 stamps
3 hats
4 books
5 pens
6 pigs
7 mats
8 roads
9 shoes

B
Answers will be individual to the children.

Prepositions

1 Sam is climbing **up** the stairs.
2 Rupa found the book **on** the shelf.
3 The cat jumped **over** the fence.
4 Raj took the dog **out** for a walk.

Proper nouns

Tim   Mrs Desai
Paul   Dan   Mr Letts

Pronouns

1 Ian felt sick because **he** had eaten too much.
2 If Tina wanted, **she** could go to the match.
3 Aunt Mary was cross with the dog because **it** had chewed the rug.

Confusing words

1 The sign pointed **to** the shops.
2 There were **two** socks on the washing line.
3 Which way do we go **to** get home?
4 The **two** bats were broken.
5 I have **to** leave in ten minutes.

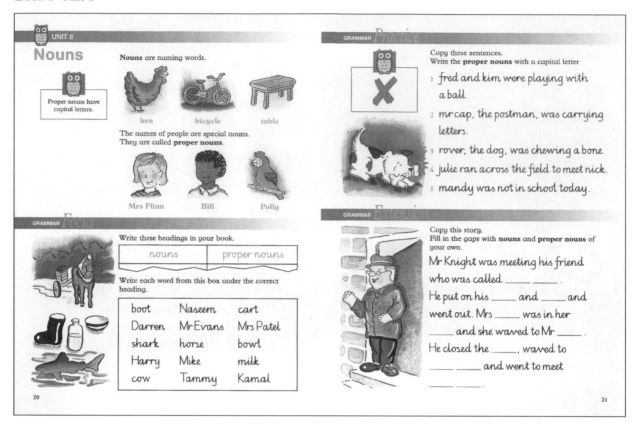

see Glossary, page 11 – Nouns

Previous work

Workbook 1
page 4
page 5
page 12
page 13

Workbook 2
page 4
page 5
page 12
page 13

Book A
pages 6/7
pages 10/11
pages 22/23
pages 36/37
pages 40/41

Book 1
pages 4/5
pages 12/13

Pupil Book answers

Focus

NOUNS	PROPER NOUNS
boot	Naseem
cart	Darren
shark	Mr Evans
horse	Mrs Patel
bowl	Harry
milk	Mike
cow	Tammy
	Kamal

Practice

1 **Fred** and **K**im were playing with a ball.
2 **Mr C**ap, the postman, was carrying letters.
3 **R**over, the dog, was chewing a bone.
4 **J**ulie ran across the field to meet **N**ick.
5 **M**andy was not in school today.

Extension

Answers will be individual to the children, for example:
*Mr Knight was meeting his friend who was called **Mr Green**. He put on his **hat** and **coat** and went out. **Mrs Flinn** was in her **garden** and she waved to **Mr Knight**. He closed the **door**, waved to **Mrs Flinn** and went to meet **Mr Green**.*

Copymaster answers

A

cart	**Sam**	**Sanjay**
flower	jump	**Mr Brown**
horse	**Tina**	sad
carpet	**Tracy**	frog
tent	singing	**Miss Swift**
wet		

B and C

Answers will be individual to the children.

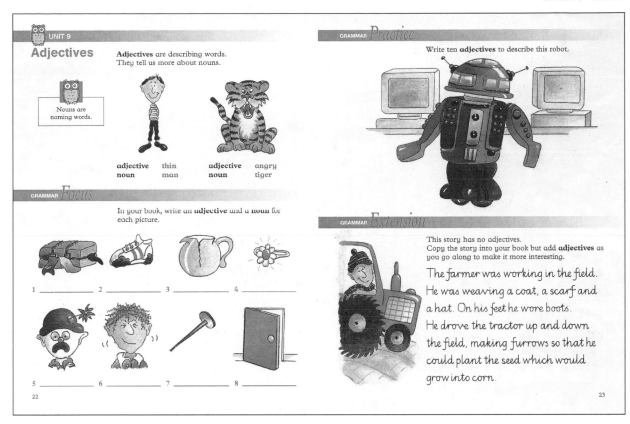

see Glossary, page 9 – Adjectives

Previous work

Workbook 1
page 6
page 7
page 13

Workbook 2
page 6
page 7
page 13

Book A
pages 8/9
pages 10/11
pages 28/29
pages 44/45

Book 1
pages 6/7

Pupil Book answers

Focus

Answers will be individual to the children, for example:
1. *a full case*　　2. *a dirty shoe*
3. *a broken jug*　4. *a sparkling ring*
5. *a sad clown*　　6. *a cold man*
7. *a sharp pin*　　8. *an open door*

Practice

Answers will be individual to the children, for example:
green, large, big, shiny, red, blue, strange, odd, frightening, yellow

Extension

Answers will be individual to the children, for example:
*The **old** farmer was working in the **muddy** field. He was wearing a **warm** coat, a **red** scarf and a **woolly** hat. On his feet he wore **large** boots. He drove the **noisy** tractor up and down the field, making **deep** furrows so that he could plant the **new** seed which would grow into **yellow** corn.*

Copymaster answers

Answers will be individual to the children.

see Glossary, page 12 – Sentences

Previous work

Book A
pages 24/25
pages 30/31
pages 34/35
pages 42/43

Pupil Book answers

Focus

1 **The** bus was late**.**
2 **The** broken glass was thrown away**.**
3 **It** rained all day**.**
4 **The** lion slept in the sun**.**
5 **The** birds made their nests in the tree**.**
6 **In** winter it is very cold**.**

Practice

1 **Flowers** begin to grow in the spring.
2 Dogs like to chase **cats**.
3 **After** tea, we went out to play.
4 Bicycles usually have **two** wheels.
5 **Today** is my birthday.

Extension

1 The man was driving his car.
2 There are flowers in the vase.
3 The food was on the table.

Copymaster answers

1 The spaceship landed on the planet.
2 The door of the spaceship opened.
3 The astronaut climbed out of the spaceship
4 The astronaut was frightened by the alien.

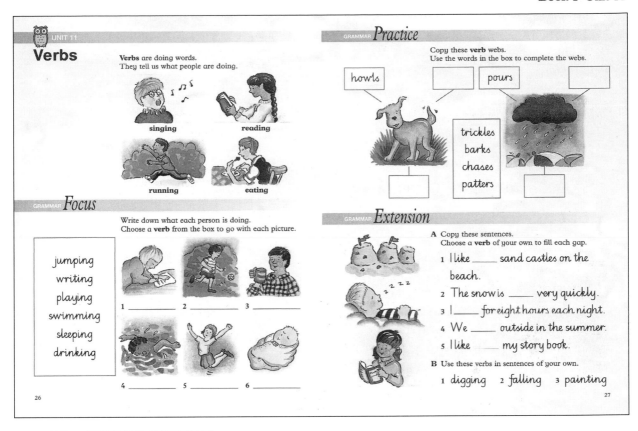

see Glossary, page 14 – Verbs

Previous work

Workbook 1
page 8
page 9
page 14
page 15

Workbook 2
page 8
page 9
page 14
page 15

Book A
pages 12/13
pages 16/17
pages 26/27
pages 38/39

Pupil Book answers

Focus

1 writing 2 playing
3 drinking 4 swimming
5 jumping 6 sleeping

Practice

dog: howls, barks, chases
rain: pours, trickles, patters

Extension

A
Answers will be individual to the children, for example:
1 *I like **making** sand castles on the beach.*
2 *The snow is **falling** very quickly.*
3 *I **sleep** for eight hours each night.*
4 *We **play** outside in the summer.*
5 *I like **reading** my story book.*

B
Answers will be individual to the children.

Copymaster answers

A

hopping	cold	making
hat	likes	window
shout	sleeping	fall
shoe	goes	green
basket	bookcase	sing

B
Answers will be individual to the children.

C
1 The ship sails on the sea.
2 I read my book until bedtime.
3 The wind blows out the candle.
4 The clock ticks loudly.
5 Many people like fish and chips.

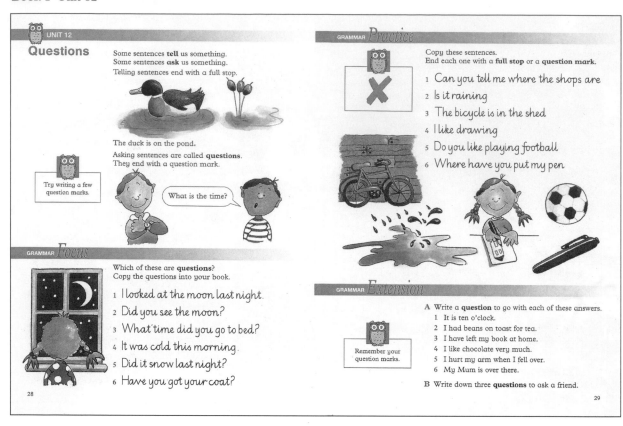

see Glossary, page 12 – Sentences

Previous work

Book A
pages 24/25
pages 30/31
pages 34/35
pages 42/43

Book 1
pages 24/25

Pupil Book answers

Focus

2 Did you see the moon?
3 What time did you go to bed?
5 Did it snow last night?
6 Have you got your coat?

Practice

1 **C**an you tell me where the shops are**?**
2 **I**s it raining**?**
3 **T**he bicycle is in the shed**.**
4 **I** like drawing**.**
5 **D**o you like playing football**?**
6 **W**here have you put my pen**?**

Extension

A

Answers will be individual to the children, for example:
1 *What time is it?*
2 *What did you have for tea?*
3 *Where have you left your book?*
4 *Do you like chocolate?*
5 *How did you hurt your arm?*
6 *Where is your Mum?*

B

Answers will be individual to the children.

Copymaster answers

A

Answers will be individual to the children, for example:
1 *Where did you go to school before?*
2 *Do you like this school?*
3 *Do you have any brothers and sisters?*

B

Answers will be individual to the children.

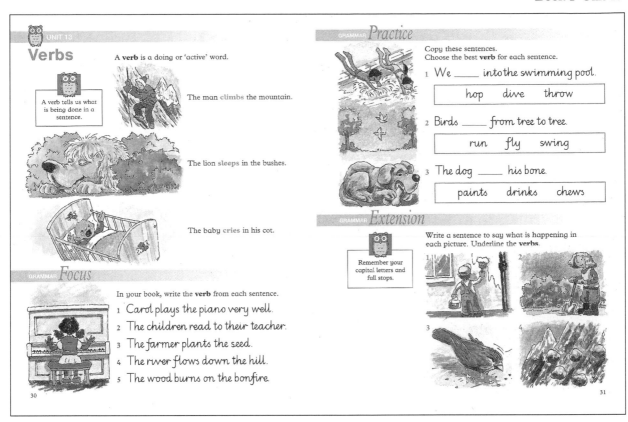

see Glossary, page 14 – Verbs

Previous work

Workbook 1
page 8
page 9
page 14
page 15

Workbook 2
page 8
page 9
page 14
page 15

Book A
pages 12/13
pages 16/17
pages 26/27
pages 38/39

Book 1
pages 26/27

Pupil Book answers

Focus

1 plays
2 read
3 plants
4 flows
5 burns

Practice

1 We **dive** into the swimming pool.
2 Birds **fly** from tree to tree.
3 The dog **chews** his bone.

Extension

Answers will be individual to the children, for example:
1 *The man <u>paints</u> the wall.*
2 *The woman <u>digs</u> the garden.*
3 *The bird <u>pecks</u> the ground.*
4 *The rocks <u>fall</u> down the mountain.*

Copymaster answers

A

1 feeds	<u>sleeps</u>	jumps
2 breaks	<u>bends</u>	shakes
3 <u>climbs</u>	runs	walks
4 sits	holds	<u>rides</u>

B

Answers will be individual to the children, for example:
1 *Sam **laughs** at the clown.*
2 *Mum **buys** bread and milk every day.*
3 *The cat **creeps** up on the bird.*
4 *The boy **shouts** at the football match.*

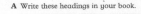

Check-up 2

Nouns

Look around the room.
Write a list of five **nouns** that you can see.
Write a list of five **proper nouns**.

Nouns and adjectives

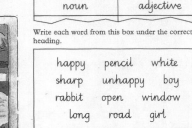

A Write these headings in your book.

noun	adjective

Write each word from this box under the correct heading.

happy	pencil	white
sharp	unhappy	boy
rabbit	open	window
long	road	girl

B Match each of the **adjectives** from your list with one of the **nouns**.
Write the pairs in your book.

Simple sentences

A Make these into **sentences** by using **capital letters** and **full stops**.

1 the children worked hard
2 the spider spun a web
3 we went out when the rain stopped
4 after tea I played a game
5 on Saturdays we go shopping

32

B Put the words in order to make **sentences**.

1 was The hungry. cat
2 white. is house My
3 the Put light on.

Verbs

A Copy these sentences.
Underline the **verbs**.

1 The teacher talks to the class.
2 The girl sings loudly.
3 My dad wakes up early.
4 You eat toast every morning.

B Use these **verbs** in sentences of your own.

1 washing 2 carrying 3 singing

Questions

A Copy these sentences.
End each one with a **full stop** or a **question mark**.

1 May I have that
2 Am I in time for the bus
3 The truck has a flat tyre
4 My window is broken
5 Is that my book

B Write a **question** to go with each answer.
1 I have been in the playground.
2 Two and two make four.
3 I am going upstairs.

33

Nouns

Answers will be individual to the children.

Nouns and adjectives

A

NOUN	ADJECTIVE
pencil	happy
boy	white
rabbit	sharp
window	unhappy
road	open
girl	long

B

sharp pencil
happy/unhappy boy
white rabbit
open window
long road
happy/unhappy girl

Simple sentences

A

1 **T**he children worked hard.
2 **T**he spider spun a web.
3 **W**e went out when the rain stopped.
4 **A**fter tea I played a game.
5 **O**n Saturdays we go shopping.

B

1 The cat was hungry.
2 My house is white.
3 Put the light on.

Verbs

A

1 The teacher <u>talks</u> to the class.
2 The girl <u>sings</u> loudly.
3 My Dad <u>wakes</u> up early.
4 You <u>eat</u> toast every morning.

B

Answers will be individual to the children.

Questions

A

1 May I have that?
2 Am I in time for the bus?
3 The truck has a flat tyre.
4 My window is broken.
5 Is that my book?

B

Answers will be individual to the children, for example:
1 *Where have you been?*
2 *What do two plus two make?*
3 *Where are you going?*

see Glossary, page 9 – Adjectives

Previous work

Workbook 1
page 6
page 7
page 13

Workbook 2
page 6
page 7
page 13

Book A
pages 8/9
pages 10/11
pages 28/29
pages 44/45

Book 1
pages 6/7
pages 22/23

Pupil Book answers

Focus

1 green grass
2 yellow daffodil
3 white snowman
4 orange carrot
5 black coal
6 red tomato

Practice

Answers will be individual to the children, for example:
1 *The **red** berries on the bush were eaten by the **black** birds.*
2 *The **yellow** bananas and the **green** apples are in the bowl.*
3 *The children played in the **blue** sea and on the **yellow** sand.*
4 *The grapes are **green** and **purple**.*

Extension

Answers will be individual to the children.

Copymaster answers

Answers will be individual to the children.

Reproduced pupil page

UNIT 15
Conjunctions

Conjunctions are words we use to join sentences.
The conjunction we use most is **and**.

When you make one sentence, you only need one capital letter and one full stop.

Sentence 1:
Mary picked an apple.

Sentence 2:
She ate it.

We can use **and** to join the two sentences:
Mary picked an apple **and** she ate it.

GRAMMAR *Focus*

Use and to join these pairs of sentences.
Write them in your book

1 The cat ran after the bird.
It flew away.
2 It rained all night.
The road was flooded.
3 The boy threw a stone.
The window was broken.
4 The day was very hot.
We went for a swim.

36

GRAMMAR *Practice*

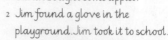

Pronouns are 'he, she, it, they'.

A Copy these sentences.
Change the red words into **pronouns**.

1 Sarah went to the shop.
Sarah bought some apples.
2 Jim found a glove in the
playground. Jim took it to school.
3 The children forgot their bags.
The children were late for school.
4 The mouse saw the cat.
The mouse ran into a hole.

B Join each pair of sentences from part A with and.

GRAMMAR *Extension*

Remember, one capital letter and one full stop for each sentence.

A Write two short sentences about each picture.

B Join each pair of sentences from part A with and.

37

---

see Glossary, page 11 –
Conjunctions

Previous work

None

Pupil Book answers

Focus

1 The cat ran after the bird **and** it flew away.
2 It rained all night **and** the road was flooded.
3 The boy threw a stone **and** the window was broken.
4 The day was very hot **and** we went for a swim.

Practice

A

1 Sarah went to the shop. **She** bought some apples.
2 Jim found a glove in the playground. **He** took it to school.
3 The children forgot their bags. **They** were late for school.
4 The mouse saw the cat. **It** ran into a hole.

B

1 Sarah went to the shop **and** she bought some apples.
2 Jim found a glove in the playground **and** he took it to school.
3 The children forgot their bags **and** they were late for school.
4 The mouse saw the cat **and** it ran into a hole.

Extension

A

Answers will be individual to the children, for example:
1 *The bird is on the nest. It is sitting on some eggs.*
2 *The girl is drinking tea. She is reading the newspaper.*
3 *The girl kicked the ball. It went into the net.*
4 *The boy has a sandwich. He is eating it.*

B

Answers will be individual to the children, for example:
1 *The bird is on the nest **and** it is sitting on some eggs.*
2 *The girl is drinking tea **and** she is reading the newspaper.*
3 *The girl kicked the ball **and** it went into the net.*
4 *The boy has a sandwich **and** he is eating it.*

Copymaster answers

A

1 <u>Last night it was very windy</u> and <u>the fence has blown down</u>.
2 <u>We had pasta for lunch</u> and <u>I ate it all</u>.
3 <u>On hot days we go to the seaside</u> and <u>we swim in the sea</u>.
4 <u>The dog barked at the postwoman</u> and <u>she dropped the letters</u>.
5 <u>I fell over</u> and <u>I hurt my knee</u>.

B

1 It rained all day **and** I got wet going to school.
2 The football went over the wall **and** we couldn't find it.
3 Two boys in our class are very tall **and** they both have brown hair.

UNIT 16

Verbs

Verbs are doing words or 'active' words.

Tammy walks quickly.

Walks tells us what Tammy does.
Verbs can be put into families.
The name of a verb family starts with **to**.

Family name	Verbs in the family
to walk	walk walks walking walked
to play	play plays playing played

GRAMMAR *Focus*

Write these **verb family names** in your book.

to look	to jump	to brush

Write each **verb** from the box under the correct family name.

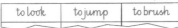

brushed looked jumps
looking jumped
brushed jumping brushes

38

GRAMMAR *Practice*

Copy these sentences.
Choose the right **verb** to finish each sentence.

1 Jim is run/running in a race.
2 Is your dad fish/fishing today?
3 We go/going to the shops every Saturday.
4 I am try/trying my best.
5 Did you put/putting the box on the table?

GRAMMAR *Extension*

A Write three **verbs** to go with each of these verb families.

1 to leap   2 to bang
3 to talk   4 to paint
5 to pray   6 to cook
7 to wish   8 to scratch

B Write the family names of these **verbs**.

1 counted   2 catches
3 drops   4 finding
5 shouted   6 sweeps

39

---

see Glossary, page 14 – Verbs

Previous work

Workbook 1
page 8 page 9 page 14 page 15
Workbook 2
page 8 page 9 page 14 page 15
Book A
pages 12/13 pages 16/17 pages 26/27 pages 38/39
Book 1
pages 26/27 pages 30/31

Pupil Book answers

Focus

TO LOOK	TO JUMP	TO BRUSH
looked	jumped	brushed
looking	jumping	brushes
	jumps	

Practice

1 Jim is **running** in a race.
2 Is your Dad **fishing** today?
3 We **go** to the shops every Saturday.
4 I am **trying** my best.
5 Did you **put** the box on the table?

Extension

A
1 leaping   leaps   leap
2 banging   bangs   banged
3 talking   talks   talked
4 painting   paints   painted
5 praying   prays   prayed
6 cooking   cooks   cooked
7 wishing   wishes   wished
8 scratching scratches scratched

B
1 to count 2 to catch 3 to drop
4 to find   5 to shout 6 to sweep

Copymaster answers

A
1 I like **to go** to the zoo.
2 **To write** neatly you must take your time.
3 If you want **to read** you must go somewhere quiet.
4 I would like **to live** in Australia.
5 I need **to find** my ticket.

B
Answers will be individual to the children, for example:
1 *rolls*   *rolled*   *rolling*
2 *picks*   *picked*   *picking*
3 *wanders*   *wandered*   *wandering*

C
1 to come
2 to find
3 to dig
4 to skip
5 to hope

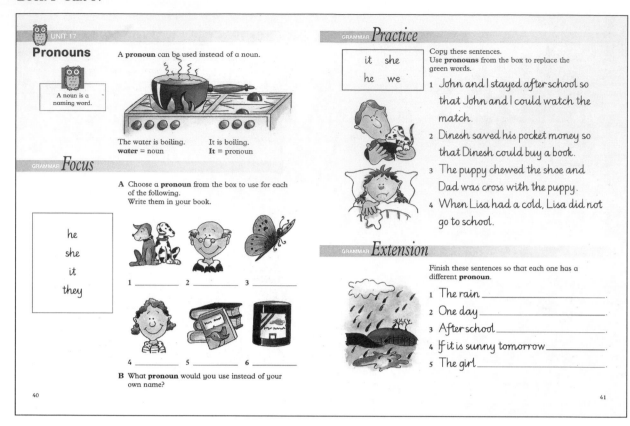

Book 1 Unit 17

UNIT 17
Pronouns

A **pronoun** can be used instead of a noun.

A noun is a
naming word.

The water is boiling.   It is boiling.
water = noun   **It** = pronoun

GRAMMAR *Focus*

A Choose a **pronoun** from the box to use for each
of the following.
Write them in your book.

he
she
it
they

1 _____   2 _____   3 _____

4 _____   5 _____   6 _____

B What **pronoun** would you use instead of your
own name?

40

GRAMMAR *Practice*

it   she
he   we

Copy these sentences.
Use **pronouns** from the box to replace the
green words.

1 John and I stayed after school so
that John and I could watch the
match.

2 Dinesh saved his pocket money so
that Dinesh could buy a book.

3 The puppy chewed the shoe and
Dad was cross with the puppy.

4 When Lisa had a cold, Lisa did not
go to school.

GRAMMAR *Extension*

Finish these sentences so that each one has a
different **pronoun**.

1 The rain _____.
2 One day _____.
3 After school _____.
4 If it is sunny tomorrow _____.
5 The girl _____.

41

---

see Glossary, page 12 – Pronouns

Previous work

Book 1
pages 14/15

Pupil Book answers

Focus

A
1 they   **2** he   **3** it
4 she   **5** they   **6** it

B
*Answers will depend on the gender of
the child, i.e. either 'he' or 'she'.*

Practice

1 John and I stayed after school so
that **we** could watch the match.
2 Dinesh saved his pocket money
so that **he** could buy a book.
3 The puppy chewed the shoe and
Dad was cross with **it**.
4 When Lisa had a cold, **she** did
not go to school.

Extension

*Answers will be individual to the
children, for example:*
1 *The rain was heavy and **it** lasted all
day.*
2 *One day **they** went to the zoo.*
3 *After school the girls went home and
they had their tea.*

4 *If it is sunny tomorrow **we** will have
a picnic.*
5 *The girl got off the bus and **she**
walked home.*

Copymaster answers

A
1 When Aziz eats jelly <u>he</u> makes a
mess.
2 I can never find my key when I
need <u>it</u>.
3 <u>We</u> must mend the broken
window.
4 <u>They</u> come to collect the rubbish
on Wednesday.
5 The floor is dirty and <u>it</u> needs
washing.

B
1 When my brother and I get our
pocket money **we** go to the
shops.
2 Sara has a bicycle and **she** cycles
to school.
3 Simon likes chocolate and **he** eats
it every day.
4 When the girls play netball **they**
like to win.

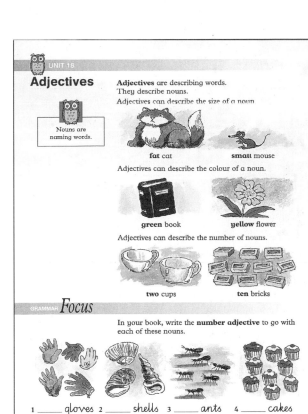

UNIT 18

Adjectives

Nouns are naming words.

Adjectives are describing words.
They describe nouns.

Adjectives can describe the size of a noun.

fat cat **small** mouse

Adjectives can describe the colour of a noun.

green book **yellow** flower

Adjectives can describe the number of nouns.

two cups **ten** bricks

GRAMMAR *Focus*

In your book, write the **number adjective** to go with
each of these nouns.

1 _____ gloves 2 _____ shells 3 _____ ants 4 _____ cakes

42

GRAMMAR *Practice*

Copy the sentences below.
Underline the **number adjective** in blue.
Underline the **colour adjective** in red.

1 I saw five white swans on the lake.
2 There are seven blue cups on the shelf.
3 Will you buy six red apples?
4 I need three black buttons.
5 Ten green bottles were standing on the wall.

GRAMMAR *Extension*

Look at this picture.

Write some sentences to describe the picture.
Use at least three **number adjectives** and three
colour adjectives.

43

---

see Glossary, page 9 – Adjectives

Previous work

Workbook 1
page 6
page 7
page 13

Workbook 2
page 6
page 7
page 13

Book A
pages 8/9
pages 10/11
pages 28/29
pages 44/45

Book 1
pages 6/7
pages 22/23
pages 34/35

Pupil Book answers

Focus

1 **five** gloves 2 **three** shells
3 **six** ants 4 **nine** cakes

Practice

NUMBER ADJECTIVES	COLOUR ADJECTIVES
1 five	white
2 seven	blue
3 six	red
4 three	black
5 ten	green

Extension

Answers will be individual to the children, for example:
1 *There are **two white** swans on the lake.*
2 ***Four red** flowers are growing by the tree.*
3 ***Three blue** birds are flying over the water.*

Copymaster answers

A

1 one	2 two
3 three	4 four
5 five	6 six
7 seven	8 eight
9 nine	10 ten

B

1 There are <u>sixteen</u> apples on the tree.
2 This plate is <u>two hundred</u> years old.
3 There are <u>eleven</u> players in a football team.
4 We have <u>five</u> cats, <u>two</u> dogs and <u>one</u> hamster.
5 <u>Twenty-five</u> people got on the bus.

C

Answers will be individual to the children, for example:
1 *There are **fifty-two** weeks in a year.*
2 *My big sister is **seventeen** on Tuesday.*

UNIT 19

Conjunctions **Conjunctions** are words we use to join sentences.

The conjunction we use most is **and**.
Give me the rubbish. I will take it outside.
Give me the rubbish and I will take it outside.
Another conjunction we often use is **but**.
The telephone rang. No one answered it.
The telephone rang but no one answered it.

GRAMMAR Focus

Use but to join each pair of sentences to make one sentence. Write the sentences in your book.

1 One of our players was hurt.
We won the match.
2 I wanted a plum.
There were none left.
3 It rained a lot today.
Josh went out to play.
4 The car crashed into the tree.
The driver was not hurt.
5 I have to go to the dentist.
I do not want to.

44

GRAMMAR Practice

A Copy these sentences.
Change the red words into **pronouns**.
1 Fred could not get to sleep.
Fred was not tired the next day.
2 Sean likes oranges. Sean does not want one now.
3 The birds built a nest. The birds did not lay any eggs.
4 My friend and I missed the train.
My friend and I got there on time.

B Use but to join each pair of sentences that you made in Part A.

GRAMMAR Extension

Use and or but to join these pairs of sentences.
1 I have lost the book. I need it.
2 Mike forgot his lunchbox. He was very hungry when he got home.
3 It was a very cold day.
My new coat kept me warm.
4 Naseem likes drawing.
He does not like painting.

45

see Glossary, page 11 – Conjunctions

Previous work

Book 1
pages 36/37

Pupil Book answers

Focus

1 One of our players was hurt **but** we won the match.
2 I wanted a plum **but** there were none left.
3 It rained a lot today **but** Josh went out to play.
4 The car crashed into the tree **but** the driver was not hurt.
5 I have to go to the dentist **but** I do not want to.

Practice

A

1 Fred could not get to sleep. **He** was not tired the next day.
2 Sean likes oranges. **He** does not want one now.
3 The birds built a nest. **They** did not lay any eggs.
4 My friend and I missed the train. **We** got there on time.

B

1 Fred could not get to sleep **but** he was not tired the next day.
2 Sean likes oranges **but** he does not want one now.
3 The birds built a nest **but** they did not lay any eggs.
4 My friend and I missed the train **but** we got there on time.

Extension

1 I have lost the book **but/and** I need it.
2 Mike forgot his lunchbox **and** he was very hungry when he got home.
3 It was a very cold day **but/and** my new coat kept me warm.
4 Naseem likes drawing **but** he does not like painting.

Copymaster answers

A

1 I hate eating sprouts but I have to have them every Sunday.
2 Shobu wanted to go out but it was too wet.
3 The runner hurt his foot but he won the race.
4 You can have an ice-cream now but you can't have one tomorrow.
5 The rain poured down but the old roof didn't leak.

B

1 Please find a pencil **and** bring it to me.
2 Take that glass into the kitchen **but** don't take the other one.
3 My bicycle got stuck in the mud **but** I managed to get it out.

Check-up 3
Nouns

A 1 Write three **nouns** beginning with the letter 's'.
2 Write three **nouns** beginning with the letter 'p'.
B Copy these sentences.
Write the **proper nouns** with capital letters.

1 mrs lock and amy have red coats.
2 My friend is called jabbar.
3 If they break the glass, harry and donna will be in trouble.

Adjectives

A Copy these sentences and fill the gaps with **adjectives**.

1 The _____ dog ran around the _____ garden.
2 Please find a _____ box for these _____ clothes.

B Copy these sentences and use a **colour adjective** to finish each one.

1 The _____ sunset was beautiful.
2 I have a _____ watch.
3 Steve wanted a _____ dog.

C Copy these sentences and complete each one with a **number adjective**.

1 There are _____ days in a week.
2 There are _____ weeks in a year.
3 There are _____ months in a year.

Nouns and adjectives

Write the headings *noun* and *adjective*.
Write the words in this box under the correct headings.

| cold | jug | red | man | purple | bag |
| three | table | big | boot | rain | |

Plurals

Choose the correct word to complete each sentence.

1 There is one comic/comics left.
2 I have two pound/pounds in my purse.
3 There were ten ticket/tickets left to sell.

Prepositions

Write a sentence using each of these **prepositions**.

1 under   2 down   3 inside
4 out   5 in   6 over

Pronouns

Copy these sentences, changing the blue words into **pronouns**.

1 Have you found the key?
2 Mum and I like ice cream.
3 The boys went to the park.
4 The old man walked with a stick.

46   47

Nouns

A

Answers will be individual to the children.

B
1 **M**rs **L**ock and **A**my have red coats.
2 My friend is called **J**abbar.
3 If they break the glass, **H**arry and **D**onna will be in trouble.

Adjectives

A

Answers will be individual to the children, for example:
1 *The **young** dog ran around the **big** garden.*
2 *Please find a **strong** box for these **old** clothes.*

B

Answers will be individual to the children, for example:
1 *The **orange** sunset was beautiful.*
2 *I have a **silver** watch.*
3 *Steve wanted a **brown** dog.*

C
1 There are **seven** days in a week.
2 There are **fifty-two** weeks in a year.
3 There are **twelve** months in a year.

Nouns and adjectives

NOUN	ADJECTIVE
jug	cold
man	red
bag	purple
table	three
boot	big
rain	

Plurals

1 There is one **comic** left.
2 I have two **pounds** in my purse.
3 There were ten **tickets** left to sell.

Prepositions

Answers will be individual to the children.

Pronouns

1 Have you found **it**?
2 **We** like ice cream.
3 **They** went to the park.
4 **He** walked with a stick.

Confusing words

Choose the correct word to complete each sentence.

1 I have to/two days to finish this work.

2 It is time to/two go out.

Simple sentences

A Put the words in the right order to make **sentences**.

1 fire. on The was house

2 go have out. I to

B Finish each sentence with a **full stop** or a **question mark**.

1 How are you today

2 My hand hurts

Conjunctions

Join each pair of sentences using and or but.

1 You can play in the snow. You must put on your coat.

2 The bird pecked at the ground. It found a worm.

Verbs

A Fill each gap with a **verb**.

1 Liz ＿＿＿ the book.

2 The badger ＿＿＿ into its hole.

B Write the **family name** of each **verb**.
1 talking   2 crying   3 makes

C Write two **verbs** to go with each **family name**.
1 to grow   2 to clean   3 to laugh

48

Confusing words

1 I have **two** days to finish this work.
2 It is time **to** go out.

Simple sentences

A
1 The house was on fire.
2 I have to go out.

B
1 How are you today**?**
2 My hand hurts**.**

Conjunctions

1 You can play in the snow **but** you must put on your coat.
2 The bird pecked at the ground **and** it found a worm.

Verbs

A
Answers will be individual to the children, for example:
1 *Liz **reads** the book.*
2 *The badger **runs** into its hole.*

B
1 to talk   2 to cry   3 to make

C
Children should have selected from the following possible answers:
1 *growing   grows   grew*
2 *cleaning   cleans   cleaned*
3 *laughing   laughs   laughed*

Book 2 – Contents/Scope and Sequence

Page/Unit		Focus	Practice
4/5	Unit 1	proper nouns – writing place names with capital letters	identifying place names
6/7	Unit 2	adjectives - making comparatives with 'er'	cloze – completing sentences with comparative adjectives
8/9	Unit 3	confusing words – using two/too	using to/too
10/11	Unit 4	conjunctions – joining sentences with 'so' and 'because'	changing nouns and proper nouns into pronouns and joining sentences
12/13	Unit 5	verbs – identifying and using present-tense verbs	changing verb family names into present-tense verbs
14/15	Unit 6	proper nouns – writing days and months	choosing day/month to complete sentences
16/17	Unit 7	verbs – cloze with present-tense verbs	choosing the correct form of the verb 'to be' to complete sentences
18/19		*Check-up 1*	*Check-up 1*
20/21	Unit 8	verbs – identifying present-tense verbs	replacing the verb family name with a present-tense verb
22/23	Unit 9	adjectives – forming superlatives	cloze – using superlatives
24/25	Unit 10	contractions – identifying contractions	expanding contractions, writing contractions
26/27	Unit 11	adverbs – identifying adverbs in sentences	classifying adverbs – how, when and where
28/29	Unit 12	prepositions – completing sentences with prepositions	writing sentences to show position
30/31	Unit 13	articles – use of 'a' and 'an'	identifying correct usage
32/33		*Check-up 2*	*Check-up 2*
34/35	Unit 14	verbs – identifying simple past-tense verbs in sentences	changing present tense to past tense in sentences
36/37	Unit 15	confusing words – identifying were/where, there/their	using where/were/we're, there/their
38/39	Unit 16	singular and plural – adding 'es'	completing a singular and plural table
40/41	Unit 17	adverbs – identifying adverb pairs	adverb pairs to improve sentences
42/43	Unit 18	verbs – matching present- and past-tense verbs	changing present-tense verbs to past tense in sentences
44/45	Unit 19	sentences – adding capital letters and full stops and identifying the verb	cloze – adding verbs to make sentences
46/48		*Check-up 3*	*Check-up 3*

Extension	Copymaster	Page/Unit	
completing sentences with proper nouns	place names	4/5	Unit 1
identifying comparatives, writing sentences	regular comparative adjectives	6/7	Unit 2
using to/too/two	using to/too/two	8/9	Unit 3
using 'and', 'but', 'so', 'because'	using 'and', 'but', 'so', 'because'	10/11	Unit 4
completing a verb table, writing sentences	using present-tense verbs	12/13	Unit 5
special days and festivals	days and months	14/15	Unit 6
correcting sentences – mistakes in noun/verb agreement	using the present tense – verb 'to be'	16/17	Unit 7
Check-up 1	*Check-up 1*	18/19	
completing a verb table, adding 'ing'	using the present tense – verb 'to be' plus 'ing'	20/21	Unit 8
completing a verb table, using superlatives	comparative and superlative adjectives	22/23	Unit 9
identifying more contractions	identifying and using contractions	24/25	Unit 10
completing sentences with adverbs, using adverbs	identifying how, when and where	26/27	Unit 11
correct usage	preposition wordsearch	28/29	Unit 12
'an' with silent 'h', 'a' before 'u' and 'eu' = 'y' sound	using the indefinite article	30/31	Unit 13
Check-up 2	*Check-up 2*	32/33	
completing a verb table	using simple past-tense verbs	34/35	Unit 14
choosing to/two/too, there/their, where/were/we're	where/were/we're	36/37	Unit 15
identifying 'es' words from written clues	plurals with 's' and 'es'	38/39	Unit 16
adverbs and adverb pairs to improve story writing	identifying and using adverb pairs	40/41	Unit 17
irregular past-tense verbs	present- and past-tense verbs	42/43	Unit 18
adding past-tense verbs, writing sentences	importance of verbs in sentences	44/45	Unit 19
Check-up 3	*Check-up 3*	46/48	

Improve your writing copymasters
1 using adjectives
2 using prepositions
3 using proper nouns and pronouns
4 using interesting verbs
5 using conjunctions
6 using adverbs
7 using adjectives and adverbs

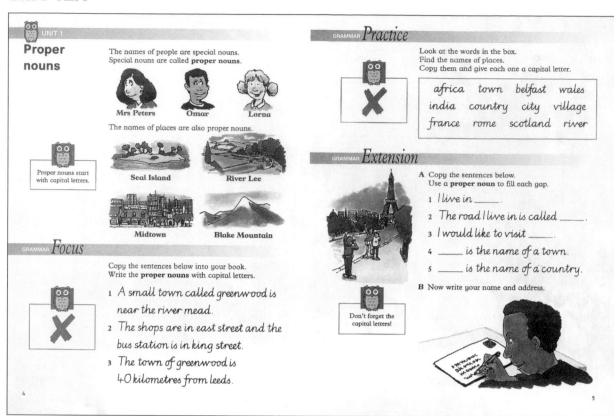

see Glossary, page 11 – Nouns

Previous work

Workbook 1
page 4
page 5
page 12
page 13

Workbook 2
page 4
page 5
page 12
page 13

Book A
pages 6/7
pages 10/11
pages 22/23
pages 36/37
pages 40/41

Book 1
pages 4/5
pages 12/13
pages 20/21

Pupil Book answers

Focus

1 A small town called **G**reenwood is near the **R**iver **M**ead.
2 The shops are in **E**ast **S**treet and the bus station is in **K**ing **S**treet.
3 The town of **G**reenwood is 40 kilometres from **L**eeds.

Practice

Africa   Belfast   Wales   India   France   Rome   Scotland

Extension

A and **B**
Answers will be individual to the children.

Copymaster answers

Answers will be individual to the children.

Adjectives

Adjectives are describing words.
They tell us more about a person or thing.

Colours and
numbers can be
adjectives as well.

enormous elephant   **old** car

We can also use adjectives to describe the difference
between two things.

big bottle   **bigger** bottle   **small** bicycle   **smaller** bicycle

Words like 'bigger' and 'smaller' are called
comparative adjectives.

Focus

Copy the sentences below into your book.
Add *er* to the end of each **adjective**.

1 This hill is (high) than that one.
2 My hands are (clean) than yours.
3 My radio is (loud) than yours.
4 This bread is (fresh) than those rolls.
5 It is (cold) today than it was
   yesterday.
6 Is the river (deep) than the pond?

6

Practice

faster
higher
warmer
harder

Copy the sentences below.
Fill each gap with a **comparative adjective** from
the box.

1 I can jump _____ than you.
2 This new car goes _____ than our
   old one.
3 It was _____ to cycle up the hill than
   it was to cycle down.
4 When the weather gets _____ than it
   has been lately, you can wear shorts.

Extension

Comparative
adjectives compare
things.

A Copy the words from the box.
Underline all the **comparative adjectives**.

cold	straight	thicker	softer
sharp	smooth	colder	straighter
great	thick	greater	soft
small	smoother	sharper	smaller

B Use these **comparative adjectives** in sentences
of your own.

1 weaker   2 shorter   3 damper
4 darker   5 lower   6 tighter

7

---

see Glossary, page 9 – Adjectives

Previous work

Workbook 1
page 6
page 7
page 13

Workbook 2
page 6
page 7
page 13

Book A
pages 8/9
pages 10/11
pages 28/29
pages 44/45

Book 1
pages 6/7
pages 22/23
pages 34/35
pages 42/43

Pupil Book answers

Focus

1 This hill is high**er** than that one.
2 My hands are clean**er** than yours.
3 My radio is loud**er** than yours.
4 This bread is fresh**er** than those
   rolls.
5 It is cool**er** today than it was
   yesterday.
6 Is the river deep**er** than the
   pond?

Practice

1 I can jump **higher** than you.
2 This new car goes **faster** than
   our old one.
3 It was **harder** to cycle up the hill
   than it was to cycle down.
4 When the weather gets **warmer**
   than it has been lately, you can
   wear shorts.

Extension

A

cold	straight	<u>thicker</u>	<u>softer</u>
sharp	smooth	<u>colder</u>	<u>straighter</u>
great	thick	<u>greater</u>	soft
small	smoother	sharper	smaller

B
*Answers will be individual to the
children.*

Copymaster answers

A

1 The people waited on the
   <u>crowded</u> platform.
2 The train was <u>late</u>.
3 "It was **later** than this yesterday,"
   said one man.
4 "We need a **faster** train," said
   another.
5 "It doesn't matter," one
   passenger said. "Even if the train
   is <u>late</u>, it is **quicker** than walking.

B

ADJECTIVE	COMPARATIVE ADJECTIVE
soft	**softer**
strong	**stronger**
large	**larger**
great	**greater**
sharp	**sharper**
old	**older**
bright	**brighter**

C
*Answers will be individual to the
children.*

UNIT 3

Confusing words

'Two' written as a number is 2.

It is easy to mix up the words **two**, **to** and **too**.

We use **two** as a number:
In two days it will be my birthday.

We use **to** like this:
I am going to the park.

To is also part of a verb family name, like:
to play   to fall   to eat

We use **too** to mean 'as well'.
I am having a cake too.
We had some presents too.

Too can also mean that we can't do something:
This hill is too hard for me to climb.
These books are too heavy for me to carry.

GRAMMAR *Focus*

Copy the sentences below into your book.
Fill each gap with *two* or *too*.

1 Please find _____ pencils for me.
2 I have _____ letters to post.
3 It is _____ far to walk to the shops.
4 It is _____ late to go out.
5 I would like an ice lolly _____ .
6 If we go to the shop, my sister wants to come _____ .

8

GRAMMAR *Practice*

Copy these sentences.
Fill each gap with *to* or *too*.

1 I want _____ play the piano.
2 I would like to play the piano _____ .
3 Do you think it will be _____ hard to learn?
4 You can learn if you really want _____ .

GRAMMAR *Extension*

A Copy these sentences.
Fill the gaps with *two*, *to* and *too*.

1 The _____ times table is easy.
2 I am going _____ a party today.
3 I am _____ tired _____ stay up late.
4 If you get _____ many wrong you will have _____ learn it again.
5 I made _____ mistakes.

B This sentence uses the words **two**, **to** and **too**:
The two dogs ran to the tree but it was too hard to climb.

Now make up your own sentence using *two*, *to* and *too*.

9

---

see Glossary, page 10 – Confusing words

Previous work

Book 1
pages 16/17

Pupil Book answers

Focus

1 Please find **two** pencils for me.
2 I have **two** letters to post.
3 It is **too** far to walk to the shops.
4 It is **too** late to go out.
5 I would like an ice lolly **too**.
6 If we go to the shop, my sister wants to come **too**.

Practice

1 I want **to** play the piano.
2 I would like to play the piano **too**.
3 Do you think it will be **too** hard to learn?
4 You can learn if you really want **to**.

Extension

A
1 The **two** times table is easy.
2 I am going **to** a party today.
3 I am **too** tired **to** stay up late.
4 If you get **too** many wrong you will have **to** learn it again.
5 I made **two** mistakes.

B
Answers will be individual to the children, for example:
On the way **to** school, the **two** boys ate **too** many cakes.

Copymaster answers

A

1 **Two** and **two** make four.
2 There are **too** many flowers in this vase.
3 Go **to** bed and read your book.
4 You must find out where we have **to** go.
5 I would like some cake **too**.
6 I you eat **too** many sweets you will have **to** go **to** the dentist.
7 I am taking **two** pounds **to** the shops **to** buy some fruit.
8 You can pack **two** pairs of shoes but you must make sure your case is not **too** heavy.

B
Answers will be individual to the children.

UNIT 4
Conjunctions

Conjunctions are words we use to join sentences.

The conjunctions **and** and **but** are often used to join sentences.

> I like chocolate cake **and** I ate a large slice.
> I like chocolate cake **but** was I too full to eat any more.

Two other useful conjunctions are **because** and **so**.

Conjunctions stick sentences together.

I don't eat liver. I don't like it.
I don't eat liver **because** I don't like it.

Put the chairs on the table. I can sweep the floor.
Put the chairs on the table **so** I can sweep the floor.

GRAMMAR *Focus*

Use *because* or *so* to join each pair of sentences to make one sentence. Write the sentences in your book.

1 Take a coat. It might rain later.
2 I climbed the tree. I could see over the roof.
3 The lion prowls around. It is hungry.
4 Close the gate. The dog will not get out.

10

GRAMMAR *Practice*

Remember, pronouns are: I, he, she, it, we, they.

A Copy the sentences.
Change the brown words into **pronouns**.

1 My brother and I woke up early. My brother and I heard a bird singing.
2 The football fans cheered. The football fans saw their team score a goal.
3 Liam lost the key. Liam could not unlock the door.

B Join each pair of sentences that you have made with *because* or *so*.

GRAMMAR *Extension*

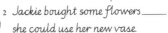

and   so
but   because

Use a **conjunction** from the box to complete each of these sentences.

1 Find a cloth ____ wipe the table.
2 Jackie bought some flowers ____ she could use her new vase.
3 I want to go home ____ it is time to eat.
4 The door was locked ____ the window was open.

11

---

see Glossary, page 11 –
Conjunctions

Previous work

Book A

pages 36/37
pages 44/45

Pupil Book answers

Focus

1 Take a coat **because** it might rain later.
2 I climbed the tree **so** I could see over the roof.
3 The lion prowls around **because** it is hungry.
4 Close the gate **so** the dog will not get out.

Practice

A

1 My brother and I woke up early. **We** heard a bird singing.
2 The football fans cheered. **They** saw their team score a goal.
3 Liam lost the key. **He** could not unlock the door.

B

1 My brother and I woke up early **because** we heard a bird singing.
2 The football fans cheered **because** they saw their team score a goal.
3 Liam lost the key **so** he could not unlock the door.

Extension

1 Find a cloth **and** wipe the table.
2 Jackie bought some flowers **so** she could use her new vase.
3 I want to go home **because** it is time to eat.
4 The door was locked **but** the window was open.

Copymaster answers

A

1 Ella wanted her tea early **because she** was hungry.
2 Kerry wanted to put her boots on **but she** could not find them.
3 The snake slithered along the ground **and it** hid under a rock.

B

Answers will be individual to the children.

73

UNIT 5
Verbs

'Tense' means 'time'.

Verbs are doing or active words.

When we use verbs to tell us about something that is happening now, we use the **present tense**.

The car speeds down the street.
The traffic lights change to red.

GRAMMAR *Practice*

Copy the sentences below.
Change each verb family name to a **present tense verb**.

1 The train (to pull) into the station.
2 The people (to get) off when it has stopped.
3 They (to meet) their friends.
4 The train (to leave) the station.

GRAMMAR *Focus*

A Copy the sentences below into your book.
Underline the **present tense verbs**.

1 I ride my bike.
2 The chain squeaks.
3 The pedals stop.
4 I push my bike.

chimes
walks
live
checks

B Use a **present tense verb** from the box to finish each sentence.

1 Kirsty _____ to school.
2 The teacher _____ the homework.
3 The clock _____ every hour.
4 Rabbits _____ in holes.

12

GRAMMAR *Extension*

A Copy the table.
Fill in the missing words.

Family name	Present tense
to know	I _____
	he _____
to _____	we climb
	she _____
_____ give	it _____
	they give
to sleep	you _____
	she _____

B 1 Choose three **verb family names** from the table and use them in sentences of your own.
2 Choose three **present tense verbs** from the table and use them in sentences of your own.

13

see Glossary, page 14 – Verbs

Previous work

Workbook 1

page 8
page 9
page 14
page 15

Workbook 2

page 8
page 9
page 14
page 15

Book A

pages 12/13
pages 16/17
pages 26/27
pages 38/39

Book 1

pages 26/27
pages 30/31
pages 38/39

Pupil Book answers

Focus
A
1 I <u>ride</u> my bike.
2 The chain <u>squeaks</u>.
3 The pedals <u>stop</u>.
4 I <u>push</u> my bike.

B
1 Kirsty **walks** to school.
2 The teacher **checks** the homework.
3 The clock **chimes** every hour.
4 Rabbits **live** in holes.

Practice
1 The train **pulls** into the station.
2 The people **get** off when it has stopped.
3 They **meet** their friends.
4 The train **leaves** the station.

Extension
A

FAMILY NAME	PRESENT TENSE
to know	I **know**
	he **knows**
to **climb**	we climb
	she **climbs**
to give	it **gives**
	they give
to sleep	you **sleep**
	she **sleeps**

B
Answers will be individual to the children.

Copymaster answers

Answers will be individual to the children.

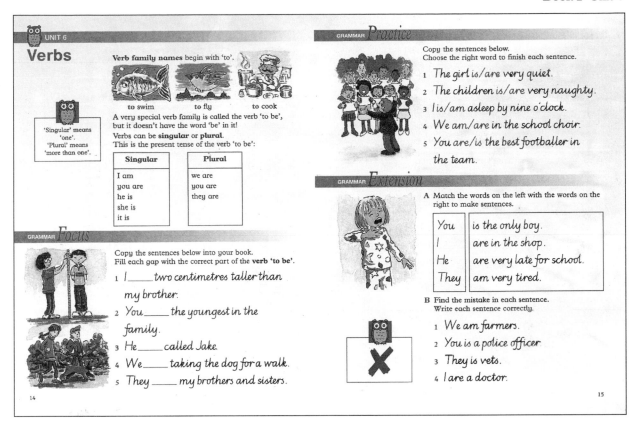

see Glossary, page 14 – Verbs

Previous work

Workbook 1	Workbook 2
page 8	page 8
page 9	page 9
page 14	page 14
page 15	page 15

Book A	Book 1
pages 12/13	pages 26/27
pages 16/17	pages 30/31
pages 26/27	pages 38/39
pages 38/39	

Book 2	
pages 12/13	

Pupil Book answers

Focus
1 I **am** two centimetres taller than my brother.
2 You **are** the youngest in the family.
3 He **is** called Jake.
4 We **are** taking the dog for a walk.
5 They **are** my brothers and sisters.

Practice
1 The girl **is** very quiet.
2 The children **are** very naughty.
3 I **am** asleep by nine o'clock.
4 We **are** in the school choir.
5 You **are** the best footballer in the team.

Extension
A
You are in the shop. *or* You are very late for school.
I am very tired
He is the only boy.
You are in the shop. *or* You are very late for school.

B
1 We **are** farmers.
2 You **are** a police officer.
3 They **are** vets.
4 I **am** a doctor.

Copymaster answers

A
1 He is very cold today. *or* He is asleep.
2 I am in the garden.
3 They are very muddy. *or* They are lost.
4 We are very muddy. *or* We are lost.
5 It is very cold today. *or* It is asleep.

B
1 I **am** going to join the school choir.
2 The dog **is** black and white.
3 You and I **are** best friends.
4 The postwoman and the milkman **are** up early every morning.
5 Sophie said, "I **am** the smallest girl in the class."
6 Louise **is** captain of the hockey team.

UNIT 7

Proper nouns

The names of people and places are **proper nouns**.
Proper nouns have capital letters.

Fatima   Sankha   United
Kingdom

Days of the week and months of the year are also
proper nouns.

Wednesday   Saturday   February

GRAMMAR *Focus*

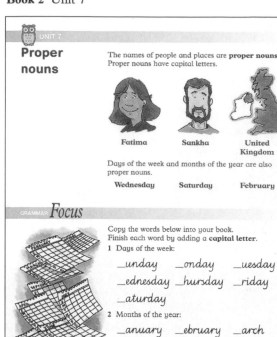

Copy the words below into your book.
Finish each word by adding a **capital letter**.

1 Days of the week:

_unday   _onday   _uesday
_ednesday _hursday   _riday
_aturday

2 Months of the year:

_anuary   _ebruary   _arch
_pril   _ay   _une
_uly   _ugust   _eptember
_ctober   _ovember   _ecember

16

GRAMMAR *Practice*

Copy the sentences below.
Use a day of the week or a month of the year to fill
each gap.

1 ____ is the first month of the year.
2 ____ is the last month of the year.
3 ____ comes after Monday.
4 ____ and ____ are called the weekend.
5 ____ is the third month of the year.
6 ____ is the middle of the week.

GRAMMAR *Extension*

Special days like festivals are also **proper nouns**:
Christmas   New Year's Eve   Ramadan

Copy these sentences.
Use capital letters for the **proper nouns**.

1 christmas day is on 25th december.
2 The 1st of january is new year's day.
3 st david's day is an important day in wales.
4 The festival of hanukkah is in december.

17

---

see Glossary, page 11 – Nouns

Previous work

Workbook 1	Workbook 2
page 4	page 4
page 5	page 5
page 12	page 12
page 13	page 13
Book A	**Book 1**
pages 6/7	pages 4/5
pages 10/11	pages 12/13
pages 22/23	pages 20/21
pages 36/37	
pages 40/41	
Book 2	
pages 4/5	

Pupil Book answers

Focus

1 **S**unday   **M**onday   **T**uesday
  Wednesday **T**hursday **F**riday
  Saturday
2 **J**anuary   **F**ebruary **M**arch
  April   **M**ay   **J**une
  July   **A**ugust   **S**eptember
  October   **N**ovember **D**ecember

Practice

1 **January** is the first month of the year.
2 **December** is the last month of the year.
3 **Tuesday** comes after Monday.
4 **Saturday** and **Sunday** are called the weekend.
5 **March** is the third month of the year.
6 **Wednesday** is the middle of the week.

Extension

1 **C**hristmas **D**ay is on the 25th **D**ecember.
2 The 1st of **J**anuary is **N**ew **Y**ear's **D**ay.

3 **S**t **D**avid's **D**ay is an important day in **W**ales.
4 The festival of **H**anukkah is in **D**ecember.

Copymaster answers

A

Saturday	Tuesday	Friday
Monday	Thursday	Wednesday
Sunday		

B

January	**February**	March
April	May	**June**
July	**August**	September
October	November	**December**

Check-up 1

Proper nouns

Copy these sentences into your book.
Write the **proper nouns** with capital letters.

1 I am going sailing on the river dee on tuesday.
2 The bus only goes to bangor on saturday.
3 We are going to america in july.

Adjectives

Copy and complete the **comparative adjectives** in this table.

This torch is bright.	That torch is _____ .
This coat is old.	That coat is _____ .
This road is long.	That road is _____ .
This man is strong.	That man is _____ .
This bag is light.	That bag is _____ .

Confusing words

Copy the sentences below.
Choose the right word to finish each sentence.

1 It is to/too late to go out.
2 I have got too/two minutes too/to catch the bus.
3 Can I come to/too?
4 The dog likes to/two bury his bone.

Conjunctions

Join each pair of sentences with a **conjunction**.

1 I hurt my hand. I cannot write.
2 The girls played very well. They won the netball match.
3 I did not feel well. I had a headache.
4 Alex was late. He missed the bus.

Verbs

A Copy the sentences below.
Change each verb family name to a **present tense verb**.

1 The tree (to grow) near the river.
2 People (to visit) the castle.
3 The owl (to hunt) at night.
4 He (to eat) cereal for breakfast.
5 She (to read) her book in bed.

B Copy the sentences below.
Choose the right word to finish each sentence.

1 The boys am/are on bicycles.
2 Some people is/are fond of animals.
3 Our cat am/is lost.
4 My brother and I is/are in the team.

18

19

Proper nouns

1 I am going sailing on the **River Dee** on **Tuesday**.
2 The bus only goes to **Bangor** on **Saturday**.
3 We are going to **America** in **July**.

Adjectives

That torch is **brighter**.
That coat is **older**.
That road is **longer**.
That man is **stronger**.
This bag is **lighter**.

Confusing words

1 It is **too** late to go out.
2 I have got **two** minutes **to** catch the bus.
3 Can I come **too**?
4 The dog likes **to** bury his bone.

Conjunctions

1 I hurt my hand **so/and** I cannot write.
2 The girls played very well **and/so** they won the netball match.
3 I did not feel well **because/and** I had a headache.
4 Alex was late **so/because/and** he missed the bus.

Verbs

A
1 The tree **grows** near the river.
2 People **visit** the castle.
3 The owl **hunts** at night.
4 She **reads** her book in bed.

B
1 The boys **are** on bicycles.
2 Some people **are** fond of animals.
3 Our cat **is** lost.
4 My brother and I **are** in the team.

UNIT 8

Verbs

This present tense tells you about an action that is still going on.

The verb 'to be' is a helper verb.

The **present tense** of a verb tells you about something that is happening now.

The dog **barks**. The girl **runs**.

Sometimes we need more than one verb to make a sentence work.

Another way to make the present tense is like this:

verb 'to be'	+ verb	+ ing	
I am	+ eat	+ ing	= I am eating.
You are	+ walk	+ ing	= You are walking.
He is	+ look	+ ing	= He is looking.
She is	+ draw	+ ing	= She is drawing.
It is	+ bark	+ ing	= It is barking.
We are	+ talk	+ ing	= We are talking.
You are	+ stand	+ ing	= You are standing.
They are	+ cry	+ ing	= They are crying.

GRAMMAR *Focus*

Copy the sentences below into your book.
Underline the two words in each sentence that make up the **present tense verb**.

1 The blackbirds are building a nest.
2 The cow is eating the grass.
3 I am walking to school.
4 The gate is swinging in the wind.
5 The boy is kicking a stone.

20

GRAMMAR *Practice*

Use the helper verb 'to be' and an 'ing' word.

Copy these sentences.
Replace each verb family name with the **present tense verb**.

1 Ann (to lick) her ice cream.
2 The mouse (to sniff) the cheese.
3 We (to play) in the park.
4 I (to read) my comic.

GRAMMAR *Extension*

Watch your spelling! You need to knock off the 'e' at the end of a word before adding 'ing'.

A Copy the table.
Fill in the missing words.

Verb family name	Present tense
to watch	he is _____
_____ buy	we are _____
to wake	you are _____
_____ _____	They _____ striking
to look	it _____ _____
_____ fall	I _____ _____

Watch your spelling!

B Add ing to each of these words.

1 wish 2 hit 3 run 4 like
5 put 6 grow 7 start 8 shine

C Add each of the words you made in part B to the verb 'to be' to make sentences of your own.

21

---

see Glossary, page 14 – Verbs

Previous work

Workbook 1	Workbook 2
page 8	page 8
page 9	page 9
page 14	page 14
page 15	page 15

Book A	Book 1
pages 12/13	pages 26/27
pages 16/17	pages 30/31
pages 26/27	pages 38/39
pages 38/39	

Book 2	
pages 12/13	
pages 14/15	

Pupil Book answers

Focus

1 The blackbirds <u>are building</u> a nest.
2 The cow <u>is eating</u> the grass.
3 I <u>am walking</u> to school.
4 The gate <u>is swinging</u> in the wind.
5 The boy <u>is kicking</u> a stone.

Practice

1 Ann **is licking** her ice cream.
2 The mouse **is sniffing** the cheese.
3 We **are playing** in the park.
4 I **am reading** my comic.

Extension

A

VERB FAMILY NAME	PRESENT TENSE
to watch	he is **watching**
to buy	we are **buying**
to wake	you are **waking**
to strike	they **are** striking
to look	it **is looking**
to fall	I **am falling**

B

1 wishing 2 hitting
3 running 4 liking
5 putting 6 growing
7 starting 8 shining

C
Answers will be individual to the children.

Copymaster answers

A

2 If you **are going** to the library, will you take back my book?
3 They **are packing** sandwiches for a picnic lunch.
4 We **are taking** boots with us in case it rains.
5 I **am doing** my homework before I go out.

B

1 smiling 2 shining
3 baking 4 driving
5 writing 6 making
7 caring 8 gliding

C
Answers will be individual to the children.

UNIT 9
Adjectives

We can use **adjectives** to describe the difference between two things.

a tall tower   a **taller** tower

We can also use adjectives to describe the difference between three or more things.

'Taller' is a comparative adjective.

small flower   smaller flower   **smallest** flower

'Smallest' is a **superlative adjective**.
We add 'est' to the end of the adjective when we compare three or more things.

GRAMMAR *Focus*

Copy these sentences into your book.
Add *est* to each **adjective**.

1 The building is the (high) in town.
2 That is the (bright) star in the sky.
3 Kim is the (young) girl in the class.
4 This is the (strong) rope we sell.
5 Tuesday was the (cold) day this week.
6 This is the (thick) rug in the house.

22

GRAMMAR *Practice*

saddest
darkest
longest

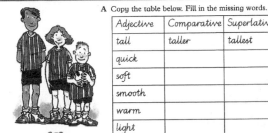

Copy the sentences below.
Fill each gap with a **superlative adjective** from the box on the left.

1 The sky was cloudy and it was the _____ night for a week.
2 We climbed the _____ mountain of the three.
3 I cried because it was the _____ story I have ever read.

GRAMMAR *Extension*

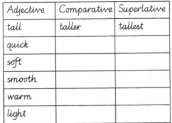

Superlative adjectives compare three or more things.

A Copy the table below. Fill in the missing words.

Adjective	Comparative	Superlative
tall	taller	tallest
quick		
soft		
smooth		
warm		
light		

B Use these **superlative adjectives** in sentences of your own.

1 plainest   2 dullest   3 largest
4 lowest   5 wettest   6 sharpest

23

---

see Glossary, page 9 – Adjectives

Previous work

Workbook 1	Workbook 2
page 6 page 7 page 13	page 6 page 7 page 13
Book A	**Book 1**
pages 8/9 pages 10/11 pages 28/29 pages 44/45	pages 6/7 pages 22/23 pages 34/35 pages 42/43
Book 2	
pages 6/7	

Pupil Book answers

Focus

1 The building is the **highest** in town.
2 That is the **brightest** star in the sky.
3 Kim is the **youngest** girl in the class.
4 This is the **strongest** rope we sell.
5 Tuesday was the **coldest** day this week.
6 This is the **thickest** rug in the house.

Practice

1 The sky was cloudy and it was the **darkest** night for a week.
2 We climbed the **highest** mountain of the three.
3 I cried because it was the **saddest** story I have ever read.

Extension
A

ADJECTIVE	COMPARATIVE	SUPERLATIVE
tall	taller	tallest
quick	**quicker**	**quickest**
soft	**softer**	**softest**
smooth	**smoother**	**smoothest**
warm	**warmer**	**warmest**
light	**lighter**	**lightest**

B
Answers will be individual to the children.

Copymaster answers

A

1 Aisha is **tall**.
2 Hasan is **small**.
3 Tom is **smaller** than Aisha and **taller** than Hasan.
4 Hasan is **smaller** than Tom and Aisha.
5 Aisha is the **tallest** of the three children.
6 Hasan is the **smallest** of the three children.

B
Answers will be individual to the children.

UNIT 10

Contractions

If something contracts it gets smaller.
Contractions are words that have been made smaller by missing out letters.
An apostrophe like this ' goes in place of the missing letter or letters.

I am looking for my gloves.
I'm looking for my gloves.

I am	=	I'm	a is missed out
you are	=	you're	a is missed out
he is	=	he's	i is missed out
she is	=	she's	i is missed out
it is	=	it's	i is missed out
we are	=	we're	a is missed out
they are	=	they're	a is missed out

GRAMMAR *Focus*

Copy these two lists into your book.
Draw lines to join each word in the first box with the correct **contraction** in the other box.

we are	he's
you are	they're
he is	she's
it is	we're
they are	it's
she is	you're

24

GRAMMAR *Practice*

A Write out the words from which these **contractions** are made.

1 she'll 2 they're 3 we're
4 it's 5 you're 6 I'm

B Copy the sentences below.
Make the coloured words into **contractions** by missing out a letter and using an apostrophe.

1 I am not happy about this.
2 If she is late she will miss the bus.
3 They are going to meet the train.
4 When you are at the shops you can buy a newspaper.
5 It is colder than it was yesterday.

GRAMMAR *Extension*

Match each word with a **contraction** from the box.
Write the contractions in your book.

1 I will
2 we were
3 can not
4 I have
5 she had
6 do not
7 would not
8 it will
9 did not
10 who is

Put the apostrophe in the space, not above a letter.

I've	didn't	it'll
	she'd	I'll
who's		wouldn't
can't	don't	we're

25

---

see Glossary, page 11 – Contractions

Previous work

None

Pupil Book answers

Focus

we are	we're
you are	you're
he is	he's
it is	it's
they are	they're
she is	she's

Practice

A
1 she will 2 they are
3 we are 4 it is
5 you are 6 I am

B
1 **I'm** not happy about this.
2 If **she's** late she will miss the bus.
3 **They're** going to meet the train.
4 When **you're** at the shops you can buy a newspaper.
5 **It's** colder than it was yesterday.

Extension

1 I'll 2 we're
3 can't 4 I've
5 she'd 6 don't
7 wouldn't 8 it'll
9 didn't 10 who's

Copymaster answers

A
2 I'm 3 We're
4 he's 5 They're
6 you're 7 it's

B
1 does not 2 is not
3 I have 4 had not
5 I will 6 would not
7 are not 8 who is
9 cannot 10 they have

Adverbs

Adverbs **add** to verbs.

An **adverb** tells us more about how, when or where the action of a verb takes place.

The boy is shouting loudly.
The adverb 'loudly' tells us **how** the boy is shouting.

Mrs Green must go today.
The adverb 'today' tells us **when** Mrs Green must go.

I have put the books here.
The adverb 'here' tells us **where** the books have been put.

Focus

Write in your book a list of the **adverbs** used in these sentences.

1 We put the cat outside when it is dark.
2 Sam carefully copied the sentences.
3 She always buys flowers in the market.
4 It rained heavily all day.
5 I get up early on a Saturday.

26

Practice

Write these headings in your book:

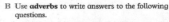

how	when	where

All the words in the box below are **adverbs**.
Put each adverb under the correct heading.

slowly   later   outside
here   angrily
never   sweetly   neatly

Extension

A Finish these sentences with **adverbs** of your own.

1 The boy sang ____.
2 The boy shouted ____.
3 The boy ran ____.
4 The boy waved ____.
5 The boy slept ____.

B Use **adverbs** to write answers to the following questions.

1 When will you do your homework?
2 How do you travel to school?
3 Where do you go shopping?
4 When can you come out to play?
5 How do you clean your teeth?
6 Where do you catch the bus?

27

---

see Glossary, page 10 – Adverbs

Previous work

None

Pupil Book answers

Focus

1 outside	2 carefully
3 always	4 heavily
5 early	

Practice

how	when	where
slowly	later	outside
angrily	never	here
sweetly		
neatly		

Extension

A
Answers will be individual to the children, for example:
1 The boy sang **quietly/outside**.
2 The boy shouted **loudly/today**.
3 The boy ran **quickly/inside**.
4 The boy waved **happily**.
5 The boy slept **peacefully/here**.

B
Answers will be individual to the children, for example:
1 I will do it **soon**.
2 I walk **quickly**.
3 I go to those shops over **there**.

4 I can come **later**.
5 I brush them **carefully** every day.
6 I catch it **here**.

Copymaster answers

A

1 Please move <u>quickly</u> to your next lesson.
2 You can tidy your books <u>later</u>.
3 I <u>often</u> go swimming.
4 Put the pencils <u>here</u> and the paper <u>there</u>.
5 I <u>never</u> eat prawns.
6 She wrote <u>slowly</u> and <u>carefully</u>.

B

HOW?	WHEN?	WHERE?
happily	soon	far
badly	then	near
swiftly	now	everywhere
angrily	early	

C

Answers will be individual to the children.

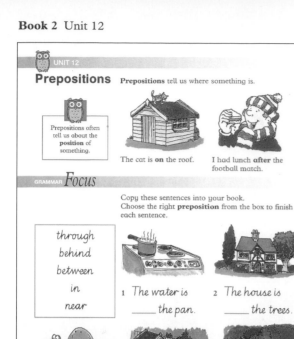

UNIT 12

Prepositions

Prepositions tell us where something is.

Prepositions often tell us about the **position** of something.

The cat is **on** the roof.

I had lunch **after** the football match.

GRAMMAR *Focus*

Copy these sentences into your book.
Choose the right **preposition** from the box to finish each sentence.

through
behind
between
in
near

1 The water is _____ the pan.
2 The house is _____ the trees.
3 The snake is _____ the rock.
4 The shed is _____ the fence.
5 The path goes _____ the wood.

28

GRAMMAR *Practice*

Look carefully at the picture.
Write some sentences, using **prepositions**, to describe where things are in the picture.

GRAMMAR *Extension*

A Copy and complete these sentences by choosing the correct **prepositions**.

1 I am very angry for/with you.
2 The medicine is good for/of you.
3 I know I can rely in/on you.

B Use these **prepositions** in sentences of your own.

1 without   2 after   3 before
4 around   5 between   6 at

29

---

see Glossary, page 12 – Prepositions

Previous work

Book 1
pages 10/11

Pupil Book answers

Focus

1 The water is **in** the pan.
2 The house is **between** the trees.
3 The snake is **behind** the rock.
4 The shed is **near** the fence.
5 The path goes **through** the wood.

Practice

Answers will be individual to the children, for example:
The teddy is in the bed.
*The shoes are **under** the bed.*
*The book is **on** the bed.*

Extension

A
1 I am very angry **with** you.
2 The medicine is good **for** you.
3 I know I can rely **on** you.

B
Answers will be individual to the children.

Copymaster answers

A
Children should find the words on the wordsearch.

B
1 rely on
2 different from
3 similar to
4 angry with
5 good for

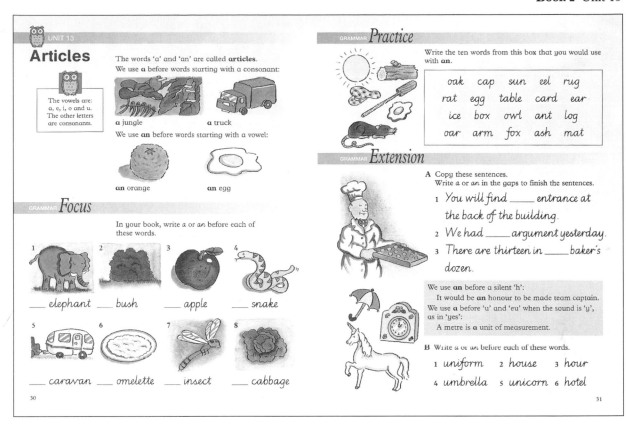

see Glossary, page 10 – Articles

Previous work

None

Pupil Book answers

Focus

1	**an** elephant	2	**a** bush
3	**an** apple	4	**a** snake
5	**a** caravan	6	**an** omelette
7	**an** insect	8	**a** cabbage

Practice

oak	eel	egg	ear	inch
owl	ant	oar	arm	ash

Extension

A

1 You will find **an** entrance at the back of the building.
2 We had **an** argument yesterday.
3 There are thirteen in **a** baker's dozen.

B

1 **a** uniform
2 **a** house
3 **an** hour
4 **an** umbrella
5 **a** unicorn
6 **a** hotel (an hotel *is also correct*)

Copymaster answers

A

1 **An** army of ants built **a** nest in the garden.
3 We have to wear **a** uniform at school.
4 **An** eel swam in the stream.
5 In **an** hour we can go home.
(2 and 6 are correct)

B

Answers will be individual to the children, for example:
a house
a cat
a pond

an egg
an ant
an umbrella

C

Answers will be individual to the children.

Book 2 Check-up 2

Check-up 2
Verbs

Write the **verb** from each sentence.

1 The curtains hang over the windows.
2 The bird is pecking at the ground.
3 I work hard at school.
4 They are waiting for the train.
5 I am talking to my friend.

Adjectives

A Write the **comparatives** of these **adjectives**.

1 sick	2 short	3 smooth
4 plain	5 small	6 green

B Write the **superlatives** of these **adjectives**.

1 sad	2 smart	3 flat
4 blunt	5 weak	6 long

C Use these **adjectives** in sentences of your own.

1 happy   2 louder   3 easiest

Contractions

Write the **contractions** for these words.

1 she is	2 we are	3 it is
4 they are	5 I am	6 you are

Adverbs

A Sort these **adverbs** into how, when and where adverbs.

> before   unhappily   often
> far   nowhere   high
> untidily   soon   quickly

B Make these sentences more interesting by adding **adverbs**.

1 The sun shone.
2 The bird flew.
3 We ran in the race.
4 They swam in the river.

Prepositions

A Write all the **prepositions** you can find in this story.

The fox ran behind the dustbin and jumped on the fence. It leaped into the tree and ran along a branch. It jumped down and disappeared through the hedge. The fox looked around, slipped inside a shed and hid between some old boxes.

B Use these **prepositions** in sentences of your own.

1 over   2 between   3 away

Articles

Write a or an before each of these words.

1 arm	2 city	3 umbrella
4 bag	5 house	6 uniform
7 aeroplane	8 bicycle	9 unicorn
10 shop	11 hour	12 oven

32   33

Verbs
1 hang
2 is pecking
3 work
4 are waiting
5 am talking

Adjectives
A
1 sicker
2 shorter
3 smoother
4 plainer
5 smaller
6 greener

B
1 saddest
2 smartest
3 flattest
4 bluntest
5 weakest
6 longest

C
Answers will be individual to the children.

Contractions
1 she's
2 we're
3 it's
4 they're
5 I'm
6 you're

Adverbs
A

HOW?	WHEN?	WHERE?
unhappily	before	far
high	often	nowhere
untidily	soon	
quickly		

Some pupils may put 'high' as a Where adverb, which is also correct (e.g. 'I searched high and low for him.').

B
Answers will be individual to the children.

Prepositions
A
behind, on, into, along, down, through, around, inside, between

B
Answers will be individual to the children.

Articles
1 **an** arm
2 **a** city
3 **an** umbrella
4 **a** bag
5 **a** house
6 **a** uniform
7 **an** aeroplane
8 **a** bicycle
9 **a** unicorn
10 **a** shop
11 **an** hour
12 **an** oven

UNIT 14
Verbs

Verbs are doing or active words.

When we use verbs to tell us about something that is happening now, we use the **present tense**.

The frog **jumps** into the pond.

or

The frog **is jumping** into the pond.

When we use verbs to tell us about something that happened in the past, we use the **past tense**.

The frog **jumped** into the pond.

To make the past tense, we usually add 'ed' to the verb family name.

If the verb family name ends in 'e', we just add 'd'.

The snowball rolled down The girl smiled.
the hill.

GRAMMAR *Focus*

Copy the sentences below into your book.
Underline the **past tense verbs**.

1 We wanted to go out on Saturday.
2 We voted to go ice skating.
3 We skated all afternoon.
4 I needed a rest when we got home.

34

GRAMMAR *Practice*

Find the verb.
Think of its family name, then add 'ed' or 'd'.

Copy the sentences below.
Change the present tense verbs to the **past tense**.

1 Ronan and Clive talk to each other on the telephone.
2 The children cook pizza for tea.
3 I decide which book to read.
4 The boys laugh at the joke.
5 They smile and wave at their friend.

GRAMMAR *Extension*

Copy this table.
Fill in the missing words.

Verb family name	Present tense	Past tense
to chew	she ＿＿＿＿ he is ＿＿＿＿	they chewed
to watch	we watch they ＿＿＿ ＿＿＿	I ＿＿＿
to ＿＿＿	I paint he ＿＿＿ painting	we ＿＿＿
to finish	you ＿＿＿ you ＿＿＿ ＿＿＿	you ＿＿＿
to ＿＿＿	they ask I am ＿＿＿	he ＿＿＿

35

see Glossary, page 14 – Verbs

Previous work

Workbook 1	Workbook 2
page 8 page 9 page 14 page 15	page 8 page 9 page 14 page 15
Book A	**Book 1**
pages 12/13 pages 16/17 pages 26/27 pages 38/39	pages 26/27 pages 30/31 pages 38/39
Book 2	
pages 12/13 pages 14/15 pages 20/21	

Pupil Book answers

Focus

1 We <u>wanted</u> to go out on Saturday.
2 We <u>voted</u> to go ice skating.
3 We <u>skated</u> all afternoon.
4 I <u>needed</u> a rest when we <u>got</u> home.

Practice

1 Ronan and Clive **talked** to each other on the telephone.
2 The children **cooked** pizza for tea.
3 I **decided** which book to read.
4 The boys **laughed** at the joke.
5 They **smiled** and **waved** at their friend.

Extension

VERB FAMILY NAME	PRESENT TENSE	PAST TENSE
to chew	she **chews** he is **chewing**	they chewed
to watch	we watch they are **watching**	I **watched**
to **paint**	I paint he **is** painting	we **painted**
to finish	you **finish** you **are finishing**	you **finished**
to **ask**	I am **asking**	he **asked**

Copymaster answers

Answers will be individual to the children.

Confusing words

We sometimes confuse words because they have similar spellings and sounds.

These three words can get mixed up:

where   **were**   **we're**

It is quite easy to tell the difference.

We use **where** when talking about a place:

Where are you going?

We use **were** when talking about something that happened in the past:

They were setting off yesterday.

We use **we're** as a contraction for 'we are':

We're not allowed on the school field if it is muddy.

Two other words that can be confusing are **there** and **their**.

There usually means a place:

The cinema is over there.

Their means 'belonging to them'. It is about people:

They made their coats dirty.

Look for the smaller word 'here' in **there**. 'Here' also means 'a place'.

'I' is in the middle of **their**. 'I' is also to do with people.

Focus

Copy the sentences below into your book.
Choose the right word to finish each sentence.

1 *Where/Were are you going?*
2 *If were/we're late we won't get in.*
3 *I think we catch the bus over there/their.*
4 *Where/We're did you find there/their hats?*

36

Practice

A Copy these sentences.
Choose *where, were* or *we're* to fill the gaps.

1 *Many people _____ queuing to see the match.*
2 *" _____ almost there," said Dad.*
3 *" _____ do we go when we get inside?" I asked.*

B Copy these sentences, choosing *there* or *their* to fill in the gaps.

1 *Max went to his friends' house and played with _____ dog.*
2 *They had a picnic for _____ tea.*
3 *"I like to go _____ ," said Max.*

Extension

Look back at Unit 3 to remind you about 'two', 'too', and 'to'.

Choose the correct words to finish these sentences.

1 *There/Their is nothing left to/two eat.*
2 *Tell me we're/where I can go too/to buy some food.*
3 *The best place to/two go is over there/their.*

37

---

see Glossary, page 10 – Confusing words

Previous work

Book 1
pages 16/17

Book 2
pages 8/9

Pupil Book answers

Focus

1 **Where** are you going?
2 If **we're** late we won't get in.
3 I think we catch the bus over **there**.
4 **Where** did you find **their** hats?

Practice

1 Many people **were** queuing to see the match.
2 "**We're** almost there," said Dad.
3 "**Where** do we go when we get inside?" I asked.

Extension

1 **There** is nothing left **to** eat.
2 Tell me **where** I can go **to** buy some food.
3 The best place **to** go is over **there**.

Copymaster answers

A

1 If **we're** quick we will see the start of the film.
2 I do not know **where** I put the newspaper.
3 The boys had climbed the tree and **were** stuck.
4 I am not sure **where** the spade is.
5 I knew you **were** in a hurry this morning.

B

1 If we go over **there** we'll be able to see more.
2 I like **their** new coats.
3 **There** are no apples left in the bowl.
4 My grandparents said I could go to **their** house for tea.
5 **There** is a pear tree in **their** garden.

C

Answers will be individual to the children.

UNIT 16
Singular and plural

Singular means 'one thing or person'.
Plural means 'more than one thing or person'.

If we are talking about more than one thing we usually add 's' to a noun. This makes it plural.

one eagle   two eagles

Some nouns need 'es' on the end to make them plural. These nouns end in:

ch sh s x

Singular	Plural
stitch	stitches
wish	wishes
bus	buses
glass	glasses
box	boxes

Nouns ending in 'zz' need 'es' to make them plural. There are very few nouns that end in 'zz'.

GRAMMAR Focus

A Make these singular nouns **plural**. Write the plural nouns in your book.

1 dish   2 trench   3 punch
4 grass   5 fox   6 cross
7 ditch   8 rash   9 gas
10 march   11 gash   12 finch

B Use five of your **plural nouns** from part A in sentences of your own.

38

GRAMMAR Practice

Be careful! Some of these nouns may only need 's'.

Copy these tables.
Fill in the missing words.

Singular	Plural
bush	
arch	
	gashes
tree	
	witches
tax	
church	
coach	

Singular	Plural
	compasses
mass	
table	
pitch	
	guesses
torch	
	carts

GRAMMAR Extension

Write the words ending in 'es' which match these descriptions.

1 We use these to tell the time.   w _ _ _ _ es
2 These books contain maps of countries.   a _ _ _ _ es
3 Places where you make sand castles by the sea.   b _ _ _ _ es
4 These are areas of swampy ground.   m _ _ _ _ es
5 Girls sometimes wear these.   d _ _ _ _ es
6 the daughters of a king and queen   p _ _ _ _ _ _ es

39

---

see Glossary, page 13 – Singular and plural

Previous work

Book A
pages 20/21

Book 1
pages 8/9

Pupil Book answers

Focus

A

1 dishes	2 trenches
3 punches	4 grasses
5 foxes	6 crosses
7 ditches	8 rashes
9 gases	10 marches
11 gashes	12 finches

B
Answers will be individual to the children.

Practice

SINGULAR	PLURAL
bush	**bushes**
arch	**arches**
gash	gashes
tree	**trees**
witch	witches
tax	**taxes**
church	**churches**
coach	**coaches**
compass	compasses
mass	**masses**
table	**tables**
pitch	**pitches**
guess	guesses
torch	**torches**
cart	carts

Extension

1 watches	2 atlases
3 beaches	4 marshes
5 dresses	6 princesses

Copymaster answers

A

desks	fox	swamp
torches	**jugs**	**boxes**
church	**floors**	wall
inches	lamp	**lunches**

B

1 glasses	2 caps
3 elephants	4 stitches
5 birds	6 taxes
7 hunches	8 hands
9 lights	10 marshes
11 hammers	12 porches

C

1 fox
2 rash
3 atlas
4 gas

UNIT 17

Adverbs

An **adverb** tells us more about how, when or where the action of a verb takes place.

How: The lightning flashed **brightly**.
When: The thunder rumbled **later**.
Where: The rain fell **here**.

Adverbs are sometimes used in pairs to make the meaning clearer.

I walked **more slowly** than my friend.

These adverbs can also tell us more about other adverbs:

quite	only	so	almost
very	rather	less	most

GRAMMAR *Focus*

Write in your book the pair of **adverbs** from each sentence.

1 The cat crept rather slowly towards the bird.
2 The bird went on quite happily pulling a worm from the ground.
3 Very quietly, the cat crept closer.
4 Almost silently, the cat jumped towards the bird.
5 The bird flew very quickly into a tree.

40

GRAMMAR *Practice*

more
very
so
rather
less
extremely

Choose a different **adverb** to improve the meaning of each sentence.
Use adverbs from the box if you wish.

1 Put away the glasses _____ carefully.
2 You need to paint _____ colourfully.
3 When we move away, we will visit _____ often.
4 The train is running _____ late.

GRAMMAR *Extension*

Find the verbs, then put an adverb or a pair of adverbs with each verb.

Improve this story by adding at least six **adverbs** or **pairs of adverbs**.

Night fell and the wood became dark and gloomy. The two friends rode along and talked. They heard rustling in the trees and stopped their horses. One of the men got off his horse and listened. There it was again. "What shall we do?" whispered the man on the horse. "I don't know," the other replied. "I think we should ride on and get out of this wood."

41

---

see Glossary, page 10 – Adverbs

Previous work

Book 2
pages 26/27

Pupil Book answers

Focus

1 rather slowly
2 quite happily
3 very quietly
4 almost silently
5 very quickly

Practice

Children may use their own adverbs or those from the box, for example:
1 *Put away the glasses* **very/extremely/more** *carefully.*
2 *You need to paint* **more/less/rather/very/ extremely** *colourfully.*
3 *When we move away, we will visit* **very/less/more** *often.*
4 *The train is running* **very/rather/extremely** *late.*

Extension

Answers will be individual to the children, for example:
Night fell **quickly** *and the wood became dark and gloomy. The two friends rode along* **rather slowly** *and talked* **quietly***. They* **suddenly** *heard rustling in the trees and stopped their horses. One of the men got off his horse* **rather nervously** *and listened* **carefully***. There it was again.*
"What shall we do?" whispered the man on the horse **very softly***.*
"I don't know," the other replied **worriedly***.*
"I think we should ride on **immediately** *and get out of this wood."*

Copymaster answers

A

2 Donisha **jumped** <u>up</u> when the bell rang.　　(where)
3 The snake **hissed** <u>suddenly</u>. (when)
4 You can **go** <u>early</u> if you finish. (when)
5 The spider **spun** <u>busily</u> to make its web.　　(how)

B

1 The time went <u>rather quickly</u>.
2 You must draw the map <u>very neatly</u>.
3 I go to that shop <u>most often</u>.
4 He spoke <u>so quietly</u> I could hardly hear him.
5 This is <u>quite firmly</u> stuck together.

C

Answers will be individual to the children.

UNIT 18

Verbs

To put a verb in the **past tense**, we usually add 'd' or 'ed' to the verb family name.

Verb family name	Past tense
to look	looked
to argue	argued

Some verbs do not follow this rule.
The verb 'to be' is one of them.
Here is the past tense of the verb 'to be'.

Singular	Plural
I was	we were
you were	you were
he was	they were
she was	
it was	

It is useful to learn the past tense of the verb 'to be'.

Sometimes, we need to change the middle vowel sound to make the past tense.

	Present tense	Past tense
	sing	sang
	write	wrote

GRAMMAR *Focus*

Match the **present tense verbs** in one box with the correct **past tense verbs** in the other box.
Write the pairs in your book.

grow	make	hike
come	throw	jump
hold	bake	draw
play	give	shine	pile

threw	drew	held	grew
played	gave	baked	
came	piled	hiked	
shone	jumped	made	

42

GRAMMAR *Practice*

Copy the sentences below.
Change the verb in brackets to the **past tense**.

1 We (arrive) at school early this morning.
2 The teacher (give) us some jobs to do.
3 I (mix) the paints.
4 My friend (clean) the paintbrushes.

GRAMMAR *Extension*

Some verbs do not seem to follow any rules to help you make the past tense. For example, the past tense of the verb 'to go' is 'went'.

A Write the **past tense** of these verbs. Use a dictionary to help you.

1 to go	2 to leave	3 to speak
4 to catch	5 to find	6 to have
7 to meet	8 to eat	9 to sleep

B Copy the sentences below.
Choose the correct verb to put the sentences into the **past tense**.

1 I am/was cross with Judy.
2 The day was/is cold and damp.
3 The children ran/run across the field.
4 Butter is make/made from milk.

43

---

see Glossary, page 14 – Verbs

Previous work

Workbook 1	Workbook 2
page 8	page 8
page 9	page 9
page 14	page 14
page 15	page 15
Book A	**Book 1**
pages 12/13	pages 26/27
pages 16/17	pages 30/31
pages 26/27	pages 38/39
pages 38/39	
Book 2	
pages 12/13	
pages 14/15	
pages 20/21	
pages 34/35	

Pupil Book answers

Focus

grow	grew	make	made
hike	hiked	come	came
throw	threw	jump	jumped
hold	held	bake	baked
draw	drew	play	played
give	gave	shine	shone
pile	piled		

Practice

1 We **arrived** at school early this morning.
2 The teacher **gave** us some jobs to do.
3 I **mixed** the paints.
4 My friend **cleaned** the paintbrushes.

Extension

A

1	went	2	left
3	spoke	4	caught
5	found	6	had
7	met	8	ate
9	slept		

B
1 I **was** cross with Judy.
2 The day **was** cold and damp.
3 The children **ran** across the field.
4 I **threw** the ball.

Copymaster answers

A

VERB FAMILY NAME	PAST TENSE
to grow	I **grew**
to play	you **played**
to swim	we **swam**
to jump	they **jumped**
to write	I **wrote**
to draw	you **drew**
to give	we **gave**
to live	they **lived**
to come	I **came**

B
1 present tense	2 past tense
3 present tense	4 past tense
5 past tense	

C
1 fought	2 met
3 bound	4 bought
5 meant	6 sought

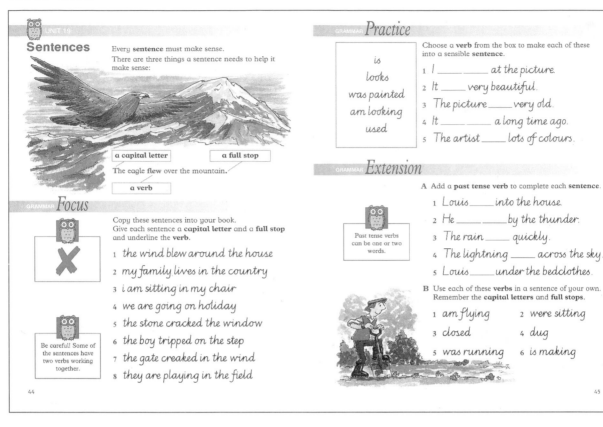

The detail reproduced from the pupil book (pages 44–45) reads:

UNIT 19

Sentences

Every **sentence** must make sense.
There are three things a sentence needs to help it make sense:

a capital letter   a full stop

The eagle **flew** over the mountain.

a verb

GRAMMAR *Focus*

Copy these sentences into your book.
Give each sentence a **capital letter** and a **full stop** and underline the **verb**.

1 the wind blew around the house
2 my family lives in the country
3 i am sitting in my chair
4 we are going on holiday
5 the stone cracked the window
6 the boy tripped on the step
7 the gate creaked in the wind
8 they are playing in the field

Be careful! Some of the sentences have two verbs working together.

44

GRAMMAR *Practice*

Choose a **verb** from the box to make each of these into a sensible **sentence**.

is
looks
was painted
am looking
used

1 I _____ at the picture.
2 It _____ very beautiful.
3 The picture _____ very old.
4 It _____ a long time ago.
5 The artist _____ lots of colours.

GRAMMAR *Extension*

A Add a **past tense verb** to complete each **sentence**.

Past tense verbs can be one or two words.

1 Louis _____ into the house.
2 He _____ by the thunder.
3 The rain _____ quickly.
4 The lightning _____ across the sky.
5 Louis _____ under the bedclothes.

B Use each of these **verbs** in a sentence of your own. Remember the **capital letters** and **full stops**.

1 am flying   2 were sitting
3 closed   4 dug
5 was running   6 is making

45

---

see Glossary, page 12 – Sentences

Previous work

Book A
pages 24/25
pages 30/31
pages 34/35
pages 42/43

Book 1
pages 24/25
pages 28/29

Pupil Book answers

Focus

1 **The** wind <u>blew</u> around the house.
2 **My** family <u>lives</u> in the country.
3 **I** am <u>sitting</u> in my chair.
4 **We** <u>are going</u> on holiday.
5 **The** stone <u>cracked</u> the window.
6 **The** boy <u>tripped</u> on the step.
7 **The** gate <u>creaked</u> in the wind.
8 **They** <u>are playing</u> in the field.

Practice

1 I **am looking** at the picture.
2 It **is** very beautiful.
3 The picture **looks** very old.
4 It **was painted** a long time ago.
5 The artist **used** lots of colours.

Extension

A
Answers will be individual to the children, for example:
1 *Louis **went** into the house.*
2 *He **was frightened** by the thunder.*
3 *The rain **fell** quickly.*
4 *The lightening **flashed** across the sky.*
5 *Louis **hid** under the bedclothes.*

B
Answers will be individual to the children.

Copymaster answers

A and *B*
Answers will be individual to the children

90

Check-up 3

Proper nouns

Copy these sentences.
Write the **proper nouns** with a **capital letter**.

1 cardiff is the capital of wales
2 new year's day is hot in australia
3 The river thames runs through london

Adjectives

A Read the passage right through then write it out adding **adjectives** to fill the gaps.

The _____ house stood by the side of the _____ road. There was a _____ garden at the front and the back. The garage was painted _____ and _____. _____ trees grew around the house making it _____ and _____.

B Make the adjectives in brackets into **comparative adjectives**.

1 That piece of cake is (small) than this one.
2 There is a (long) piece of string in the drawer.
3 The river by the other bank is (deep).

C Make the adjectives in brackets into **superlative adjectives**.

1 This is the (high) of all the hills.
2 This is the (proud) moment of my life.
3 Use the (clean) cloth you can find.

Confusing words

Choose the correct words to complete the passage.

In too/two days time were/we're going to/too visit our cousins. There/Their house is in the country and we're/where taking a taxi from the station. Were/Where they live is very beautiful because their/there is a river and a lake two/too.

Verbs

A Change these sentences from the present tense to the **past tense**.

1 We swim in the sea.
2 I run for the bus.
3 The cows chew the grass.

B Change these sentences from the past tense to the **present tense**.

1 Many people played golf.
2 The children sang every morning.
3 The elephants liked the water.

46   47

Proper nouns

1 **Cardiff** is the capital of **Wales**.
2 **New Year's Day** is hot in **Australia**.
3 The **River Thames** runs through **London**.

Adjectives

A

Answers will be individual to the children.

B

1 That piece of cake is **smaller** than this one.
2 There is a **longer** piece of string in the drawer.
3 The river by the other bank is **deeper**.

C

1 This is the **highest** of all the hills.
2 This is the **proudest** moment of my life.
3 Use the **cleanest** cloth you can find.

Confusing words

In **two** days time **we're** going **to** visit our cousins. **Their** house is in the country and **we're** taking a taxi from the station. **Where** they live is very beautiful because **there** is a river and a lake **too**.

Verbs

A

1 We **swam** in the sea.
2 I **ran** for the bus.
3 The cows **chewed** the grass.

B

1 Many people **are playing/play** golf.
2 The children **are singing/sing** every morning.
3 The elephants **like** the water.

C Choose the right word to finish each sentence.

1 The plants is/are growing well.

2 I am/is writing a letter.

3 We was/were allowed to go outside.

Contractions

Put the apostrophe in the correct place in these **contractions**.

1 Im 2 youre 3 hes 4 shes

5 its 6 were 7 theyre 8 dont

Adverbs

Copy these sentences and add **adverbs** to fill the gaps.

1 The clowns juggled _____.

2 The ringmaster cracked his whip _____.

3 The crowd clapped _____ _____.

Prepositions

Use these **prepositions** in sentences of your own.

1 between 2 over 3 through

4 in 5 under 6 near

Articles

Write a or an before each word.

1 bush 2 antelope 3 hour

4 umpire 5 hero 6 island

7 donkey 8 uniform

48

C
1 The plants **are** growing well.
2 I **am** writing a letter.
3 We **were** allowed to go outside.

Contractions

1 I'm
2 you're
3 he's
4 she's
5 it's
6 we're
7 they're
8 don't

Adverbs

Answers will be individual to the children, for example:
1 *The clowns juggled* **expertly**.
2 *The ringmaster cracked his whip* **loudly**.
3 *The crowd clapped* **very enthusiastically**.

Prepositions

Answers will be individual to the children.

Articles

1 **a** bush
2 **an** antelope
3 **an** hour
4 **an** umpire
5 **a** hero
6 **an** island
7 **a** donkey
8 **a** uniform

**Improve Your Writing
copymaster 1**

*Answers will be individual to the
children, for example:*
*The **fierce** dragon is breathing fire.*
*The dragon has a **frightening** roar.*
*The dragon's **huge** body is **scaly**.*
*The dragon has a long tail, **big**,
sharp claws and **huge pointed**
teeth.*

**Improve Your Writing
copymaster 2**

The cat is **on** the shed roof.
The spade is **in** the ground.
The chair is **on** the lawn.
The dog is jumping **over** the fence.
The man is **up/on** a ladder.
The book is **under** the chair.

**Improve Your Writing
copymaster 3**

*Answers will be individual to the
children.*

**Improve Your Writing
copymaster 4**

A

*Answers will be individual to the
children, for example:*
cry – sob, weep, snivel, howl
eat – gobble, nibble, chew, gorge, guzzle,
chomp
go – depart, leave, move, travel, walk
laugh – chuckle, titter, guffaw, snigger,
cackle, giggle

B

*Answers will be individual to the
children.*

**Improve Your Writing
copymaster 5**

A

*Answers will be individual to the
children, for example:*
1 *I have finished this book
although/and/but I did not like
it.*
2 *Naomi bought some apples **and** she
bought some cakes.*

B

*Answers will be individual to the
children.*

**Improve Your Writing
copymaster 6**

A

*Answers will be individual to the
children, for example:*
1 *The teacher smiled **kindly** at the
boy.*
2 *The book fell **noisily** to the floor.*
3 *The dog barked **furiously** at the
stranger.*

B

*Answers will be individual to the
children, for example:*
1 *I go swimming **often**.*
2 *It rained **constantly**.*
3 ***Sometimes** we walk to school.*

C

*Answers will be individual to the
children, for example:*
1 *Put the box **there**.*
2 *I can't find the cat **anywhere**.*
3 *I saw someone I knew **yesterday**.*

D

*Answers will be individual to the
children.*

**Improve Your Writing
copymaster 7**

*Answers will be individual to the
children.*

Book 3 – Contents/Scope and Sequence

Page/Unit		Focus	Practice
4/5	Unit 1	proper nouns – names of people	writing book, film and play titles with capital letters
6/7	Unit 2	matching number and number-order adjectives	identifying number and number-order adjectives with nouns
8/9	Unit 3	revision of plurals	plurals with 'y', using plurals
10/11	Unit 4	identifying prepositions, prepositions as opposites	choosing the correct preposition
12/13	Unit 5	identifying the subject and object of sentences	adding interesting objects
14/15	Unit 6	using pronouns in sentences	choosing the correct pronoun
16/17	Unit 7	identifying direct speech, using inverted commas	punctuating conversation
18/19	Unit 8	choosing appropriate collective nouns	identifying groups
20/21		*Check-up 1*	*Check-up 1*
22/23	Unit 9	plurals for 'f' and 'fe' words	using 'f' and 'fe' plurals
24/25	Unit 10	adjectives – completing a comparative/superlative table	making adjectives into comparative and superlative
26/27	Unit 11	verbs – identifying past-tense verbs ('to be' plus 'ing')	using past-tense verbs in sentences
28/29	Unit 12	nouns – singular possessive, identifying owner	using an apostrophe to show ownership
30/31	Unit 13	sentences – identifying subject and predicate	joining subjects and predicates
32/33	Unit 14	identifying future-tense verbs	changing present and past tense into future tense
34/35	Unit 15	noun and verb agreement – is/are	have/has, choosing the correct verb
36/37	Unit 16	singular and plural – 'o' words and irregular plurals	verb and plural agreement
38/39		*Check-up 2*	*Check-up 2*
40/41	Unit 17	writing compound nouns from picture clues	joining nouns to make compound nouns
42/43	Unit 18	writing comparative and superlative adverbs	changing adverbs into comparatives and superlatives
44/45	Unit 19	identifying and writing contractions	contractions in conversation
46/47	Unit 20	singular possessive nouns	plural possessive nouns
48/49	Unit 21	choosing comparative or superlative adjectives	completing an adjective table
50/51	Unit 22	identifying the subject and predicate	writing interesting subjects
52/53	Unit 23	using inverted commas	punctuating direct speech
54/55	Unit 24	completing a past-/present-/future-tense verb table	identifying past-, present- and future-tense verbs
56/57	Unit 25	sentences – adding negative words	identifying negative words, writing opposite meanings
58/59	Unit 26	identifying abstract nouns	identifying common and abstract nouns
60/64		*Check-up 3*	*Check-up 3*

Extension	Copymaster	Page/Unit
adding capital letters to continuous prose	punctuating sentences with book/film titles	4/5 Unit 1
completing sentences with number-order adjectives	identifying and using number and number-order adjectives	6/7 Unit 2
identifying plurals from clues	singular and plural crossword	8/9 Unit 3
cloze – using prepositions	identifying and using prepositional phrases	10/11 Unit 4
adding adjectives to objects, writing sentences	identifying subject and object, writing sentences	12/13 Unit 5
changing nouns and proper nouns into pronouns	identifying pronouns, using pairs of pronouns	14/15 Unit 6
using other words instead of 'said'	converting a cartoon strip into written conversation	16/17 Unit 7
completing sentences with collective nouns	collective noun crossword, definitions of compound nouns	18/19 Unit 8
Check-up 1	*Check-up 1*	20/21
identifying 'f' and 'fe' plurals from clues	using plurals in sentences	22/23 Unit 9
using comparative and superlative adjectives	using comparatives and superlatives in sentences	24/25 Unit 10
completing a verb table, cloze – completing sentences	forming and using the past tense	26/27 Unit 11
writing possessive nouns	identifying and using singular possessive nouns	28/29 Unit 12
writing interesting subjects and predicates	identifying and using subjects and predicates	30/31 Unit 13
completing a verb table, alternative use of shall/will	identifying and using the future tense	32/33 Unit 14
correcting verb mistakes in continuous prose	subject and verb agreement	34/35 Unit 15
irregular plurals	revision of plural forms	36/37 Unit 16
Check-up 2	*Check-up 2*	38/39
identifying and using compound nouns	forming compound nouns	40/41 Unit 17
using adverbs	using comparative and superlative adverbs	42/43 Unit 18
writing conversation	forming contractions and using them in direct speech	44/45 Unit 19
using the apostrophe, using plural possessive nouns	using possessive adjectives	46/47 Unit 20
identifying and using comparative and superlative adjectives	using comparative and superlative adjectives	48/49 Unit 21
use of 'I' and 'me'	writing interesting predicates	50/51 Unit 22
punctuating conversation	correcting punctuation and layout of direct speech	52/53 Unit 23
changing sentences into past and future tense	identifying and using verb tenses	54/55 Unit 24
correcting double negatives	correcting double negatives	56/57 Unit 25
forming abstract nouns	identifying and using noun forms	58/59 Unit 26
Check-up 3	*Check-up 3*	60/64

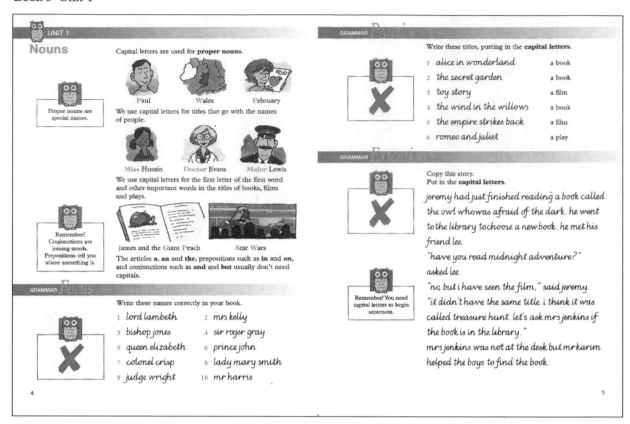

see Glossary, page 11 – Nouns

Previous work

Workbook 1	Workbook 2
page 4	page 4
page 5	page 5
page 12	page 12
page 13	page 13
Book A	**Book 1**
pages 6/7	pages 4/5
pages 10/11	pages 12/13
pages 22/23	pages 20/21
pages 36/37	
pages 40/41	
Book 2	
pages 4/5	
pages 16/17	

Pupil Book answers

Focus

1 Lord Lambeth
2 Mrs Kelly
3 Bishop Jones
4 Sir Roger Gray
5 Queen Elizabeth
6 Prince John
7 Colonel Crisp
8 Lady Mary Smith
9 Judge Wright
10 Mr Harris

Practice

1 Alice in Wonderland
2 The Secret Garden
3 Toy Story
4 The Wind in the Willows
5 The Empire Strikes Back
6 Romeo and Juliet

Extension

Jeremy had just finished reading a book called **The Owl Who Was Afraid of the Dark. He** went to the library to choose a new book. **He** met his friend **Lee.**
  "**Have** you read **Midnight** Adventure?" asked **Lee.**
  "**No,** but **I** have seen the film," said Jeremy. "**It** didn't have the same title. **I** think it was called **Treasure Hunt. Let's** ask **Mrs Jenkins** if the book is in the library.
Mrs Jenkins was not at the desk but **Mr Karim** helped the boys to find the book.

Copymaster answers

A

1 I have finished reading The Wind in the Willows.
2 Did you see the film Batman?
3 Fantastic Mr Fox and James and the Giant Peach are books by Roald Dahl.
4 I watched a TV programme called Wildlife in Africa last night.
5 Our school play is called Little Red Riding Hood.

B *Answers will be individual to the children.*

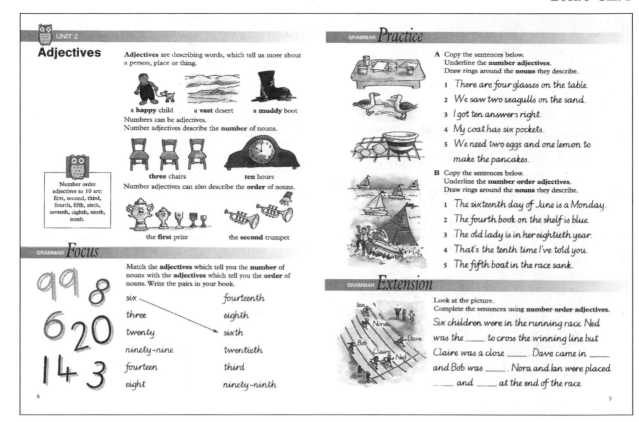

see Glossary, page 9 – Adjectives

Previous work

Workbook 1	Workbook 2
page 6	page 6
page 7	page 7
page 13	page 13
Book A	**Book 1**
pages 8/9	pages 6/7
pages 10/11	pages 22/23
pages 28/29	pages 34/35
pages 44/45	pages 42/43
Book 2	
pages 6/7	
pages 22/23	

Pupil Book answers

Focus

six	sixth
three	third
twenty	twentieth
ninety-nine	ninety-ninth
fourteen	fourteenth
eight	eighth

Practice

A

1 There are four **glasses** on the table.
2 We saw <u>two</u> **seagulls** on the sand.
3 I got <u>ten</u> **answers** right.
4 My coat has <u>six</u> **pockets**.
5 We need <u>two</u> **eggs** and <u>one</u> **lemon** to make the pancakes.

B

1 The <u>sixteenth</u> **day** of June is a Monday.
2 The <u>fourth</u> **book** on the shelf is blue.
3 The old lady is in her <u>eightieth</u> **year**.
4 That's the <u>tenth</u> **time** I've told you.
5 The <u>fifth</u> **boat** in the race sank.

Extension

Six children were in the running race. Ned was the **first** to cross the winning line but Claire was a close **second**. Dave came in **third** and Bob was **fourth**. Nora and Ian were placed **fifth** and **sixth** at the end of the race.

Copymaster answers

A

1 King Henry's <u>sixth</u> **wife** outlived him.
2 There are <u>one hundred</u> **pence** in a pound.
3 Please go through the <u>second</u> **door** on the right.
4 Can you find <u>five</u> **buttons** that are the same?
5 The <u>first</u> **Queen Elizabeth** ruled about <u>four hundred</u> **years** ago.

B *Answers will be individual to the children.*

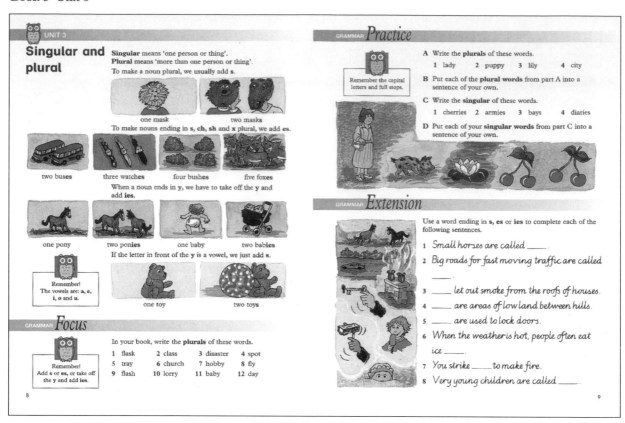

see Glossary, page 13 – Singular and plural

Previous work

Book A
pages 20/21

Book 1
pages 8/9

Book 2
pages 38/39

Pupil Book answers

Focus

1 flasks	2 classes
3 disasters	4 spots
5 trays	6 churches
7 hobbies	8 flies
9 flashes	10 lorries
11 babies	12 days

Practice

A
1 ladies
2 puppies
3 lilies
4 cities

B
Answers will be individual to the children.

C
1 cherry
2 army
3 bay
4 diary

D
Answers will be individual to the children.

Extension

1 Small horses are called **ponies**.
2 Big roads for fast moving traffic are called **motorways**.
3 **Chimneys** let out smoke from the roofs of houses.
4 **Valleys** are areas of low land between hills.
5 **Keys** are used to lock doors.
6 When the weather is hot, people often eat ice **lollies**.
7 You strike **matches** to make fire.
8 Very young children are called **babies**.

Copymaster answers

A

Across	Down
2 atlases	1 flashes
3 cities	2 armies
4 bays	5 toys
6 hutches	

B
Answers will be individual to the children.

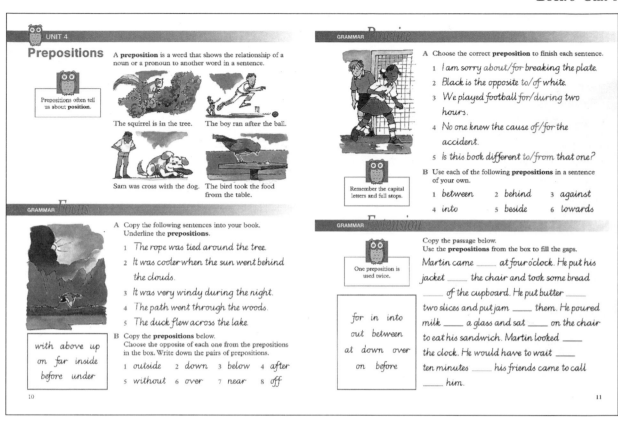

see Glossary, page 12 –
Prepositions

Previous work

Book 1
pages 10/11
Book 2
pages 28/29

Pupil Book answers

Focus

A
1 The rope was tied <u>around</u> the tree.
2 It was cooler when the sun went <u>behind</u> the clouds.
3 It was very windy <u>during</u> the night.
4 The path went <u>through</u> the woods.
5 The duck flew <u>across</u> the lake.

B
1	outside	inside
2	down	up
3	below	above
4	after	before
5	without	with
6	over	under
7	near	far
8	off	on

Practice

A
1 I am sorry **about** breaking the plate.
2 Black is the opposite **of** white.
3 We played football **for** two hours.
4 No one knew the cause **of** the accident.
5 Is this book different **from** that one?

B
Answers will be individual to the children.

Extension

Martin came **in** at four o'clock. He put his jacket **over** the chair and took some bread **out** of the cupboard. He put butter **on** two slices and put jam **between** them. He poured milk **into** a glass and sat **down** on the chair to eat his sandwich. Martin looked **at** the clock. He would have to wait **for** ten minutes **before** his friends came to call **for** him.

Copymaster answers

A
1 I walked <u>behind my brother</u>.
2 The show lasted <u>for three hours</u>.
3 We flew <u>over the Atlantic Ocean</u>.
4 The flowers grow <u>in good, rich soil</u>.
5 I'll be there <u>in five minutes</u>.

B
Answers will be individual to the children.

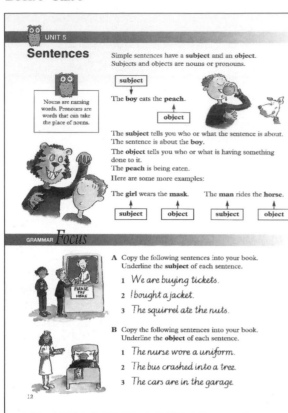

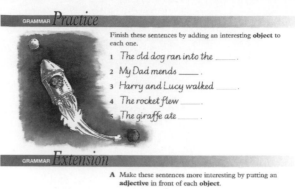

UNIT 5

Sentences

Simple sentences have a **subject** and an **object**.
Subjects and objects are nouns or pronouns.

Nouns are naming words. Pronouns are words that can take the place of nouns.

subject

The **boy** eats the **peach**.

object

The **subject** tells you who or what the sentence is about.
The sentence is about the **boy**.
The **object** tells you who or what is having something done to it.
The **peach** is being eaten.
Here are some more examples:

The **girl** wears the **mask**. The **man** rides the **horse**.

subject object subject object

GRAMMAR Focus

A Copy the following sentences into your book.
Underline the **subject** of each sentence.

1 We are buying tickets.
2 I bought a jacket.
3 The squirrel ate the nuts.

PLEASE PAY HERE

B Copy the following sentences into your book.
Underline the **object** of each sentence.

1 The nurse wore a uniform.
2 The bus crashed into a tree.
3 The cars are in the garage.

12

GRAMMAR Practice

Finish these sentences by adding an interesting **object** to each one.

1 The old dog ran into the ____.
2 My Dad mends ____.
3 Harry and Lucy walked ____.
4 The rocket flew ____.
5 The giraffe ate ____.

GRAMMAR Extension

A Make these sentences more interesting by putting an **adjective** in front of each **object**.

Adjectives are describing words.

1 I saw a snake.
2 Mum bought a pillow.
3 The man escaped from the prison.
4 The wind blew around the house.
5 Ella broke the window.

B Write sentences of your own using these pairs of **subjects** and **objects**.

	Subject	Object
1	we	ball
2	the rain	garden
3	the crowd	train
4	the children	park
5	they	kitten

13

see Glossary, page 12 – Sentences

Previous work

Book A
pages 24/25 pages 30/31 pages 34/35 pages 42/43
Book 1
pages 24/25 pages 28/29
Book 2
pages 44/45

Pupil Book answers

Focus

A

1 We are buying tickets.
2 I bought a jacket.
3 The squirrel ate the nuts.

B

1 The nurse wore a uniform.
2 The bus crashed into a tree.
3 The cars are in the garage.

Practice

Answers will be individual to the children, for example:

1 *The old dog ran into the* ***forest****.*
2 *My Dad mends* ***watches****.*
3 *Harry and Lucy walked over* ***the bridge****.*
4 *The rocket flew to* ***Mars****.*
5 *The giraffe ate* ***the woman's hat****.*

Extension

A

Answers will be individual to the children, for example:

1 *I saw a* ***poisonous*** *snake.*
2 *Mum bought a* ***feather*** *pillow.*
3 *The man escaped from the* ***gloomy*** *prison.*
4 *The wind blew around the* ***eerie*** *house.*
5 *Ella broke the* ***enormous*** *window.*

B

Answers will be individual to the children.

Copymaster answers

A

1 The teacher piled up the **books**.
2 Mr Smith cleaned the **windows**.
3 The gardener cut off the **branches**.
4 Three children forgot their **packed lunches**.
5 Larry rode the winning **horse**.

B

Answers will be individual to the children, for example:

1a) *The* ***car*** *was parked in the street.*
b) *The boys cleaned the* ***car****.*

2a) *My* ***house*** *is the one at the end of the road.*
b) *I would like to live in that* ***house****.*

3a) *The* ***traffic warden*** *gave the driver a ticket.*
b) *I saw a* ***traffic warden*** *near the car.*

UNIT 6

Pronouns

A **pronoun** can be used instead of a noun.

The candle is burning.
It is burning.

Rex hates cabbage.
He hates cabbage.

Here is a list of useful pronouns:

I	you	he	she	it	we	they
me	yourself	him	her	itself	us	them
myself	yourselves	himself	herself		ourselves	themselves

Focus

Choose **pronouns** from the box to replace the brown words in the sentences below.
Write the correct pronouns in your book.

them	him	they	it	she

1 The vase fell on the floor and the **vase** broke.
2 The zebras wanted to drink so the **zebras** went to the water hole.
3 I told the children we would meet the **children** at ten o'clock.
4 The headmaster said I should come in to see the **headmaster**.
5 Denise ate quickly so **Denise** could go out early.

14

Practice

Use a **pronoun** from the box to finish each sentence.

myself
yourself
himself
herself
itself

1 Tara wants to paint the cottage _____ .
2 The dog stretched _____ in front of the fire.
3 The postman hurt _____ when he fell off his bike.
4 I want to go to the shops by _____ .
5 You almost cut _____ with that knife.

Extension

A Change the **nouns** and **proper nouns** in these sentences into **pronouns**.
The first one is done for you.

1 Paula and Alex saw the ghost.
   They saw _it_ .

2 Rachel waited for the milkman.
   _____ waited for _____ .

3 Nigel and I waved to Scott.
   _____ waved to _____ .

4 Edward met his friends.
   _____ met _____ .

B Use each of these **pronouns** in sentences of your own.

1 yourself   2 they   3 myself
4 her   5 us   6 itself

15

---

see Glossary, page 12 – Pronouns

Previous work

Book 1
pages 14/15
pages 40/41

Pupil Book answers

Focus
1 The vase fell on the floor and **it** broke.
2 The zebras wanted to drink so **they** went to the water hole.
3 I told the children we would meet **them** at ten o'clock.
4 The headmaster said I should come in to see **him**.
5 Denise ate quickly so **she** could go out early.

Practice
1 Tara wants to paint the cottage **herself**.
2 The dog stretched **itself** in front of the fire.
3 The postman hurt **himself** when he fell off his bike.
4 I want to go to the shops by **myself**.
5 You almost cut **yourself** with that knife.

Extension
A
2 **She** waited for **him**.
3 **We** waved to **him**.
4 **He** met **them**.

B
Answers will be individual to the children.

Copymaster answers

A
1 <u>He</u> is very upset with <u>himself</u> for missing the goal.
2 <u>I</u> would do it <u>yourself</u> if <u>I</u> were <u>you</u>.
3 Go and tell <u>them</u> that <u>we</u> are ready.
4 If <u>we</u> can find the paint, <u>we</u> will do it <u>ourselves</u>.
5 They bought <u>themselves</u> umbrellas.

B
Answers will be individual to the children, for example:
1 *You told me I could go out today.*
2 *I banged myself on the cupboard door.*
3 *They rang up while we were out.*
4 *I told him to feed the dog himself.*
5 *If you see them tell them it is teatime.*

UNIT 7

Sentences

Inverted commas are also called speech marks.

Direct speech is when we write the actual words that someone has spoken.
Direct speech can be written in speech bubbles like this:

Lovely fresh cabbages!

I'll have two please.

If we want to write this as conversation, we need to use **inverted commas**.
We put **"** at the beginning of the words that are spoken and **"** at the end.

"Lovely fresh cabbages!" shouted the man.
"I'll have two please," said the woman.

GRAMMAR *Focus*

A Find the **spoken words** in each sentence.
Copy them into your book.

1 "I must cut the grass today," said Mum.
2 "I'll be lucky to finish this homework," said Toby.
3 Mr Visram said, "My leg is very painful."
4 "Stick out your tongue," said the doctor.

B Copy these sentences.
Put **inverted commas** around the **spoken words**.

Find the words that are spoken. Put " in front of them and " at the end.

1 This window is broken, said the angry man.
2 I have lost my lunchbox, said the girl.
3 Marion said, I want a drink.
4 The clown said, I like making people laugh.

16

GRAMMAR *Practice*

Look at this conversation:
"Are you frightened?" asked the ghost.
"No," said the little boy.
"You should be frightened. I'm a ghost. I frighten people."
"Well, you don't frighten me," said the boy.
The spoken words have **inverted commas** around them.
When a different person speaks, we **start a new line**.

Copy the conversation below.
Put **inverted commas** around the spoken words and **start a new line** when a different person speaks.

Did you see the rabbit go down that hole? said the farmer. No, said Mary. Look over there by that big tree, said the farmer. Oh yes! The rabbit has just popped out again, said Mary. It might not be the same one. There are lots of rabbits in that hole, said the farmer.

GRAMMAR *Extension*

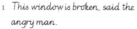

Remember to put inverted commas around the spoken words.

Always using the word **said** in conversations is not very interesting.

Below are some words you can use instead of **said**.
Write a **direct speech sentence** using each one.

1 cried   2 called   3 shouted
4 asked   5 muttered   6 whispered

17

---

see Glossary, page 12 – Sentences

Previous work

Book A
pages 24/25
pages 30/31
pages 34/35
pages 42/43
Book 1
pages 24/25
pages 28/29
Book 2
pages 44/45
Book 3
pages 12/13

Pupil Book answers

Focus

A

1 "I must cut the grass today,"
2 "I'll be lucky to finish this homework,"
3 "My leg is very painful."
4 "Stick out your tongue,"

B

1 "This window is broken," said the angry man.
2 "I have lost my lunchbox," said the girl.
3 Marion said, "I want a drink."
4 The clown said, "I like making people laugh."

Practice

"Did you see the rabbit go down that hole?" said the farmer.
"No," said Mary.
"Look over there by that big tree," said the farmer.
"Oh yes! The rabbit has just popped out again," said Mary.
"It might not be the same one. There are lots of rabbits in that hole," said the farmer.

Extension

Answers will be individual to the children, for example:
1 *"I can't find my teddy,"* **cried** *the little boy.*
2 *"Are you there?"* **called** *the old lady.*
3 *Brian* **shouted,** *"Look out!"*
4 *"Could you tell me the time?" Dennis* **asked**.
5 *"I didn't do it," Seth* **muttered**.
6 *"Shall I tell you a secret?" the girl* **whispered**.

Copymaster answers

Answers will be individual to the children, for example:
"Have you got your PE kit?" Freddy asked.
"What for?" demanded Jane.
"We are practising for Sports Day today," replied Freddy.
"I forgot!" Jane wailed, "What races are you in?"
"I'm doing the hundred metres and the long jump," Freddy informed her. "What are you doing?"
"Just the high jump, I think," said Jane.

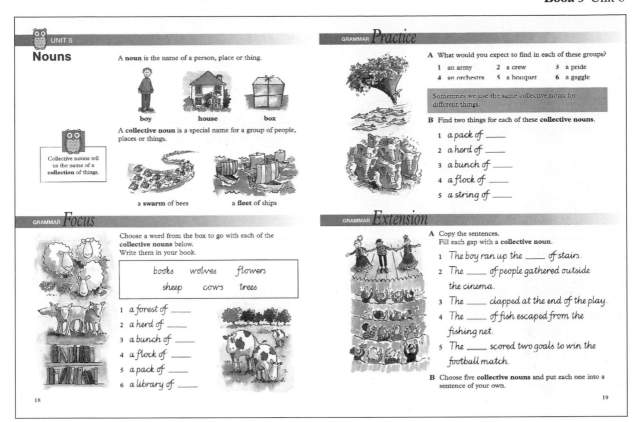

see Glossary, page 11 – Nouns

Previous work

Workbook 1	Workbook 2
page 4	page 4
page 5	page 5
page 12	page 12
page 13	page 13

Book A	Book 1
pages 6/7	pages 4/5
pages 10/11	pages 12/13
pages 22/23	pages 20/21
pages 36/37	
pages 40/41	

Book 2	Book 3
pages 4/5	pages 4/5
pages 16/17	

Pupil Book answers

Focus

1 a forest of **trees**
2 a herd of **cows**
3 a bunch of **flowers**
4 a flock of **sheep**
5 a pack of **wolves**
6 a library of **books**

Practice

A
1 soldiers   2 sailors
3 lions   4 musicians
5 flowers   6 geese

B
There are several possible answers for each collective noun, for example:
1 *a pack of **wolves/cards***
2 *a herd of **cows/elephants***
3 *a bunch of **flowers/grapes***
4 *a flock of **sheep/birds***
5 *a string of **beads/excuses***

Extension

A
1 The boy ran up the **flight** of stairs.
2 The **crowd/queue** of people gathered outside the cinema.
3 The **audience** clapped at the end of the play.
4 The **school** of fish escaped from the fishing net.
5 The **team** scored two goals to win the football match.

B
Answers will be individual to the children.

Copymaster answers

A

Across	Down
2 bouquet	1 pride
4 school	2 bunch
5 team	3 flock
6 army	4 swarm

B
1 A peal is a group of **bells**.
2 An archipelago is a group of **islands**.
3 A constellation is a group of **stars**.
4 A range is a group of **mountains**.
5 Clergy is a group of **church ministers**.

Check-up 1

Proper nouns

A In your book, write these names correctly.

1 *tina robinson* 2 *richard smith*
3 *kamal khan* 4 *doctor finch*

B Write these book titles correctly.

1 *a tale of two cities* 2 *the twits*
3 *the railway children* 4 *the silver sword*

Adjectives

A Copy the sentences below.
Underline the **number adjectives**.

1 *Five ponies are in the field.*
2 *Six thousand people watched the match.*
3 *I planted twenty trees.*

B Use these **number order adjectives** in sentences of your own.

1 *eighth* 2 *fortieth* 3 *thirty-second*

Singular and plural

Write the **plurals** of these words.

1 berry 2 key 3 post
4 penny 5 ruby 6 kidney

Prepositions

A Copy the sentences below.
Fill each gap with a **preposition**.

1 *The bird flew _____ the trees.*
2 *I will hide _____ the shed.*
3 *"It is very cold _____." said Mum.*

B Use each of these **prepositions** in a sentence of your own.

1 *beneath* 2 *around* 3 *during*

20

Sentences

A Copy the following sentences.
Underline the **subject** of each sentence.

1 *The goat ate the grass.*
2 *We like to ride our bicycles.*
3 *The circus came to town.*

B Copy the following sentences.
Underline the **object** of each sentence.

1 *Mrs Potter cleaned the windows.*
2 *Freda ate an ice cream.*
3 *I like oranges.*

C Copy these sentences.
Put **inverted commas** around the **spoken words**.

1 *Let me bathe that cut, said the nurse.*
2 *The boy muttered, I always get the blame.*
3 *What a mess, Mum shouted.*
4 *I'm very cold, moaned the little girl.*

Pronouns

Copy the sentences below.
Underline the **pronouns**.

1 *I am going to tidy the garage myself.*
2 *He watched the seagull as it dived for the fish.*
3 *When you go out, see if you can see it.*
4 *You must get yourself ready in good time.*

Collective nouns

Use the following **collective nouns** in sentences of your own.

1 *herd* 2 *band* 3 *bundle* 4 *queue*

21

Proper nouns

A
1 Tina Robinson
2 Richard Smith
3 Kamal Khan
4 Doctor Finch

B
1 A Tale of Two Cities
2 The Twits
3 The Railway Children
4 The Silver Sword

Adjectives

A
1 Five ponies are in the field.
2 Six thousand people watched the match.
3 I planted twenty trees.

B *Answers will be individual to the children.*

Singular and plural

1 berries
2 keys
3 posts
4 pennies
5 rubies
6 kidneys

Prepositions

A
Answers will be individual to the children, for example:
1 *The bird flew **over/into** the trees.*
2 *I will hide **in/behind** the shed.*
3 *"It is very cold **outside**," said Mum.*

B
Answers will be individual to the children.

Sentences

A
1 The goat ate the grass.
2 We like to ride our bicycles.
3 The circus came to town.

B
1 Mrs Potter cleaned the windows.
2 Freda ate an ice cream.
3 I like oranges.

C
1 "Let me bathe that cut," said the nurse.
2 The boy muttered, "I always get the blame."
3 "What a mess," Mum shouted.
4 "I'm very cold," moaned the little girl.

Pronouns

1 I am going to tidy the garage myself.
2 He watched the seagull as it dived for the fish.
3 When you go out, see if you can see it.
4 You must get yourself ready in good time.

Collective nouns

Answers will be individual to the children.

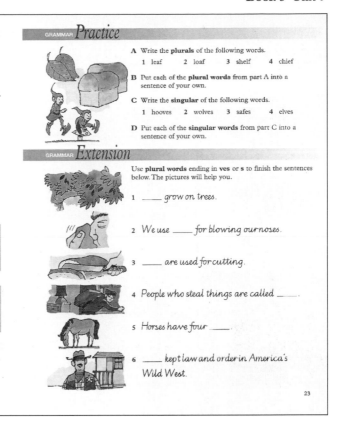

UNIT 9

Singular and plural

Singular means 'one person or thing'.
Plural means 'more than one person or thing'.

To make a noun plural, we usually add **s**.
shadow – shadows   rabbit – rabbits

To make nouns ending in **s**, **ch**, **sh** and **x** plural, we add **es**.
glass – **glasses**   match – matches
flash – flashes   box – boxes

When a noun ends in **y**, we take off the **y** and add **ies**.
body – **bodies**   lorry – lorries

If the letter in front of the **y** is a vowel, we just add **s**.
chimney – chimneys   guy – guys

Words ending in **f** and **fe** can be made plural by changing the **f** or **fe** to **v** and adding **es**.

wolf – wolves

shelf – shelves   knife – knives

Some nouns ending in **f** or **fe** can have an **s** or a **ves** ending: **wharf** can be **wharfs** or **wharves**. **hoof** can be **hoofs** or **hooves**.

Learn these examples:
calf – calves   elf – elves   half – halves
knife – knives   loaf – loaves   life – lives
scarf – scarves   sheaf – sheaves   shelf – shelves
thief – thieves   leaf – leaves   wolf – wolves

For some **f** and **fe** words, we just add **s**.

Learn these examples:
chief – chiefs   cliff – cliffs   dwarf – dwarfs
gulf – gulfs   sheriff – sheriffs   waif – waifs
oaf – oafs   reef – reefs   roof – roofs
muff – muffs   handkerchief – handkerchiefs

GRAMMAR *Focus*

In your book, write the **plurals** of these words.
1 scarf   2 reef   3 sheaf   4 life
5 thief   6 cliff   7 half   8 wife

22

GRAMMAR *Practice*

A Write the **plurals** of the following words.
1 leaf   2 loaf   3 shelf   4 chief

B Put each of the **plural words** from part A into a sentence of your own.

C Write the **singular** of the following words.
1 hooves   2 wolves   3 safes   4 elves

D Put each of the **singular words** from part C into a sentence of your own.

GRAMMAR *Extension*

Use **plural words** ending in **ves** or **s** to finish the sentences below. The pictures will help you.

1 ____ grow on trees.

2 We use ____ for blowing our noses.

3 ____ are used for cutting.

4 People who steal things are called ____.

5 Horses have four ____.

6 ____ kept law and order in America's Wild West.

23

---

see Glossary, page 13 – Singular and plural

Previous work

Book A
pages 20/21

Book 1
pages 8/9

Book 2
pages 38/39

Book 3
pages 8/9

Pupil Book answers

Focus

1 scarves   2 reefs
3 sheaves   4 lives
5 thieves   6 cliffs
7 halves   8 wives

Practice

A
1 leaves   2 loaves
3 shelves   4 chiefs

B *Answers will be individual to the children.*

C
1 hoof   2 wolf
3 safe   4 elf

D *Answers will be individual to the children.*

Extension

1 **Leaves** grow on trees.
2 We use **handkerchiefs** for blowing our noses.
3 **Knives** are used for cutting.
4 People who steal things are called **thieves**.
5 Horses have four **hooves/hoofs**.
6 **Sheriffs** kept law and order in America's Wild West.

Copymaster answers

A
1 The police caught the **thieves**.
2 There were six **handkerchiefs** in the drawer.
3 The **roofs** were covered with snow.
4 The **wolves** prowled in the forest.
5 A horse has four **hoofs/hooves**.

B
1 calves
2 halves
3 shelves
4 safes
5 dwarfs

UNIT 10

Adjectives

Adjectives are words that describe nouns.

long   small   short   cold

We use a **comparative adjective** to compare **two** things. To make an adjective into a comparative adjective, we usually add **er**.

This rope is longer than that rope.

We use a **superlative adjective** to compare **three or more** things. To make an adjective into a superlative adjective, we usually add **est**.

This rope is the longest of the three.

For adjectives that end in **y**, we have to change the **y** to **i** before we add **er** or **est**.

windy	windier	windiest
sleepy	sleepier	sleepiest
lazy	lazier	laziest

If the adjective is a long word and does not end in **y**, we put the word '**more**' in front of it when we are comparing two things and '**most**' in front of it when we are comparing three or more things.

important	more important	most important
modern	more modern	most modern
frightening	more frightening	most frightening

GRAMMAR *Focus*

Copy this table into your book. Fill in the missing words.

Adjective	Comparative	Superlative
round		roundest
___	shorter	shortest
___	heavier	
beautiful		most beautiful
___	more terrible	___

24

GRAMMAR *Practice*

A Copy the sentences below.
Make the red **adjectives** into **comparative adjectives**.

1 That question is easy than the last one.
2 It is cloudy than yesterday.
3 Our dog is intelligent than our cat.

B Copy the sentences below.
Make the red **adjectives** into **superlative adjectives**.

1 This is the smelly of all the cheeses.
2 He is the lazy boy in the school.
3 This is the peaceful place I have ever been.

GRAMMAR *Extension*

A Use the **comparative** or **superlative** of an adjective from the box to compare each set of things below. The first one has been done for you.

sunny	heavy	bumpy	tidy	ancient

1 compare the weight of two loaves

The white loaf is heavy.
The brown loaf is heavier.

2 compare the surface of two roads
3 compare the weather on three days
4 compare the age of three fossils
5 compare the neatness of two rooms

B Use these **comparative** and **superlative adjectives** in sentences of your own.

1 messier   2 more nervous
3 cheekiest   4 most dangerous

25

---

see Glossary, page 9 – Adjectives

Previous work

Workbook 1	Workbook 2
page 6	page 6
page 7	page 7
page 13	page 13

Book A	Book 1
pages 8/9	pages 6/7
pages 10/11	pages 22/23
pages 28/29	pages 34/35
pages 44/45	pages 42/43

Book 2	Book 3
pages 6/7	pages 6/7
pages 22/23	

Pupil Book answers

Focus

ADJECTIVE	COMPARATIVE	SUPERLATIVE
round	**rounder**	roundest
short	shorter	shortest
foggy	foggier	**foggiest**
beautiful	**more beautiful**	most beautiful
terrible	more terrible	**most terrible**

Practice

A

1 That question is **easier** than the last one.
2 It is **cloudier** than yesterday.
3 Our dog is **more intelligent** than out cat.

B

1 This is the **smelliest** of all the cheeses.
2 He is the **laziest** boy in the school.
3 This is the **most peaceful** place I have ever been.

Extension

Answers will be individual to the children, for example:
2 *This road is **bumpy**.*
   *That road is **bumpier**.*

3 *It was **sunny** on Monday.*
   *It was **sunnier** on Tuesday.*
   *Today is the **sunniest** day.*
4 *The fossil is **ancient**.*
   *This fossil is **more ancient**.*
   *That fossil is the **most ancient**.*
5 *My room is **tidy**.*
   *Your room is **tidier**.*

B
Answers will be individual to the children.

Copymaster answers

A

1 She is the **grumpiest** person I know.
2 My left hand is **weaker** than my right one.
3 This is the **most isolated** island of the three.
4 Chris is **more dependable** than Jack.
5 Come on Monday or Tuesday, whichever is **more convenient**.

B
Answers will be individual to the children.

UNIT 11

Verbs

Tense comes from the Latin word 'tempus', meaning 'time'.

When we use **verbs** to tell us about something that has happened in the past, we use the **past tense**.

To make the past tense, we usually add **ed** or **d** to the verb family name.

I combed my hair.   I washed my face.
I walked downstairs.   I picked up my bag.

Another way to make the past tense is like this:

Past tense of the verb 'to be'	+ verb	+ ing	
I was	sing	ing	= I **was singing**
you were	point	ing	= you **were pointing**
he was	help	ing	= he **was helping**
she was	laugh	ing	= she **was laughing**
it was	rain	ing	= it **was raining**
we were	jump	ing	= we **were jumping**
you were	shout	ing	= you **were shouting**
they were	fight	ing	= they **were fighting**

We use this way of writing the past tense when an action goes on for some time or something else happens at the same time.

I **was walking** to the shops when it started to rain.
We **were playing** football for three hours.
She **was reading** when the telephone rang.

GRAMMAR *Focus*

Copy the following sentences into your book.
Underline the two words in each sentence that make up the **past tense**.

1 The birds were flying around the garden.
2 The tree was bending in the wind.
3 The ducks were quacking for some food.
4 The dog was scattering leaves everywhere.

26

GRAMMAR *Practice*

Remember! Use the past tense of the verb 'to be' and an 'ing' word.

Copy the sentences below.
Use the **past tense** instead of the verb family name.

1 Jill (to post) a letter when she saw her friend.
2 The children (to talk) until the teacher came in.
3 I (to hope) to cut the grass but it started to rain.
4 We had a power cut while we (to watch) the television.

GRAMMAR *Extension*

A Copy this table and fill in the missing **verbs**.

Verb family name	Past tense with 'ed or 'd'	Past tense with verb 'to be' + 'ing'
to look	looked	I was looking
to save		we were ____
____	laughed	he was ____
to show	____	they ____ showing
____	borrowed	he was ____
to follow		she ____ following
to stroll		I was ____
____	smiled	you were

B Complete these sentences by adding **past tense** verbs.

1 I ____ when it began to snow.
2 We ____ when we saw the accident.
3 She ____ all day.
4 He ____ breakfast when the post came.

27

---

see Glossary, page 14 – Verbs

Previous work

Workbook 1	Workbook 2
page 8	page 8
page 9	page 9
page 14	page 14
page 15	page 15

Book A	Book 1
pages 12/13	pages 26/27
pages 16/17	pages 30/31
pages 26/27	pages 38/39
pages 38/39	

Book 2	
pages 12/13	
pages 14/15	
pages 20/21	
pages 34/35	
pages 42/43	

Pupil Book answers

Focus

1 The birds <u>were flying</u> around the garden.
2 The tree <u>was bending</u> in the wind.
3 The ducks <u>were quacking</u> for some food.
4 The dog <u>was scattering</u> leaves everywhere.

Practice

1 Jill **was posting** a letter when she saw her friend.
2 The children **were talking** until the teacher came in.
3 I **was hoping** to cut the grass but it started to rain.
4 We had a power cut while we **were watching** the television.

Extension

A

VERB FAMILY NAME	PAST TENSE WITH 'ED' OR 'D'	PAST TENSE WITH VERB 'TO BE' AND 'ING'
to look	looked	I was looking
to save	**saved**	we were **saving**
to laugh	laughed	he was **laughing**
to show	**showed**	they **were** showing
to borrow	borrowed	he was **borrowing**
to follow	**followed**	she **was** following
to stroll	**strolled**	I was **strolling**
to smile	smiled	you were **smiling**

B
Answers will be individual to the children.

Copymaster answers

A

2	they saved	there were saving
3	we talked	we were talking
4	you jumped	you were jumping
5	he frowned	he was frowning
6	she managed	she was managing
7	it barked	it was barking

B
Answers will be individual to the children.

UNIT 12

Nouns

Possessive nouns tell you who owns something. They have an apostrophe ' and an s at the end.

Ruth's bicycle
Ruth is the owner.
'Ruth's bicycle' means the same as 'the bicycle belonging to Ruth'.
Ruth's is the **possessive noun**.

Roger's book
Roger is the owner.
'Roger's book' means the same as 'the book belonging to Roger'.
Roger's is the **possessive noun**.

The **'s** tells you who or what is the owner.

GRAMMAR *Focus*

Copy the following into your book.
Underline the name of the **owner** in each one.

1 Deepak's football
2 the girl's laugh
3 the flower's stem
4 the doctor's coat
5 the dog's lead
6 the car's engine
7 Nigel's shoe
8 the farmer's field
9 the captain's ship
10 the boy's hair

28

GRAMMAR *Practice*

Copy the sentences below.
Add an **apostrophe** to the name of the owner in each sentence.

1 Garys homework was very hard.
2 Graham found the dogs lead in the park.
3 That mans tie has red and blue spots.
4 The cats claws were very sharp.
5 In the autumn, that trees leaves fall off.
6 The books cover was torn.
7 The reporters notebook was in her pocket.
8 Nadias wish came true.
9 Tamara didn't like Amandas coat.
10 The old mans gloves were lost.

GRAMMAR *Extension*

A Write these in a shorter way, using **possessive nouns**.
  1 the hand belonging to the girl
  2 the dinner belonging to the boy
  3 the tail belonging to the mouse
  4 the song belonging to the bird
  5 the wheels belonging to the tractor
B Write five sentences of your own, using a **possessive noun** in each one.

29

---

see Glossary, page 11 – Nouns

Previous work

Workbook 1	Workbook 2
page 4	page 4
page 5	page 5
page 12	page 12
page 13	page 13

Book A	Book 1
pages 6/7	pages 4/5
pages 10/11	pages 12/13
pages 22/23	pages 20/21
pages 36/37	
pages 40/41	

Book 2	Book 3
pages 4/5	pages 4/5
pages 16/17	pages 18/19

Pupil Book answers

Focus

1 <u>Deepak</u>'s football
2 the <u>girl</u>'s laugh
3 the <u>flower</u>'s stem
4 the <u>doctor</u>'s coat
5 the <u>dog</u>'s lead
6 the <u>car</u>'s engine
7 <u>Nigel</u>'s shoe
8 the <u>farmer</u>'s field
9 the <u>captain</u>'s ship
10 the <u>boy</u>'s hair

Practice

1 Gary's homework was very hard.
2 Graham found the dog's lead in the park.
3 That man's tie has red and blue spots.
4 The cat's claws were very sharp.
5 In the autumn, that tree's leaves fall off.
6 The book's cover was torn.
7 The reporter's notebook was in her pocket.
8 Nadia's wish came true.
9 Tamara didn't like Amanda's coat.
10 The old man's gloves were lost.

Extension

A
1 The girl's hand
2 the boy's dinner
3 the mouse's tail
4 the bird's song
5 the tractor's wheels

B
Answers will be individual to the children.

Copymaster answers

A
1 I found my <u>brother's</u> **football** in the ditch.
2 The <u>flower's</u> **petals** had fallen off.
3 The <u>teacher's</u> **car** wouldn't start.
4 The <u>sun's</u> **rays** can be harmful.
5 The <u>doctor's</u> **surgery** was full.

B
1 the clown's hat
2 the ship's sails
3 the musician's guitar
4 the man's voice
5 the bird's wings

C
Answers will be individual to the children.

UNIT 13
Sentences

A sentence needs a capital letter and a full stop or a question mark.

A sentence has two parts.
The **subject** is the thing or person that the sentence is about.
The **predicate** is the rest of the sentence.

Subject	Predicate
The eagle	is a large bird.
My bucket	has a hole in it.
Rabbits	live in burrows.
I	would like a kitten.

GRAMMAR *Focus*

A Copy the following sentences into your book.
Underline the **subject** in each sentence.

1 I have hurt my knee.
2 Sharks live in the sea.
3 The Queen lives in a palace.
4 The horses are in the stable.

B Copy the sentences below.
Underline the **predicate** in each sentence.

1 The bakery opens at nine o'clock.
2 We decided to go to the park.
3 The river burst its banks.
4 Our garage is big enough for two cars.

30

GRAMMAR *Practice*

Join each **subject** with the right **predicate** to make a sentence.
Write the five sentences in your book.

	Subject	Predicate
1	The cottage	watched the match.
2	I	was very exciting.
3	The race	was near the stream.
4	A large crowd	wrote the answers carefully.
5	Sam	am paddling a canoe.

GRAMMAR *Extension*

A Write an interesting **subject** for each of these predicates.

1 _____ fell into the pond.
2 _____ were afraid of the dark.
3 _____ frightened my brother.
4 _____ left her bag on the bus.

B Write an interesting **predicate** for each of these subjects.

1 The rotting apple _____ .
2 The huge forest _____ .
3 They _____ .
4 Some birds _____ .

31

---

see Glossary, page 12 – Sentences

Previous work

Book A
pages 24/25
pages 30/31
pages 34/35
pages 42/43

Book 1
pages 24/25
pages 28/29
pages 38/39

Book 2
pages 44/45

Book 3
pages 12/13
pages 16/17

Pupil Book answers

Focus

A
1 <u>I</u> have hurt my knee.
2 <u>Sharks</u> live in the sea.
3 <u>The Queen</u> lives in a palace.
4 <u>The horses</u> are in the stable.

B
1 The bakery <u>opens at nine o'clock</u>.
2 We <u>decided to go to the park</u>.
3 The river <u>burst its banks</u>.
4 Our garage <u>is big enough for two cars</u>.

Practice

1 The cottage was near the stream.
2 I am paddling a canoe.
3 The race was very exciting.
4 A large crowd watched the match.
5 Sam wrote the answers carefully.

Extension

A and **B**
Answers will be individual to the children.

Copymaster answers

A
1 <u>The cows</u> **were lying down in the field**.
2 <u>The cricket ball</u> **was hit for six runs**.
3 <u>A large audience</u> **came to see the concert**.
4 <u>Our house</u> **has a broken window**.
5 <u>These chips</u> **are not cooked**.

B
Answers will be individual to the children, for example:
1a) *The cake had gone very stale.*
  b) *I ate the last piece of cake.*
2a) *My bicycle has a flat tyre.*
  b) *Sam borrowed my bicycle.*
3a) *This letter came yesterday morning.*
  b) *I forgot to post this letter.*

UNIT 14
Verbs

Verbs tell us what action is happening.
The **tense** of a verb tells us when an action happened.
If the action is happening in the present, we use the
present tense.

> She **knits** a jumper.
> or
> She **is knitting** a jumper.

If the action happened in the past, we use the **past tense**.

> He **climbed** the mountain.
> or
> He **was climbing** the mountain.

If we want to write about what is going to happen in the
future, we use the **future tense**.
The future tense is made up of two parts:
Part 1: **shall** after **I** and **we**
    will after **you, he, she, it** and **they**
Part 2: the verb family name.

> I **shall** swim to the steps.
> She **will** dive into the pool.

GRAMMAR

Copy the following sentences into your book.
Underline the **future tense verbs**.

1 I shall go at seven o'clock.
2 If it rains, we will take an umbrella.
3 He will wrap the present in a minute.
4 The children will know when to sing.
5 We shall catch the bus to town.

32

GRAMMAR

A Copy the sentences below.
Change the **present tense verbs** to the **future tense**.

1 Sanjay answers the question.
2 Mandy is paying for the apples.
3 We are walking to school.

B Copy the sentences below.
Change the **past tense verbs** to the **future tense**.

1 Freddy strolled along the beach.
2 The teacher was talking to the class.
3 The cars raced around the track.

GRAMMAR

A Copy this table and fill in the missing words.

Verb family name	Present tense	Past tense	Future tense
to believe	I believe	I believed	I shall believe
to _____	they argue	they _____	they _____
to work	she _____	she _____	she _____
to _____	we notice	we _____	we _____

If we want to make a strong statement, we put **will** after
I and **we**, and **shall** after **you, he, she, it** and **they**.

> I will not eat that cabbage!
> You shall eat this meal!

B Put *shall* or *will* in each gap to make these into strong
statements.

1 You _____ go to bed at nine o'clock!
2 I _____ ride my bike down the lane!
3 He _____ not go to the pictures!

33

---

see Glossary, page 14 – Verbs

Previous work

Workbook 1	Workbook 2
page 8	page 8
page 9	page 9
page 14	page 14
page 15	page 15

Book A	Book 1
pages 12/13	pages 26/27
pages 16/17	pages 30/31
pages 26/27	pages 38/39
pages 38/39	

Book 2	Book 3
pages 12/13	pages 26/27
pages 14/15	
pages 20/21	
pages 34/35	
pages 42/43	

Pupil Book answers

Focus

1 I shall go at seven o'clock.

2 If it rains, we will take an umbrella.
3 He will wrap the present in a minute.
4 The children will know when to sing.
5 We shall catch the bus to town.

Practice

A
1 Sanjay **will answer** the question.
2 Mandy **will pay** for the apples.
3 We **shall walk** to school.

B
1 Freddy **will stroll** along the beach.
2 The teacher **will talk** to the class.
3 The cars **will race** around the track.

Extension

A

VERB FAMILY NAME	PRESENT TENSE
to believe	I believe
to **argue**	they argue
to work	she **works**
to **notice**	we notice

PAST TENSE	FUTURE TENSE
I believed	I shall believe
they **argued**	they **will argue**
she **worked**	she **will work**
we **noticed**	we **shall notice**

B
1 You **shall** go to bed at nine o'clock!
2 I **will** ride my bike down the lane!
3 He **shall** not go to the pictures!

Copymaster answers

A
1 We shall go out in five minutes.
2 After tea I shall read my book.
3 The wheels will squeak if you don't oil them.
4 My Mum will meet you at three o'clock.
5 The dog will bark when someone knocks on the door.

B
2 Tomorrow we shall visit the museum.
3 Tomorrow he will mend his bicycle.
4 Tomorrow they will plant some seeds.
5 Tomorrow I shall go to the library.

UNIT 15

Nouns and verbs

English can be very strange! When we want a plural noun, we usually add **s**, **es** or **ies**. When we want a plural verb, we usually take off the **s**.

Nouns can be **singular** or **plural**.
Verbs can also be **singular** or **plural**.
When we use a singular noun, we must also use a singular verb.

The **garage needs** painting.

| singular noun | singular verb |

When we use a plural noun, we must use a plural verb.

The **garages need** painting.

| plural noun | plural verb |

The verb families '**to be**' and '**to have**' can be tricky. Learn these:

	Present tense		Past tense	
	singular	plural	singular	plural
To be	I am you are he is she is it is	we are you are they are	I was you were he was she was it was	we were you were they were
To have	I have you have he has she has it has	we have you have they have	I had you had he had she had it had	we had you had they had

GRAMMAR *Focus*

Copy the following sentences into your book. Choose the correct **verb** to finish each one.

1 The cottages is/are empty.
2 We is/are going to buy them.
3 I is/am going to live in one of them.

34

GRAMMAR *Practice*

A Put each of these nouns into a sentence, followed by have or has.

1 crowd   2 children   3 team
4 girls   5 mice   6 everyone
7 oxen   8 herd   9 women

B Copy the sentences below.
Choose the correct **verb** to finish each one.

1 The cake crumble/crumbles when you cut it.
2 The icing is/are very soft.
3 I like/likes to eat this cake.
4 We buy/buys this cake every week.

GRAMMAR *Extension*

Copy this passage, correcting the mistakes.

We goes to the library on a Saturday morning. I likes to read adventure stories but my sister like books about animals. We takes three books home every week. The man in the library are very helpful. If he haven't got the book I wants, he order it for next time.

35

---

see Glossary, page 11 – Nouns and page 14 – Verbs

Previous work

Nouns

Verbs

Pupil Book answers

Focus

1 The cottages **are** empty
2 We **are** going to buy them.
3 I **am** going to live in one of them.

Practice

A
Sentences will be individual to the children. The verbs should be as follows:

1 crowd **has**   2 children **have**
3 team **has**   4 girls **have**
5 mice **have**   6 everyone **has**
7 oxen **have**   8 herd **has**
9 women **have**

B
1 The cake **crumbles** when you cut it.
2 The icing **is** very soft.
3 I **like** to eat this cake.
4 We **buy** this cake every week.

Extension

We **go** to the library on a Saturday morning. I **like** to read adventure stories but my sister **likes** books about animals. We **take** three books home every week. The man in the library **is** very helpful. If he **hasn't** got the book I **want**, he **orders** it for next time.

Copymaster answers

Answers will be individual to the children, for example:
1 *This **porridge is** cold.*
2 *The **rubbish has** burst out of the bag.*
3 *The **snakes were** slithering over the rock.*
4 *The **trees have** been cut down.*
5 *Our **drinks are** on the table.*
6 *The **garden was** very overgrown.*

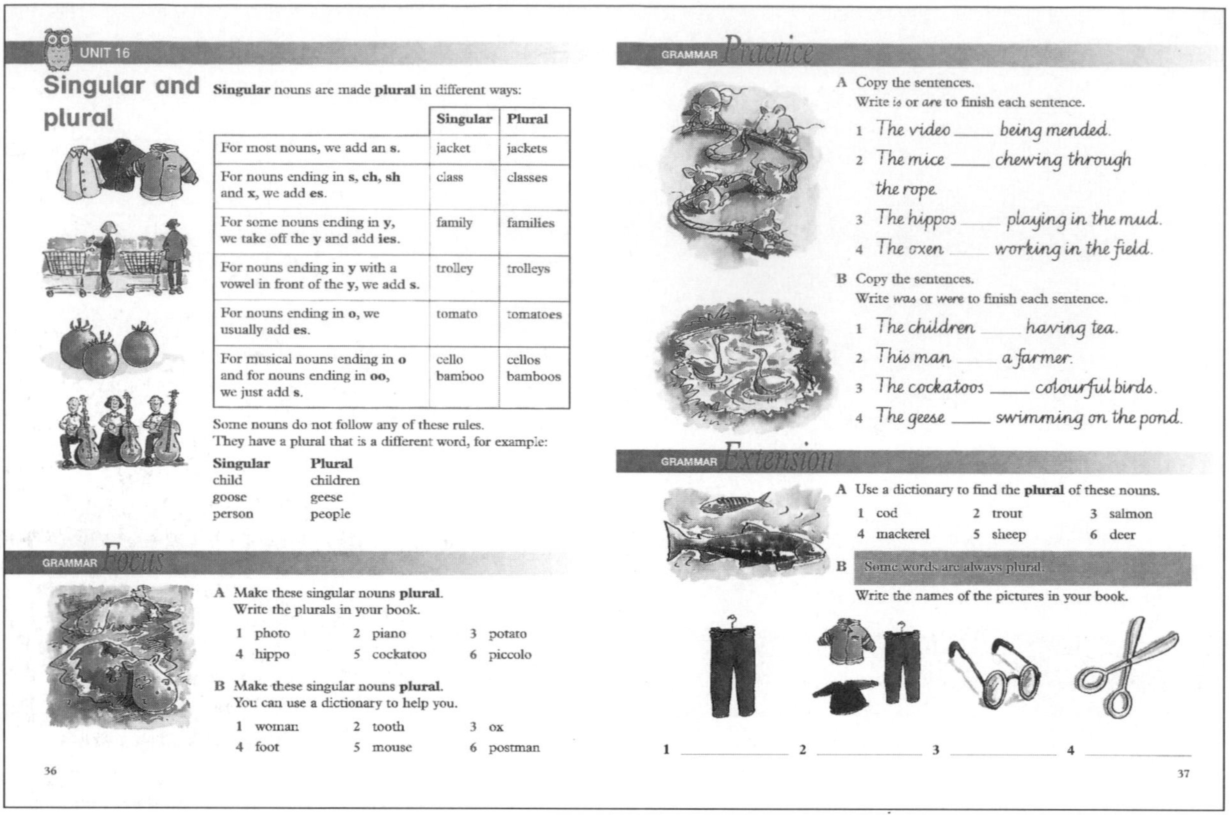

UNIT 16

Singular and plural

Singular nouns are made **plural** in different ways:

	Singular	Plural
For most nouns, we add an **s**.	jacket	jackets
For nouns ending in **s**, **ch**, **sh** and **x**, we add **es**.	class	classes
For some nouns ending in **y**, we take off the **y** and add **ies**.	family	families
For nouns ending in **y** with a vowel in front of the **y**, we add **s**.	trolley	trolleys
For nouns ending in **o**, we usually add **es**.	tomato	tomatoes
For musical nouns ending in **o** and for nouns ending in **oo**, we just add **s**.	cello bamboo	cellos bamboos

Some nouns do not follow any of these rules.
They have a plural that is a different word, for example:

Singular	**Plural**
child	children
goose	geese
person	people

GRAMMAR Focus

A Make these singular nouns **plural**.
Write the plurals in your book.

1 photo 2 piano 3 potato
4 hippo 5 cockatoo 6 piccolo

B Make these singular nouns **plural**.
You can use a dictionary to help you.

1 woman 2 tooth 3 ox
4 foot 5 mouse 6 postman

36

GRAMMAR Practice

A Copy the sentences.
Write *is* or *are* to finish each sentence.

1 The video ____ being mended.
2 The mice ____ chewing through the rope.
3 The hippos ____ playing in the mud.
4 The oxen ____ working in the field.

B Copy the sentences.
Write *was* or *were* to finish each sentence.

1 The children ____ having tea.
2 This man ____ a farmer.
3 The cockatoos ____ colourful birds.
4 The geese ____ swimming on the pond.

GRAMMAR Extension

A Use a dictionary to find the **plural** of these nouns.

1 cod 2 trout 3 salmon
4 mackerel 5 sheep 6 deer

B Some words are always plural.
Write the names of the pictures in your book.

1 ____ 2 ____ 3 ____ 4 ____

37

see Glossary, page 13 – Singular and plural

Previous work

Book A
pages 20/21
Book 1
pages 8/9
Book 2
pages 38/39
Book 3
pages 8/9 pages 22/23

Pupil Book answers

Focus

A

1 photos **2** pianos
3 potatoes **4** hippos
5 cockatoos **6** piccolos

B

1 women **2** teeth
3 oxen **4** feet
5 mice **6** postmen

Practice

A

1 The video **is** being mended.
2 The mice **are** chewing through the rope.
3 The hippos **are** playing in the mud.
4 The oxen **are** working in the field.

B

1 The children **were** having tea.
2 This man **was** a farmer.
3 The cockatoos **were** colourful birds.
4 The geese **were** swimming on the pond.

Extension

A

1 cod **2** trout
3 salmon **4** mackerel
5 sheep **6** deer

B

1 trousers
2 clothes
3 glasses (*or* spectacles)
4 scissors

Copymaster answers

ADD S	ADD 'ES'	TAKE OFF 'Y' AND ADD 'IES'	CHANGE THE WORD
baths	potatoes	rubies	geese
trolleys	matches	babies	children
desks	bushes	factories	feet
pianos	glasses	puppies	men
shoes	foxes		
valleys			
bamboos			

Check-up 2

Singular and plural

Write the **plurals** of these nouns.
1 calf 2 life 3 loaf 4 gulf
5 dwarf 6 knife 7 thief 8 cliff
9 goose 10 piano 11 mouse 12 deer

Adjectives

A Write the **comparative** of each adjective.
1 calm 2 loud 3 bumpy 4 sleepy
5 funny 6 marvellous 7 white 8 terrifying

B Write the **superlative** of each adjective.
1 happy 2 lonely 3 hard 4 ancient
5 dirty 6 dangerous 7 muddy 8 enjoyable

Verbs

Copy the sentences.
Underline the **past tense verb** in each sentence.
1 The clown was tumbling in the ring.
2 We quickly scrambled up the hill.
3 Rita strolled to the shops.
4 The children were grumbling all the time.
5 I was working hard all day.

Nouns

A Copy the sentences.
Underline the **owner** in each sentence.
1 The dog's ball was lost in the bushes.
2 Maisie's umbrella was bright yellow.
3 The manager's car had broken down.
4 The giraffe's neck is very long.
5 The giant's feet are enormous.

B Copy these sentences.
In each sentence, add the **apostrophe** to the owner's name.
1 The ghosts scream was frightening.
2 The alligators teeth were very sharp.
3 The kittens fur is very soft.

C Copy these sentences.
Put the verbs into the **future tense**.
1 Gran is knitting a jumper for me.
2 I wrapped the present in shiny paper.
3 The bells are jingling in the wind.

Sentences

A Copy these sentences.
Underline the **subject** in each sentence.
1 I catch a bus to school every day.
2 Swallows fly south for the winter.
3 The icy path was very dangerous.

B Finish these sentences with interesting **predicates**.
1 The old wreck _____.
2 My younger brother _____.
3 The grey clouds _____.

Nouns and verbs

Correct these sentences.
1 My friend and I is going for a walk.
2 Everyone have gone out.
3 My sister were in the school choir.
4 The mice lives in the barn.

38   39

Singular and plural

1 calves	2 lives
3 loaves	4 gulfs
5 dwarfs	6 knives
7 thieves	8 cliffs
9 geese	10 pianos
11 mice	12 deer

Adjectives

A
1 calmer
2 louder
3 bumpier
4 sleepier
5 funnier
6 more marvellous
7 whiter
8 more terrifying

B
1 happiest
2 loneliest
3 hardest
4 most ancient
5 dirtiest
6 most dangerous
7 muddiest
8 most enjoyable

Verbs

1 The clown <u>was tumbling</u> in the ring.
2 We quickly <u>scrambled</u> up the hill.
3 Rita <u>strolled</u> to the shops.
4 The children <u>were grumbling</u> all the time.
5 I <u>was working</u> hard all day.

Nouns

A
1 The <u>dog</u>'s ball was lost in the bushes.
2 <u>Maisie</u>'s umbrella was bright yellow.
3 The <u>manager</u>'s car had broken down.
4 The <u>giraffe</u>'s neck is very long.
5 The <u>giant</u>'s feet are enormous.

B
1 The ghost's scream was frightening.
2 The alligator's teeth were very sharp.
3 The kitten's fur is very soft.

C

1 Tina's skirt
2 Bill's birthday present
3 Mum's car
4 the rat's tail
5 Julie's birthday

Sentences

A
1 <u>I</u> catch a bus to school every day.
2 <u>Swallows</u> fly south for the winter.
3 <u>The icy path</u> was very dangerous.

B *Answers will be individual to the children.*

Nouns and verbs

1 My friend and I **are** going for a walk.
2 Everyone **has** gone out.
3 My sister **was** in the school choir.
4 The mice **live** in the barn.

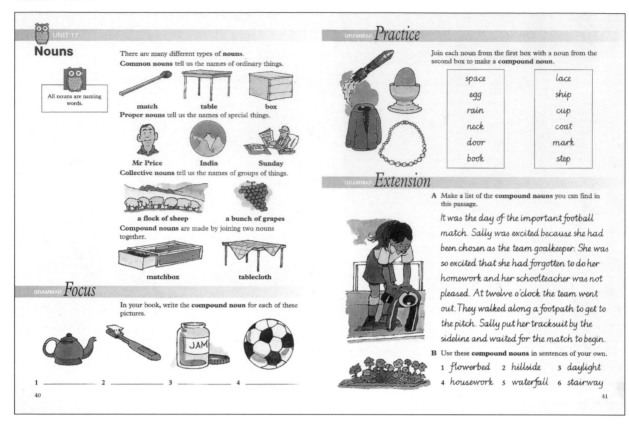

see Glossary, page 11 – Nouns

Previous work

Workbook 1	Workbook 2
page 4	page 4
page 5	page 5
page 12	page 12
page 13	page 13
Book A	**Book 1**
pages 6/7	pages 4/5
pages 10/11	pages 12/13
pages 22/23	pages 20/21
pages 36/37	
pages 40/41	
Book 2	**Book 3**
pages 4/5	pages 4/5
pages 16/17	pages 18/19
	pages 28/29
	pages 34/35

Pupil Book answers

Focus

1 teapot
2 toothbrush
3 jamjar
4 snowman

Practice

spaceship
eggcup
raincoat
necklace
doorstep
bookmark

Extension

A

It was the day of the important **football** match. Sally was excited because she had been chosen as the team **goalkeeper**. She was so excited that she had forgotten to do her **homework** and her **schoolteacher** was not pleased. At twelve o'clock the team went out. They had to go along a **footpath** to get to the pitch. Sally put her **tracksuit** by the **sideline** and waited for the match to begin.

B *Answers will be individual to the children.*

Copymaster answers

Answers will be individual to the children, but might include:

1 *rainbow, raindrop, rainfall, raincoat, rainwater, rainstorm*
2 *bedroom, bedside, bedtime, bedclothes, bedspread*
3 *fireman, fireside, firework, firelight, firewood, fireplace*
4 *snowball, snowdrop, snowman*
5 *moonbeam, moonlight, moonshine*
6 *eyebrow, eyelash, eyelid, eyesight, eyeball*
7 *waterfall, watermark, waterproof, waterway, watercress*
8 *farmstead, farmyard, farmhouse*
9 *bookcase, bookmark, bookshop, bookworm*
10 *sunbeam, sunflower, sunshine, sunburn, sunshade, sunlight*

UNIT 18

Adverbs

An **adverb** tells us more about **how**, **when** or **where** the action of a verb takes place.

How?	Sam clapped **loudly**.
When?	Mandy fell off her bicycle **yesterday**
Where?	I put the flowers **outside**.

Some adverbs tell us more about other adverbs.

I walked **very quickly** to catch the bus.

It rained **quite heavily** during the night.

Comparative adverbs compare two things. **Superlative** adverbs compare three or more things.

We can use **comparative** and **superlative** adverbs to compare actions, just as we use adjectives to compare nouns.

We add the words '**more**' and '**most**' for adverbs ending in **ly**.

Adverb	Comparative	Superlative
quickly	more quickly	most quickly
clearly	more clearly	most clearly
loudly	more loudly	most loudly

We add **er** and **est** to adverbs that do not end in **ly**.

Adverb	Comparative	Superlative
hard	harder	hardest
high	higher	highest

Some adverbs don't follow this pattern and we have to learn them.

Be careful! A few adverbs do not follow these rules.

Adverb	Comparative	Superlative
well	better	best
badly	worse	worst

GRAMMAR *Focus*

In your book write the **comparatives** and **superlatives** of these adverbs.

1 easily 2 happily 3 patiently 4 early
5 seriously 6 late 7 widely 8 badly

42

GRAMMAR *Practice*

A Write these sentences, changing the brown **adverbs** into **comparatives**.

1 When it snows we will be able to use the sledge often.

2 The donkeys trotted quickly when it began to rain.

3 The vegetables grew well after we watered them.

B Change the brown **adverb** into a **superlative** in each sentence.

1 Ben tried hard and won the race.

2 The last choir to perform was tuneful

3 You have scored badly in your test.

GRAMMAR *Extension*

The second brown word in each sentence gives you a clue to the adverb you need.

A Replace each brown word with a **single adverb**.

1 The nurse dealt with the emergency with calmness.

2 Sam dribbled the ball with skill.

3 Lisa answered the question with truth.

B Use these **comparative** and **superlative** adverbs in sentences of your own.

1 worse 2 more dishonestly
3 widest 4 most clearly
5 more neatly 6 earliest

43

---

see Glossary, page 10 – Adverbs

Previous work

Book 2
pages 26/27
pages 40/41

Pupil Book answers

Focus

ADVERB	COMPARATIVE	SUPERLATIVE
easily	more easily	most easily
happily	more happily	most happily
patiently	more patiently	most patiently
early	earlier	earliest
seriously	more seriously	most seriously
late	later	latest
widely	more widely	most widely
badly	more badly	most badly

Practice

A

1 When it snows we will be able to use the sledge **more often**.
2 The donkeys trotted **more quickly** when it began to rain.
3 The vegetables grew **better** after we watered them.

B

1 Ben tried **hardest** and won the race.
2 The last choir to perform was **most tuneful**.
3 You have scored **worst** in the test.

Extension

A

1 The nurse dealt with the emergency **calmly**.
2 Sam dribbled the ball **skilfully**.
3 Lisa answered the question **truthfully**.

B

Answers will be individual to the children.

Copymaster answers

Answers will be individual to the children.

Contractions

UNIT 19

Contractions are words that have been made smaller by missing out letters.

I am = I'm   you are = you're

We usually use contractions when we are speaking or when we are writing direct speech.

An apostrophe ' replaces the missing letter or letters in a contraction.

"That's not right," explained John. "A rectangle doesn't have five corners."

That's = that is   doesn't = does not

GRAMMAR *Focus*

A In your book, write these **contractions** in full.

1 who's   2 they'll   3 he's
4 you're   5 doesn't   6 there's
7 who'd   8 shouldn't 9 we've

B Write the **contractions** for these pairs of words.

1 would not   2 have not   3 she has
4 we are   5 we shall   6 has not
7 who would   8 will not   9 let us

GRAMMAR *Practice*

Copy this conversation, changing the green words into **contractions**.

"I cannot find my book anywhere," shouted Justin. "I have seen it in my room but it is not there now."

"If you would put things away you would be able to find them," said his mother. "I shall come and help you when I have finished writing this letter."

"I shall ask Trevor," said Justin. "He will know where it is. I bet he has got it."

GRAMMAR *Extension*

A Write the **contraction** from each of the sentences below.
Next to it, write the two words which it replaces.

1 "The ball's gone into the pond," shouted Philip.

2 "We'll need a long stick to get it out," said Luke.

3 "I'll go and look in the shed," said Philip.

B Write a conversation between two or three people, using as many of the following **contractions** as you can.

| can't | he'll | she's | haven't |
| it's | they've | won't | don't |

Remember to use inverted commas for direct speech.

44   45

---

see Glossary, page 11 – Contractions

Previous work

Book 2
pages 24/25

Pupil Book answers

Focus

A

1 who is *or* who has   2 they will
3 he is *or* he has   4 you are
5 does not   6 there is *or* there has
7 who would   8 should not
9 we have

B

1 wouldn't   2 haven't   3 she's
4 we're   5 we'll   6 hasn't
7 who'd   8 won't   9 let's

Practice

"I **can't** find my book anywhere," shouted Justin. "**I've** seen it in my room but it **isn't** there now."

"If **you'd** put things away **you'd** be able to find them," said his mother.

"**I'll** come and help you when **I've** finished writing this letter."

"**I'll** ask Trevor," said Justin. "**He'll** know where it is. I bet **he's** got it."

Extension

A

1 ball's   ball has
2 we'll   we shall
3 I'll   I shall

B

Answers will be individual to the children.

Copymaster answers

A

1 shouldn't   2 won't
3 we're   4 can't
5 mustn't   6 I'm
7 here's   8 we're
9 let's   10 you're

B

Answers will be individual to the children.

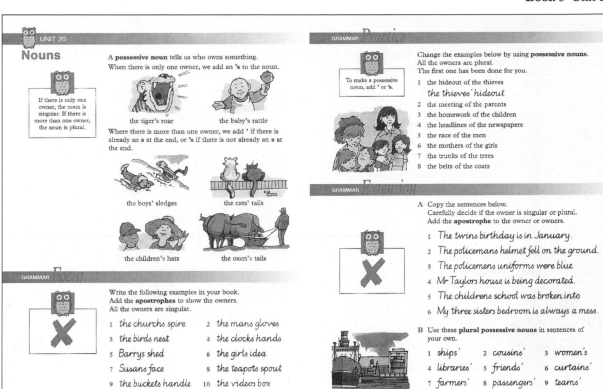

Previous work

Workbook 1	Workbook 2
page 4	page 4
page 5	page 5
page 12	page 12
page 13	page 13
Book A	**Book 1**
pages 6/7	pages 4/5
pages 10/11	pages 12/13
pages 22/23	pages 20/21
pages 36/37	
pages 40/41	
Book 2	**Book 3**
pages 4/5	pages 4/5
pages 16/17	pages 18/19
	pages 28/29
	pages 34/35
	pages 40/41

Pupil Book answers

Focus

1 the church's spire
2 the man's gloves
3 the bird's nest
4 the clock's hands
5 Barry's shed
6 the girl's idea
7 Susan's face
8 the teapot's spout
9 the bucket's handle
10 the video's box

Practice

2 the **parents'** meeting
3 the **children's** homework
4 the **newspapers'** headlines
5 the **men's** race
6 the **girls'** mothers
7 the **trees'** trunks
8 the **coats'** belts

Extension

A

1 The twins' birthday is in January.
2 The policeman's helmet fell on the ground.
3 The policemen's uniforms were blue.

4 Mr Taylor's house is being decorated.
5 The children's school was broken into.
6 My three sisters' bedroom is always a mess.

B

Answers will be individual to the children.

Copymaster answers

Answers will be individual to the children, for example:

2 *I can see the **alligator's** sharp teeth.*
3 *The **man's** car is stuck in the mud.*
4 ***Susan's** racket is broken.*
5 *That **girl's** bedroom is really messy.*
6 *The **boy's** broken arm is in a sling.*

UNIT 21

Adjectives

Adjectives describe and compare nouns.
We can describe a jumper using an **adjective**.

a **dirty** jumper

We can compare two jumpers using a **comparative adjective**.

a **dirty** jumper   a **dirtier** jumper

We can compare three or more jumpers using a **superlative adjective**.

a **dirty** jumper   a **dirtier** jumper   the **dirtiest** jumper

A few adjectives change completely in their comparative and superlative forms. You need to learn them.

Adjective	Comparative	Superlative
bad	worse	worst
good	better	best
little	less	least
much	more	most
many	more	most
some	more	most

GRAMMAR *Focus*

Choose the correct **adjective** to complete each sentence. Write the sentences in your book.

1 This is the better/best birthday party I have ever had.

2 You can get more/most water in this jug than in that one.

3 Today's weather made it the worse/worst day of the holiday.

48

GRAMMAR *Practice*

Comparative adjectives can be made by adding **er**, **ier** or '**more**'. Superlative adjectives can be made by adding **est**, **iest** or '**most**'.

Copy this table and fill in the missing words.

Adjective	Comparative	Superlative
silly	————	silliest
formal	more formal	————
good		————
beautiful	———— ————	most beautiful
	less	
		happiest
wonderful	———— ————	————
	merrier	
some		
		worst
	more comfortable	————
new	————	————
old	————	————
		wisest

GRAMMAR *Extension*

Write sentences using the following **adjectives**.

1 the comparative of **important**
2 the superlative of **good**
3 the superlative of **frightening**
4 the superlative of **small**
5 the comparative of **some**
6 the superlative of **bad**
7 the superlative of **sleepy**
8 the comparative of **heavy**

49

---

see Glossary, page 9 – Adjectives

Previous work

Workbook 1	Workbook 2
page 6	page 6
page 7	page 7
page 13	page 13

Book A	Book 1
pages 8/9	pages 6/7
pages 10/11	pages 22/23
pages 28/29	pages 34/35
pages 44/45	pages 42/43

Book 2	Book 3
pages 6/7	pages 6/7
pages 22/23	pages 24/25

Pupil Book answers

Focus

1 This is the **best** birthday party I have ever had.
2 You can get **more** water in this jug than in that one.
3 Today's weather made it the **worst** day of the holiday.

Practice

ADJECTIVE	COMPARATIVE	SUPERLATIVE
silly	**sillier**	silliest
formal	more formal	**most formal**
good	**better**	**best**
beautiful	**more beautiful**	most beautiful
little	less	**least**
happy	**happier**	happiest
wonderful	**more wonderful**	**most wonderful**
merry	merrier	**merriest**
some	**more**	**most**
bad	**worse**	worst
comfortable	more comfortable	**most comfortable**
new	**newer**	**newest**
old	**older**	**oldest**
wise	**wiser**	wisest

Extension

Sentences should include these words:

1 more important	2 best	
3 most frightening	4 smaller	
5 more	6 worst	
7 sleepiest	8 heavier	

Copymaster answers

2 I went the **longer** way round.
   I went the **longest** way round.

3 I have **more important** news for you.
   I have **most important** news for you.

4 He needs **less** help.
   He needs **the least** help.

5 The weather has been **worse** today.
   The weather has been **the worst** today.

6 I had **a better** day today.
   I had **the best** day today.

7 This is **more** than I can eat.
   This is **the most** I can eat.

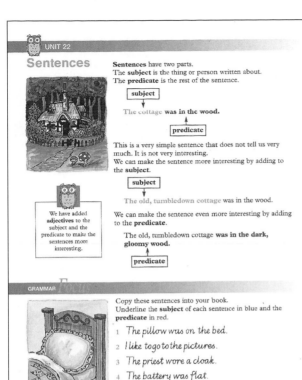

see Glossary, page 12 – Sentences

Previous work

Book A
pages 24/25
pages 30/31
pages 34/35
pages 42/43
Book 1
pages 24/25
pages 28/29
Book 2
pages 44/45
Book 3
pages 12/13
pages 16/17
pages 30/31

Pupil Book answers

Focus

The subject is underlined, the predicate is in bold type:
1 The pillow **was on the bed**.
2 I **like to go to the pictures**.
3 The priest **wore a cloak**.
4 The battery **was flat**.
5 Robin **is cooking the dinner**.

Practice

A
1 The butterfly sat on a leaf.
2 Monkeys live in the jungle.
3 A package was delivered.

Rewritten sentences will be individual to the children, for example:
1 **The beautiful, delicate** butterfly sat on a leaf.
2 **Many kinds of** monkeys live in the jungle.
3 **A large, mysterious package** was delivered.

B
1 The flag was hoisted up the pole.
2 I went to the shop.
3 Rafique has a bicycle.

Rewritten sentences will be individual to the children, for example:
1 The flag was **slowly and carefully** hoisted up the pole.
2 I went to the shop **which sold all kinds of musical instruments.**
3 Rafique has a **very old and shabby** bicycle.

Extension

1 **I** saw a ghost in the old house.
2 Will you get **me** a drink?
3 Katy and **I** are going swimming.
4 The dog frightened Becky and **me**.

Copymaster answers

Answers will be individual to the children.

Sentences

Direct speech is when we write the actual words that someone has spoken.

I feel cold.

We use **inverted commas** to show the actual words spoken.
"I feel cold," said Nick.

We begin a new line when a different person speaks.
"I feel cold," said Nick.
"So do I," replied Maggie.

After the spoken words, you need some punctuation. Usually we use a comma.
"I feel cold," said Tom.

We can also use a question mark.
"Do you feel cold?" asked Mum.

We can also use an exclamation mark.
"I'm frozen!" shouted the boy.

The punctuation after the spoken words always comes **before** the inverted commas.

GRAMMAR *Focus*

Copy the following sentences into your book.
Put **inverted commas** around the spoken words.

1 The police are coming soon, said Anne.
2 What is the time? asked Richard.
3 Watch out! yelled the farmer.
4 Don't make any noise, whispered the girl.
5 I'm bored, complained Bridget.

52

GRAMMAR *Practice*

Copy the sentences below.
Put in any missing **punctuation**.

1 Grab this rope shouted the climber
2 May I have an apple asked Tara
3 That building over there is the museum said the guide
4 I have lost my purse sobbed Kathy
5 Have you got your ticket asked the bus driver

GRAMMAR *Extension*

Sometimes the words that tell us who is speaking come before the spoken words.
Dad said, "You can watch a video tonight."

We always divide the spoken words from the words telling us who is speaking with a comma.
The boy mumbled, "I don't know the answer."
The teacher said, "Please learn it for tomorrow."

Put in the missing punctuation – inverted commas, full stops, commas, question marks and exclamation marks.

Copy the sentences below.
Put in the missing **punctuation**.

1 Where is the treasure hidden asked the pirate
2 Billy said I have got the map
3 Let me see it demanded the pirate
4 Billy asked What will you give me in return
5 With a cruel laugh, the pirate replied Nothing
6 That's not fair gasped Billy

53

---

see Glossary, page 12 – Sentences

Previous work

Book A
pages 24/25
pages 30/31
pages 34/35
pages 42/43

Book 1
pages 24/25
pages 28/29

Book 2
pages 44/45

Book 3
pages 12/13
pages 16/17
pages 30/31
pages 50/51

Pupil Book answers

Focus

1 "The police are coming soon," said Anne.
2 "What is the time?" asked Richard.
3 "Watch out!" yelled the farmer.
4 "Don't make any noise," whispered the girl.
5 "I'm bored," complained Bridget.

Practice

1 "Grab this rope!" shouted the climber.
2 "May I have an apple?" asked Tara.
3 "That building over there is the museum," said the guide.
4 "I have lost my purse," sobbed Kathy.
5 "Have you got your ticket?" asked the bus driver.

Extension

1 "Where is the treasure hidden?" asked the pirate.
2 Billy said, "I have got the map."
3 "Let me see it," demanded the pirate.
4 Billy asked, "What will you give me in return?"
5 With a cruel laugh, the pirate replied, "Nothing!"
6 "That's not fair!" gasped Billy.

Copymaster answers

"Today we are going to learn about how to begin a story. The beginning of a story is very important. Can anyone tell me why?" said the teacher.

"I know why. It has to make the reader want to go on and find out what happens," said Jenny.

"Yes, that is one reason. Why else is the beginning of a story important?" asked the teacher.

"It can tell us where the story is set," said Barry.

"Anything else?"

"It can introduce us to the characters," said Vera.

UNIT 24
Verbs

Remember, if we are using he, she or it in the present tense, we add 's' to the verb family name.

Verbs tell us what is happening.

The **tense** of a verb tells us when something happens – in the **past**, in the **present** or in the **future**.

We usually make the **past tense** by adding **d** or **ed** to the verb family name.

Hannah talk**ed** to her friend.

Some verbs have **irregular** past tenses.

Hannah **told** him about her holiday.

We can also make the **past tense** by using the verb 'to be' and an **ing** word.

She **was talking** to her friend.

We make the **present tense** by using the **verb family name** or the verb 'to be' and an **ing** word.

I **walk** to school.
or I **am walking** to school.

We make the **future tense** by using the verb 'to be' and the **verb family name**.

I **will go** at ten o'clock.

GRAMMAR *Focus*

Copy this table into your book.
Fill in the missing **verb tenses**.

Family name	Past tense	Present tense	Future tense
to walk	I walked	I walk	I shall walk
	I was walking	I am walking	
to grow	he ____	he ____	he ____
	he ____ ____	he ____ ____	
to bring	you ____	you ____	you ____ ____
	you ____ ____	you ____ ____	
to see	we ____	we ____	we ____
	we ____ ____	we ____ ____	

54

GRAMMAR *Practice*

Copy the sentences below.
After each sentence write whether it is **past tense**, **present tense** or **future tense**.

1 I am sewing seven buttons on to my jacket.
2 The army wore bright red uniforms.
3 Your helmet will protect you.
4 She was making a cake when the doorbell rang.
5 I believe everything you say.

GRAMMAR *Extension*

A Write these sentences in the **past tense**.
1 My neighbour is working in the garden.
2 This is a valuable vase.
3 The giant is frightening the villagers.
4 The dog steals the sausages.
5 I go to the shops every morning.

B Write these sentences in the **future tense**.
1 The siren sounded at midnight.
2 It happens every day at four o'clock.
3 I ate my tea very quickly.
4 The dog washes her new puppies.
5 The match was cancelled because of the bad weather.

55

---

see Glossary, page 14 – Verbs

Previous work

Workbook 1	Workbook 2
page 8	page 8
page 9	page 9
page 14	page 14
page 15	page 15
Book A	**Book 1**
pages 12/13	pages 26/27
pages 16/17	pages 30/31
pages 26/27	pages 38/39
pages 38/39	
Book 2	**Book 3**
pages 12/13	pages 26/27
pages 14/15	pages 32/33
pages 20/21	pages 34/35
pages 34/35	
pages 42/43	

Practice

1 present tense
2 past tense
3 future tense
4 past tense
5 present tense

Pupil Book answers

Focus

FAMILY NAME	PAST TENSE	PRESENT TENSE	FUTURE TENSE
to walk	I walked	I walk	I shall walk
	I was walking	I am walking	
to grow	he **grew**	he **grows**	he **will grow**
	he **was growing**	he **is growing**	
to bring	you **brought**	you **bring**	you **will bring**
	you **were bringing**	you **are bringing**	
to see	we **saw**	we **see**	we **shall see**
	we **were seeing**	we **are seeing**	

Extension

A
1 My neighbour **was working** in the garden.
2 This **was** a valuable vase.
3 The giant **was frightening** the villagers.
4 The dog **stole** the sausages.
5 I **went** to the shops every morning.

B
1 The siren **will sound** at midnight.
2 It **will happen** every day at four o'clock.
3 I **shall eat** my tea very quickly.
4 The dog **will wash** her new puppies.
5 The match **will be cancelled** because of the bad weather.

Copymaster answers

A

PAST TENSE	PRESENT TENSE	FUTURE TENSE
was going	am reading	will fly
rowed	help	shall have
broke	are seeing	will go
were catching	look	will buy

B
Answers will be individual to the children.

UNIT 25

Sentences

Contractions which end in **n't** and the words **no, not, nothing, never** and **nowhere** are **negative** words.

By using these words, we can change the meaning of a sentence.

He has an ice cream.
Positive

He **does** **not** have an ice cream.
Negative

If there are two negative words in one sentence, they cancel each other out and the meaning becomes positive.

I do not have no money.   Two negatives = positive

The two negative words make the sentence mean 'I do have some money.'

The correct sentence would be:

I do not have any money.

*When two negative words are used in the same sentence, it is called a **double negative**.*

GRAMMAR *Focus*

Add a **negative word** to each sentence to make it mean the opposite.

Write the sentences in your book.

1 I _____ have an apple for lunch.
2 She has _____ time to tidy her room.
3 The children do _____ want to go to the park.
4 There is _____ space in the cupboard.
5 I _____ lift this heavy box.
6 Greg _____ goes to the library on Saturday.

56

GRAMMAR *Practice*

Copy the sentences below.
Underline the **negative** words.
Write the sentences again, so that they have the opposite meaning.

1 The thief said he knew nothing about the burglary.
2 He did not have a ticket to get in.
3 The boys had nowhere to go.
4 "I mustn't feed the cat," said Dad.

GRAMMAR *Extension*

A Write the **contractions** of these **negative words**.

1 cannot	2 will not	3 shall not
4 must not	5 have not	6 should not
7 would not	8 does not	9 do not
10 is not	11 could not	12 has not

B All these sentences have **two negative words**, so they do not mean what the writer intended.
Write each sentence again so that it means what the writer wanted.
The first one has been done for you.

1 I wanted to win the race but I didn't have no luck.

I wanted to win the race but I didn't have any luck.

2 Pam didn't want to go nowhere.
3 I mustn't throw nothing away.
4 Mum will not get no bus today.

57

---

see Glossary, page 12 – Sentences

Previous work

Book A
pages 24/25
pages 30/31
pages 34/35
pages 42/43

Book 1
pages 24/25
pages 28/29

Book 2
pages 44/45

Book 3
pages 12/13
pages 16/17
pages 30/31
pages 50/51
pages 52/53

Pupil Book answers

Focus

1 I **don't/didn't/can't/won't** have an apple for lunch.
2 She has **no** time to tidy her room.
3 The children do **not** want to go to the park.
4 There is **no/never** space in the cupboard.
5 I **can't/won't/didn't** lift this heavy box.
6 Greg **never** goes to the library on a Saturday.

Practice

1 The thief said he knew <u>nothing</u> about the burglary.
The thief said he knew about the burglary.
2 He did <u>not</u> have a ticket to get in.
He did have a ticket to get in.
or He had a ticket to get in.
3 The boys had <u>nowhere</u> to go.
The boys had somewhere to go.
4 "I <u>mustn't</u> feed the cat," said Dad.
"I must feed the cat," said Dad.

Extension

A

1 can't	2 won't
3 shan't	4 mustn't
5 haven't	6 shouldn't
7 wouldn't	8 doesn't
9 don't	10 isn't
11 couldn't	12 hasn't

B

2 Pam didn't want to go anywhere.
3 I mustn't throw anything away.
4 Mum will not get a bus today.

Copymaster answers

A

1 He doesn't want any more soup.
2 The tiger will find no food tonight. *or* The tiger will not find any food tonight.
3 I'm not going to the cinema ever again. *or* I am never going to the cinema again.
4 I could not go anywhere today.

B

Answers will be individual to the children.

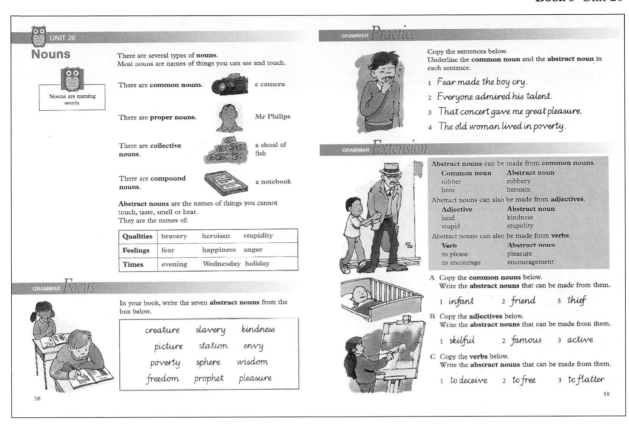

see Glossary, page 11 – Nouns

Previous work

Workbook 1	Workbook 2
page 4	page 4
page 5	page 5
page 12	page 12
page 13	page 13
Book A	**Book 1**
pages 6/7	pages 4/5
pages 10/11	pages 12/13
pages 22/23	pages 20/21
pages 36/37	
pages 40/41	
Book 2	**Book 3**
pages 4/5	pages 4/5
pages 16/17	pages 18/19
	pages 28/29
	pages 34/35
	pages 40/41
	pages 46/47

Pupil Book answers

Focus

slavery, kindness, envy, poverty,
wisdom, freedom, pleasure

Practice

*The common nouns are underlined, the
abstract nouns are in bold type:*
1 **Fear** made the <u>boy</u> cry.
2 <u>Everyone</u> admired his **talent**.
3 That <u>concert</u> gave me great
   pleasure.
4 The old <u>woman</u> lived in **poverty**.

Copymaster answers

Extension

A
1 infancy
2 friendship
3 theft

B
1 skill
2 fame
3 action

C
1 deception
2 freedom
3 flattery

A

COMMON NOUNS	PROPER NOUNS	COLLECTIVE NOUNS	ABSTRACT NOUNS
table	Karen	bunch	generosity
garden	David	herd	laughter
cart	Paris	gaggle	sympathy
elephant	Mars	congregation	pity
water	Cardiff	pack	idea

B
1 selfishness 2 stupidity 3 brightness 4 poverty
5 gratitude 6 wisdom

C
1 flattery 2 pleasure 3 action 4 robbery 5 hatred 6 satisfaction

Check-up 3

Proper nouns

Write these film titles correctly.

1 gone with the wind
2 mary poppins
3 the hunchback of notre dame

Adjectives

A Copy the sentences below.
Underline the **number order adjectives**.

1 Astronauts landed on the Moon in the twentieth century.
2 That is the second time I have warned you.
3 The family gave Dad a surprise party on his thirty-fifth birthday.

B Write the **comparative** and the **superlative** of each of these adjectives.

1 loud	2 immense	3 bad
4 shabby	5 good	6 tidy
7 little	8 terrifying	9 important
10 honest	11 much	12 kind
13 many	14 grumpy	15 some

Singular and plural

Write the **plurals** of these nouns.

1 pony	2 foot	3 loaf
4 piano	5 donkey	6 baby
7 banjo	8 half	9 wharf
10 scarf	11 berry	12 tooth

60

Prepositions

Copy the sentences below.
Underline the **preposition** in each sentence.

1 The rat hid behind the shed.
2 The ball was thrown over the fence.
3 I went into the shop to buy some bread.
4 The tree was growing near the water.

Sentences

A Copy the sentences below.
Underline the **subject** in each sentence.

1 This door needs painting.
2 I have hurt my leg.
3 The noisy children were chasing each other.
4 The violent storm frightened the animals.

B Copy the sentences below.
Underline the **object** in each sentence.

1 I would like a banana.
2 The torn umbrella did not keep off the rain.
3 All the books have colourful covers.
4 We need to mend the gate.

C Add interesting **predicates** to complete these sentences.

1 The lonely man _____.
2 Every flower _____.
3 The two goats _____.
4 These shabby curtains _____.

61

Proper nouns

1 **G**one **W**ith the **W**ind
2 **M**ary **P**oppins
3 The **H**unchback of **N**otre **D**ame

Adjectives

A

1 Astronauts landed on the moon in the <u>twentieth</u> century.
2 That is the <u>second</u> time I have warned you.
3 The family gave Dad a surprise party on his <u>thirty-fifth</u> birthday.

B

ADJECTIVE	COMPARATIVE	SUPERLATIVE
1 loud	louder	loudest
2 immense	more immense	most immense
3 bad	worse	worst
4 shabby	shabbier	shabbiest
5 good	better	best
6 tidy	tidier	tidiest
7 little	least	less
8 terrifying	more terrifying	most terrifying
9 important	more important	most important
10 honest	more honest	most honest
11 much	more	most
12 kind	kinder	kindest
13 many	more	most
14 grumpy	grumpier	grumpiest
15 some	more	most

Singular and plural

1 ponies
2 feet
3 loaves
4 pianos
5 donkeys
6 babies
7 banjos
8 halves
9 wharfs *or* wharves
10 scarves
11 berries
12 teeth

Prepositions

1 The rat hid <u>behind</u> the shed.
2 The ball was thrown <u>over</u> the fence.
3 I went <u>into</u> the shop to buy some bread.
4 The tree was growing <u>near</u> the water.

Sentences

A

1 <u>This door</u> needs painting.
2 <u>I</u> have hurt my leg.
3 <u>The noisy children</u> were chasing each other.
4 <u>The violent storm</u> frightened the animals.

B

1 I would like <u>a banana</u>.
2 The torn umbrella did not keep off <u>the rain</u>.
3 All the books have <u>colourful covers</u>.
4 We need to mend <u>the gate</u>.

C

Answers will be individual to the children.

D Copy the sentences below and add the missing **punctuation**.

1 I will carry that for you offered Jake
2 Will you come for tea asked Danny
3 Mark said I can't find my jumper
4 Elizabeth shouted Look out

Pronouns

Use these **pronouns** in sentences of your own.

1 myself 2 yourself 3 ourselves
4 itself 5 himself 6 herself
7 yourselves 8 themselves

Collective nouns

A Write the **collective noun** for each of these.

1 soldiers 2 flowers 3 books
4 geese 5 lions 6 birds
7 musicians 8 sheep 9 cows

B Join each noun from the first box with a noun from the second box to make a **compound noun**.

rain	shade
fire	light
sun	man
sea	drop
day	shore

C Copy these sentences.
Add the **apostrophe** to the owner or owners.

1 The giraffes neck is long and thin.
2 Where is this childs coat?
3 Birds feathers help them to fly.

62

D Copy the sentences below.
Underline the **abstract nouns**.

1 The pain in my arm made me cry.
2 The escape was planned for midnight.
3 "My memory is not what it used to be," said Mum.
4 It's a mystery where that book has gone.

E Use these **abstract nouns** in sentences of your own.

1 generosity 2 joy 3 pain
4 misery 5 knowledge 6 wisdom

Verbs

A Copy the sentences below.
Use the **past tense** – the verb 'to be' and **ing** – instead of the verb family name.

1 I to talk to my friend when the telephone rang.
2 She to run for the bus when she tripped.
3 Sam to post a letter when it began to rain.
4 I did my homework while my brother to read his book.

B Write these sentences as though they will happen in the **future**.

1 The candle burned all night.
2 The bells jingled in the wind.
3 I listen to the radio on Saturday morning.
4 The cabbage is rotting in the vegetable basket.
5 The palace was built of stone.

63

D

1 "I will carry that for you," offered Jake.
2 "Will you come for tea?" asked Greg.
3 Mark said, "I can't find my jumper."
4 Elizabeth shouted, "Look out!"

Pronouns

Answers will be individual to the children.

Nouns

A

1 an **army/batallion/platoon /company** of soldiers
2 a **bunch/bouquet/posy/vase** of flowers
3 a **library/shelf** of books
4 a **gaggle** of geese
5 a **pride** of lions
6 a **flock** of birds
7 an **orchestra/quartet/quintet/trio** of musicians
8 a **flock** of sheep
9 a **herd** of cows

B

raindrop
fireman
sunshade
seashore
daylight

C

1 The giraffe's neck is long and thin.
2 Where is this child's coat?
3 Birds' feathers help them to fly.

D

1 The <u>pain</u> in my arm made me cry.
2 The <u>escape</u> was planned for midnight.
3 "My <u>memory</u> is not what it used to be," said Mum.
4 It's a <u>mystery</u> where that book has gone.

E

Answers will be individual to the children.

Verbs

A

1 I **was talking** to my friend when the telephone rang.
2 She **was running** for the bus when she tripped.
3 Sam **was posting** a letter when it began to rain.
4 I did my homework while my brother **was reading** his book.

B

1 The candle **will burn** all night.
2 The bells **will jingle** in the wind.
3 I **shall listen** to the radio on Saturday morning.
4 The cabbage **will rot** in the vegetable basket.
5 The palace **will be built** of stone.

C

1 The children **go** to the park to play.
2 Ben **finds/found** his ball in the long grass.
3 I **want** my tea now.
4 Cats **like** milk to drink.
5 The foal **gallops** around the field.

125

C Copy and correct these sentences.

1 The children goes to the park to play.

2 Ben find his ball in the long grass.

3 I wants my tea now.

4 Cats likes milk to drink.

5 The foal gallop around the field.

Contractions

Copy the sentences below.
Add the **apostrophes** to the **contractions**.

1 "I cant go out this evening," said Debbie.

2 "We wont get there in time if we dont hurry," said Mum.

3 "Sharon mustnt leave her book at home again," said the teacher.

4 "Why shouldnt you cross the road here?" asked the policewoman.

5 "I couldnt do the long jump and I wouldnt do the high jump," said Megan.

Double negatives

Write these sentences again so they say what the writer wanted.

1 Hamish did not get no lunch today.

2 I never go nowhere on a Sunday.

3 The boys couldn't find nowhere to play.

4 The cat didn't climb no trees in the park.

5 Can't I not go out today?

64

Contractions

1 "I can't go out this evening," said Debbie.
2 "We won't get there in time if we don't hurry," said Mum.
3 "Sharon mustn't leave her book at home again," said the teacher.
4 Why shouldn't you cross the road here?" asked the policewoman.
5 "I couldn't do the long jump and I wouldn't do the high jump," said Megan.

Double negatives

1 Hamish did not get any lunch today.
   or Hamish got no lunch today.
2 I never go anywhere on Saturday.
3 The boys couldn't find anywhere to play.
   or The boys could find nowhere to play.
4 The cat didn't climb any trees in the park.
5 Can I not go out today?
   or Can I go out today?

Book 4 – Contents/Scope and Sequence

Page/Unit	Focus	Practice
4/5 Unit 1	identifying adjective phrases	using adjective phrases
6/7 Unit 2	making opposites with prefixes	meanings of words with prefixes
8/9 Unit 3	identifying auxiliary verbs	using am, are, is, was, were
10/11 Unit 4	substituting pronouns with possessive pronouns	completing sentences with possessive pronouns
12/13 Unit 5	identifying nouns from verbs	completing sentences with nouns made from verbs
14/15 Unit 6	identifying noun and verb agreement	correcting sentences
16/17 Unit 7	identifying adverb phrases	using adverb phrases
18/19	*Check-up 1*	*Check-up 1*
20/21 Unit 8	direct and indirect speech	using direct and indirect speech
22/23 Unit 9	identifying active and passive verbs	changing active to passive and passive to active
24/25 Unit 10	'ed', 'ing', 'er' suffixes	adding suffixes
26/27 Unit 11	identifying main clauses in sentences	identifying clauses
28/29 Unit 12	identifying possessive adjectives	using possessive adjectives
30/31 Unit 13	identifying adjective clauses	using 'who' and 'which'
32/33 Unit 14	identifying auxiliary verbs	using 'can' and 'may'
34/35 Unit 15	identifying adverb clauses	completing adverb clauses
36/37 Unit 16	identifying how adjectives are formed	adjectives formed from verbs and nouns
38/39	*Check-up 2*	*Check-up 2*
40/41 Unit 17	suffixes – 'ful', 'tion', 'ness'	adding suffixes
42/43 Unit 18	adding commas in lists	punctuating sentences
44/45 Unit 19	pronouns – using 'who' and 'which'	joining sentences with relative pronouns
46/47 Unit 20	identifying main clauses in sentences	identifying adverb and adjective clauses
48/49 Unit 21	identifying past-tense verbs	completing a verb table
50/51 Unit 22	identifying spoken words in sentences	punctuating direct speech
52/53 Unit 23	making compound sentences	identifying main clauses in compound sentences
54/55 Unit 24	identifying main clauses in complex sentences	making complex sentences
56/57 Unit 25	improving sentences by replacing words	expanding sentences with detail
58/59 Unit 26	writing paragraphs	main idea in paragraphs
60/64	*Check-up 3*	*Check-up 3*

UNIT 1

Adjectives

Sometimes, a single **adjective** is not enough to describe a noun or pronoun.
We need to use a **phrase** (a group of words) to describe a thing so that the reader has a clear picture of what we are writing about.
We could describe the picture on the left by saying:

An **old** lady is crossing the road.

A reader would have a much clearer picture of the old lady if we wrote:

An **old** lady **with a big floppy hat** is crossing the road.

'Old' is a single adjective.
'With a big floppy hat' is an **adjective phrase**.
Joining two adjectives makes an adjective phrase.

A phrase is a group of words that does not contain a verb.

The garden, **silent and deserted**, was covered with snow.
The adjective phrase 'silent and deserted' describes the garden.

GRAMMAR *Focus*

Look for more than one adjective.

Copy the following sentences into your book.
Underline the **adjective phrase** in each sentence.

1 The weather, cold and wet, kept us in all day.

2 The handsome but sulky prince was in a bad mood.

3 The wood was dark and frightening in the moonlight.

4 Five small blue flowers had grown on the rubbish heap.

4

GRAMMAR *Practice*

A Use these **adjective phrases** in sentences of your own.

1 sleek and graceful 2 with no shoes
3 frozen and slippery 4 with loud cries
5 old but useful
6 without an umbrella

B Write a sentence with an **adjective phrase** to describe each of these nouns.

1 meadow 2 feathers 3 cough
4 photograph 5 shepherd 6 dolphin

GRAMMAR *Extension*

Remember, a phrase is a group of words that does not contain a verb.

Three of the examples below are **adjective phrases** and three are sentences.
Find the three adjective phrases.
Add a verb and any other words you need to make each one into a sentence.
Find the three sentences and write them with their correct punctuation.

1 thank you said Jim
2 Janet ran home
3 the poor injured duck
4 a shivering and frightened
5 give me that
6 with a heavy bag

5

---

see Glossary, page 9 – Adjectives

Previous work

Workbook 1	Workbook 2
page 6	page 6
page 7	page 7
page 13	page 13
Book A	**Book 1**
pages 8/9	pages 6/7
pages 10/11	pages 22/23
pages 28/29	pages 34/35
pages 44/45	pages 42/43
Book 2	**Book 3**
pages 6/7	pages 6/7
pages 22/23	pages 24/25
	pages 48/49

Pupil Book answers

Focus

1 The weather, **cold and wet**, kept us in all day.
2 The **handsome but sulky** prince was in a bad mood.
3 The wood was **dark and frightening** in the moonlight.
4 **Five small blue** flowers had grown on the rubbish heap.

Practice

A and **B**
Answers will be individual to the children.

Extension

The sentences are:
1 "Thank you," said Jim.
2 Janet ran home.
5 Give me that.

*The adjective phrases are **3**, **4** and **6**. Children will make these into sentences in their own way.*

Copymaster answers

A

1 The noise, <u>eerie and frightening</u>, came from the forest.
2 This cat <u>with four white paws</u> is called Socks.
3 <u>Seven large black</u> crows landed on the lawn.
4 The lady <u>with the hat</u> is old Mrs Cotton.
5 We saw a <u>large, brightly coloured</u> balloon in the sky.

B

Answers will be individual to the children, for example:
1 *The worn but beautiful carpet was quite valuable.*
2 *The road, twisting and narrow, led to a remote farmhouse.*
3 *The picture with the thick gold frame is very old.*
4 *A huge, powerful whale leaped out of the water.*

The pupil book page (reproduced)

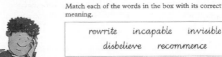

UNIT 2
Prefixes

'Pre' comes from the Latin word 'prae', meaning 'before'.

Letters added to the front of a word are called a **prefix**.
Some prefixes can change a word so it means the opposite.

happy	**un**happy	wise	**un**wise
visible	**in**visible	sane	**in**sane
possible	**im**possible	patient	**im**patient
appear	**dis**appear	trust	**dis**trust
legal	**il**legal	legible	**il**legible
clockwise	**anti**clockwise	climax	**anti**climax

Prefixes have special meanings.
Here are some more common prefixes and their meanings.

Prefix	Meaning	Examples	
bi	two	**bi**cycle	**bi**lingual
ex	out of	**ex**port	**ex**it
inter	between	**inter**val	**inter**national
mis	wrong	**mis**behave	**mis**judge
re	again	**re**place	**re**turn
sub	under	**sub**marine	**sub**way

Like 'pre', many prefixes come from Latin.

GRAMMAR Focus

*The opposite of a word is called its **antonym**.*

A Use a **prefix** to make the opposite of each of these words. Write the words in your book and check them in a dictionary.
1 true   2 loyal   3 movable   4 secure
5 honour   6 pure   7 well   8 mobile
9 approve   10 logical   11 agree   12 active

B Copy the sentences below.
Add a **prefix** to one word in each sentence so that the sentence has the opposite meaning.
1 Did you obey the rules?
2 Will you lock the door?
3 What you want to do is possible.

6

GRAMMAR Practice

Match each of the words in the box with its correct meaning.

rewrite   incapable   invisible
disbelieve   recommence

1 to begin again
2 to think that something is not true
3 not able to do something
4 not able to be seen
5 to put words on paper again

GRAMMAR Extension

A Use a dictionary to find one word that begins with each of the following **prefixes**.
1 inter   2 bi   3 pro   4 pre
5 mono   6 sub   7 post   8 auto
9 al   10 re   11 ex   12 trans

B Put each word that you made in part A into a sentence of your own.

C Use a dictionary to help you to write the meaning of each of these words.
1 explosion   2 extension   3 invasion
4 preparation   5 biped   6 international
7 mistake   8 revise   9 submerge

7

---

see Glossary, page 12 – Prefixes

Previous work

None

Pupil Book answers

Focus

A
1 **un**true   2 **dis**loyal
3 **im**movable   4 **in**secure
5 **dis**honour   6 **im**pure
7 **un**well   8 **im**mobile
9 **dis**approve   10 **il**logical
11 **dis**agree   12 **in**active

B
1 Did you **dis**obey the rules?
2 Will you **un**lock the door?
3 What you want to do is **im**possible.

Practice

1 recommence
2 disbelieve
3 incapable
4 invisible
5 rewrite

Extension

A
Answers will be individual to the children, but might include the following:
1 *interchange, intertwine, interlock*
2 *bicycle, biped, bikini*
3 *propose, propel, provide*
4 *prefix, prepare, presume*
5 *monologue, monopoly, monopolize*
6 *submarine, submerge, subdue*
7 *postpone, postscript, posture*
8 *automatic, autobiography, autograph*
9 *alcove, album, always*
10 *reassure, recover, return*
11 *expand, expel, exterior*
12 *translate, transform, transplant*

B
Answers will be individual to the children.

C
Precise answers will depend on the dictionary used.

Copymaster answers

1
a biplane
b biped
c bisect

2
a precede
b preface (*or* preamble)
c prehistoric

3
a submarine
b suburb(s)
c subside

4
a redeliver
b rewrite
c reform

5
a exit
b extend
c exterior

UNIT 3

Verbs

Auxiliary verbs are 'helper' verbs.

Sometimes we need more than one **verb** to make a sentence work properly.
We need to use an **auxiliary verb** to help the main verb. The verb 'to be' is often used as an auxiliary verb and tells us when something happens.

He was **teaching** me how to do this.
His is **teaching** me how to do this.
He will **teach** me how to do this.

Here are some more auxiliary verbs.

has	She has **gone** out.
have	I have **forgotten** my dinner money.
had	We had **seen** the fox many times.
must	You must **clean** the floor.
might	I might **catch** the early train.
could	I could **meet** you at twelve o'clock.
should	You should **wear** a helmet on your bike.
would	They would **enjoy** a picnic today.

GRAMMAR *Focus*

Copy the following sentences into your book.
Underline the **auxiliary verb** in each sentence.

1 She is feeling unwell today.
2 We would like to discuss the problem.
3 The telephone has rung seven times.
4 I must leave at six o'clock.
5 I could find the station on the map.
6 The photographs were taken last summer.

8

GRAMMAR *Practice*

Copy the sentences below.
Use the **auxiliary verbs** am, are, is, was or were to fill the gaps.

1 Cowslips _____ growing in the meadow last year.
2 I _____ spreading butter on my bread before I put on the jam.
3 She _____ going abroad for her holidays.
4 We _____ hoping to finish this before we go.
5 He _____ playing tennis when he hurt his hand.

GRAMMAR *Extension*

A The sentences below are written in the present tense. Change the **two auxiliary verbs** in each sentence so that they are in the past tense.

1 I am thinking about what I am going to do.
2 We are walking to the town and then we are going to catch a bus.
3 They are wondering what they are going to find.

B The sentences below are written in the past tense. Change the **auxiliary verb** and the **main verb** so that each sentence is in the future tense.

1 I was meeting a friend after lunch.
2 We were hoping for sunny weather.
3 She was going outside for a few minutes.

9

---

see Glossary, page 14 – Verbs

Previous work

Workbook 1	Workbook 2
page 8	page 8
page 9	page 9
page 14	page 14
page 15	page 15
Book A	**Book 1**
pages 12/13	pages 26/27
pages 16/17	pages 30/31
pages 26/27	pages 38/39
pages 38/39	
Book 2	**Book 3**
pages 12/13	pages 26/27
pages 14/15	pages 32/33
pages 20/21	pages 34/35
pages 34/35	pages 54/55
pages 42/43	

Pupil Book answers

Focus

1 She <u>is</u> feeling unwell today.
2 We <u>would</u> like to discuss the problem.
3 The telephone <u>has</u> rung seven times.
4 I <u>must</u> leave at six o'clock.
5 I <u>could</u> find the station on the map.
6 The photographs <u>were</u> taken last summer.

Practice

1 Cowslips **were** growing in the meadow last year.
2 I **am** spreading butter on my bread before I put on the jam.
3 She **is/was** going abroad for her holidays.
4 We **are/were** hoping to finish this before we go.
5 He **was** playing tennis when he hurt his hand.

Extension

A

1 I **was** thinking about what I **was** going to do.
2 We **were** walking to the town and then we **were** going to catch a bus.
3 They **were** wondering what they **were** going to find.

B

1 I **shall meet** a friend after lunch.
2 We **shall hope** for sunny weather.
3 She **will go** outside for a few minutes.

Copymaster answers

A

1 I **shall walk** five miles on Saturday.
2 The tickets **will sell** very well.
3 You **will write** that letter before tea.

B

Answers will be individual to the children.

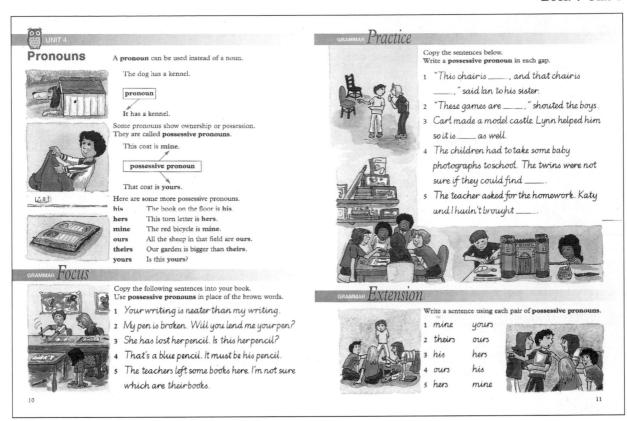

see Glossary, page 12 – Pronouns

Previous work

Book 1
pages 14/15 pages 40/41
Book 3
pages 14/15

Pupil Book answers

Focus

1 Your writing is neater than **mine**.
2 My pen is broken. Will you lend me **yours**?
3 She has lost her pencil. Is this **hers**?
4 That's a blue pencil. It must be **his**.
5 The teachers left some books here. I'm not sure which are **theirs**.

Practice

1 "This chair is **mine/yours**, and that chair is **yours/mine**," said Ian to his sister.
2 "These games are **ours**," shouted the boys.
3 Carl made a model castle. Lynn helped him so it is **hers** as well.
4 The children had to take some baby photographs to school. The twins were not sure if they could find **theirs**.
5 The teacher asked for the homework. Katy and I hadn't brought **ours**.

Extension

Answers will be individual to the children.

Copymaster answers

A

2 It is **ours**.
3 It is **mine**.
4 They are **his**.
5 They are **hers**.
6 It is **yours**.

B

Answers will be individual to the children.

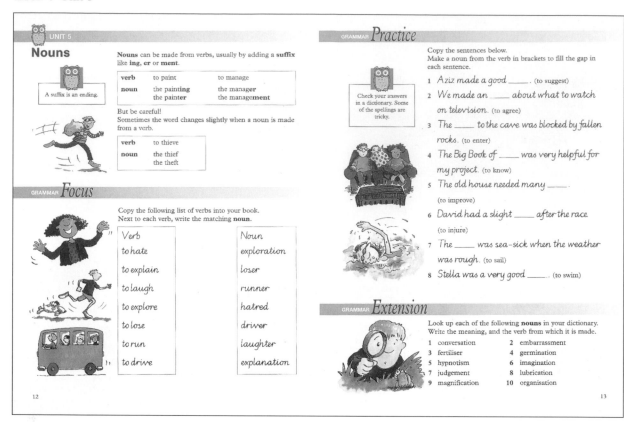

see Glossary, page 11 – Nouns

Previous work

Workbook 1	Workbook 2
page 4	page 4
page 5	page 5
page 12	page 12
page 13	page 13

Book A	Book 1
pages 6/7	pages 4/5
pages 10/11	pages 12/13
pages 22/23	pages 20/21
pages 36/37	
pages 40/41	

Book 2	Book 3
pages 4/5	pages 4/5
pages 16/17	pages 18/19
	pages 28/29
	pages 34/35
	pages 40/41
	pages 46/47
	pages 58/59

Pupil Book answers

Focus

VERB	NOUN
to hate	hatred
to explain	explanation
to laugh	laughter/laugh
to explore	exploration
to lose	loser/loss
to run	runner/run
to drive	driver/drive

Practice

1 Aziz made a good **suggestion**.
2 We made an **agreement** about what to watch on television.
3 The **entrance** to the cave was blocked by fallen rocks.
4 The Big Book of **Knowledge** was very helpful for my project.
5 The old house needed many **improvements**.
6 David had a slight **injury** after the race.
7 The **sailor** was sea-sick when the weather was rough.
8 Stella was a very good **swimmer**.

Extension

Meanings the children give will depend on the dictionary used. The nouns are derived from the following verbs:

1	to converse	2	to embarrass
3	to fertilise	4	to germinate
5	to hypnotise	6	to imagine
7	to judge	8	to lubricate
9	to magnify	10	to organise

Copymaster answers

A

1 encouragement
2 satisfaction
3 actor/actress/action
4 freedom
5 runner/run
6 deceiver/deception

B

1 to collect
2 to discover
3 to predict
4 to obstruct
5 to teach
6 to donate

C *Answers will be individual to the children.*

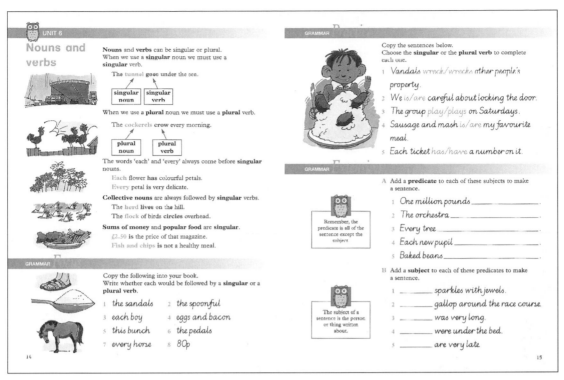

see Glossary, page 11 – Nouns and page 14 – Verbs

Previous work

Nouns

Workbooks 1 and 2
pages 4, 5, 12, 13

Book A
pages 6/7, 10/11, 22/23, 36/37, 40/41

Book 1
pages 4/5, 12/13, 20/21

Book 2
pages 4/5, 16/17

Book 3
pages 4/5, 18/19, 28/29, 34/35, 40/41, 46/47, 58/59

Book 3
pages 12/13

Verbs

Workbooks 1 and 2
pages 8, 9, 14, 15

Book A
pages 12/13, 16/17, 26/27, 38/39

Book 1
pages 26/27, 30/31, 38/39

Book 2
pages 12/13, 14/15, 20/21, 34/35, 42/43

Book 3
pages 26/27, 32/33, 34/35, 54/55

Book 4
pages 8/9

Pupil Book answers

Focus

1 plural verb 2 singular verb
3 singular verb 4 singular verb
5 singular verb 6 plural verb
7 singular verb 8 singular verb

Practice

1 Vandals **wreck** other people's property.
2 We **are** careful about locking the door.
3 The group **plays** on Saturdays.
4 Sausage and mash **is** my favourite meal.
5 Each ticket **has** a number on it.

Extension

A and **B**
Answers will be individual to the children.

Copymaster answers

A
1 The crowd **is** huge.
2 The flowers **are** wilting.
3 The cows **are** brown.
4 The herd **is** grazing.
5 The army **is** attacking.
6 The soldiers **are** marching.
7 The orchestra **is** playing.
8 The musicians **are** practising.
9 Every book **is** damaged.
10 The library **is** closed.

B
1 The queue of people **was** very long.
2 A swarm of bees **was** flying across our garden.
3 The puppies **were** born last night.

C
Answers will be individual to the children.

UNIT 7
Adverbs

Sometimes, a single **adverb** is not enough to tell us how, when or where something happens.

We need to use two or three words to describe how, when or where something happens so that the reader has a clear picture of what we are writing about.

We could write about the picture on the left by saying:

The rocket took off quickly.

A reader would have a much clearer picture of what happened if we wrote:

The rocket took off in a huge burst of flame.

'In a huge burst of flame' is an **adverb phrase**, telling us **how** the rocket took off.

We could write:

The rocket took off on Thursday night.

'On Thursday night' is an **adverb phrase**, telling us **when** the rocket took off.

We could write:

The rocket took off into the dark night sky.

'Into the dark night sky' is an **adverb phrase**, telling us **where** the rocket took off.

A phrase is a group of words that does not contain a verb.

GRAMMAR Focus

Copy the following sentences into your book. Underline the **adverb phrase** in each one.

Look for the words which tell you **how**, **when** or **where** the action takes place.

1 The giant approached the village with loud, thudding footsteps.
2 Yesterday morning, I planted some seeds.
3 The painter climbed to the top of the ladder to paint the window frame.
4 We ran as quickly as we could.
5 The eagle built its nest on the mountain top.

16

GRAMMAR Practice

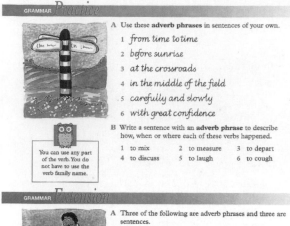

A Use these **adverb phrases** in sentences of your own.

1 from time to time
2 before sunrise
3 at the crossroads
4 in the middle of the field
5 carefully and slowly
6 with great confidence

You can use any part of the verb. You do not have to use the verb family name.

B Write a sentence with an **adverb phrase** to describe how, when or where each of these verbs happened.

1 to mix   2 to measure   3 to depart
4 to discuss   5 to laugh   6 to cough

GRAMMAR Extension

A Three of the following are adverb phrases and three are sentences.
Copy the **adverb phrases** and add a verb and any other words you need to make them into sentences.

1 before the first lesson
2 we'll meet at the corner
3 in front of the cinema
4 gasping for breath
5 simon rang the bell repeatedly
6 you must find that letter

B Find the three sentences from part A. Write them with their correct punctuation.

17

---

see Glossary, page 10 – Adverbs

Previous work

Book 2
pages 26/27 pages 40/41
Book 3
pages 42/43

Pupil Book answers

Focus

1 The giant approached the village with loud, thudding footsteps.
2 Yesterday morning, I planted some seeds.
3 The painter climbed to the top of the ladder to paint the window frame.
4 We ran as quickly as we could.
5 The eagle built its nest on the mountain top.

Practice

A and **B**
Answers will be individual to the children.

Extension

A *Questions 2, 5 and 6 are sentences. Questions 1, 3 and 4 are adverb phrases. Children will make these into sentences in their own way.*

B
2 We'll meet at the corner.
5 Simon rang the bell repeatedly.
6 You must find that letter.

Copymaster answers

A

1 The car came to a halt with a loud screeching noise.
2 Late last night there was a knock on the door.
3 I left my bicycle outside the shop.
4 I drew the picture slowly and carefully.
5 We will meet in the morning.

B
Answers will be individual to the children.

Check-up 1

Nouns

Write a **noun** that can be made from each verb.
1 to manage   2 to free   3 to paint
4 to laugh   5 to walk   6 to encourage

Adjectives

A Copy these sentences.
Underline the **adjective phrases**.

1 Antarctica is a cold and frozen land.
2 The bicycle with the punctured tyre is mine.
3 The birds pecked at the newly mown lawn.
4 The angry, wounded tiger ran into the jungle.

B Use these **adjective phrases** in sentences of your own.
1 brightly coloured   2 dirty and smelly
3 in the old coat   4 blue and still

Prefixes

Use a **prefix** to make the opposite of each word.

1 legal   2 accurate   3 perfect
4 respect   5 enjoyable   6 decided

Verbs

Copy these sentences.
Underline the **auxiliary verbs**.

1 I am drawing a flower and a tree.
2 The dolphin might jump out of the water.
3 The pollution of this river must stop.
4 We should plough the field tomorrow.
5 The lions have drunk at the water hole.

18

Pronouns

A Copy these sentences.
Underline the **possessive pronouns**.

1 This towel is mine.
2 That dog of theirs is very noisy.
3 I'm taking this book back to the library. Do you want me to take yours?
4 I like his painting better than hers.

B Use each of these **possessive pronouns** in a sentence of your own.

1 his   2 hers   3 mine
4 ours   5 theirs   6 yours

Nouns and verbs

A Use these words in sentences of your own.
Underline the **nouns** in red and the **verbs** in blue.

1 penguin   2 hospital   3 needles
4 students   5 is   6 have
7 croaks   8 were

B Use these **collective nouns** in sentences of your own.
1 queue   2 gang   3 forest

Adverbs

Copy these sentences and underline the **adverb phrases**.

1 The class listened in complete silence.
2 Tomorrow at midday the parade will begin.
3 From the top of the tree, I could see the old mill.
4 Dad was preparing a meal in the kitchen.
5 I could not get to sleep last night.

19

Nouns

1 manager/management
2 freedom
3 painting/painter/paint
4 laughter/laugh
5 walker/walk
6 encouragement

Adjectives

A
1 Antarctica is a <u>cold and frozen</u> land.
2 The bicycle <u>with the punctured tyre</u> is mine.
3 The birds pecked at the <u>newly mown</u> lawn.
4 The <u>angry, wounded</u> tiger ran into the jungle.

B *Answers will be individual to the children.*

Prefixes

1 **il**legal
2 **in**accurate
3 **im**perfect
4 **dis**respect
5 **un**enjoyable
6 **un**decided

Verbs

1 I <u>am</u> drawing a flower and a tree.
2 The dolphin <u>might</u> jump out of the water.
3 The pollution of this river <u>must</u> stop.
4 We <u>should</u> plough the field tomorrow.
5 The lions <u>have</u> drunk at the water hole.

Pronouns

A
1 This towel is <u>mine</u>.
2 That dog of <u>theirs</u> is very noisy.
3 I'm taking this book back to the library. Do you want me to take <u>yours</u>?
4 I like his painting better than <u>hers</u>.

B *Answers will be individual to the children.*

Nouns and verbs

A
Sentences will be individual to the children. 1, 2, 3 and 4 are nouns; 5, 6, 7 and 8 are verbs.

B
Answers will be individual to the children.

Adverbs

1 The class listened <u>in complete silence</u>.
2 <u>Tomorrow at midday</u> the parade will begin.
3 <u>From the top of the tree</u>, I could see the old mill.
4 Dad was preparing a meal <u>in the kitchen</u>.
5 I could not get to sleep <u>last night</u>.

UNIT 8

Sentences

Direct speech is when we write the actual words that someone has spoken.
Inverted commas go around the spoken words.
Punctuation at the end of the spoken words goes before the inverted commas.
When a different person speaks we begin a new line.

"The driver got the bus stuck on the bridge today," said Meg.
"What happened?" asked Mum.
"The police came and sent for a tow truck. It took them ages to get it free. We were late for school!" replied Meg.

Indirect speech is when we write about what a person has said.
We don't use the actual spoken words so we don't need inverted commas.

Meg told her Mum that the bus had got stuck on the bridge. Mum wanted to know what happened and Meg said that the police and a tow truck came to free the bus but it took so long they were late for school.

Indirect speech is sometimes called **reported speech** because we report what somebody has said.

GRAMMAR *Focus*

In your book, write which of these sentences use **direct speech** and which use **indirect speech**.

1 "Look at my swimming certificate," said Len.
2 Sonia said that she couldn't find the newspaper.
3 "Stop, thief!" shouted the policewoman as the burglar ran away.
4 Rob told his Dad that the computer was broken.
5 The doctor asked how long I had been feeling unwell.

20

GRAMMAR *Practice*

A Write each of these sentences using **indirect speech**.

1 "Would all passengers go to platform 8," boomed the voice over the loudspeaker.
2 "I like porridge for breakfast," said Dad.
3 "How long do I have to wait to be served?" snapped the customer.
4 "I've forgotten my lines!" groaned the actor.

B Write each of these sentences using **direct speech**.

1 Chris said that his book was very dull.
2 Owen wanted to know how far they still had to go.
3 The singer asked if many people had come to the show.
4 Martha encouraged Sandy to tell her what had happened.

GRAMMAR *Extension*

A Write a conversation in **direct speech** between Malcolm and Emma about what they watched on television last night.
Remember to use inverted commas, punctuation and to begin a new line when a different person speaks.

B Write the same conversation between Malcolm and Emma in **indirect speech**.
Remember that you do not need inverted commas because you are not writing the words that were actually spoken.

21

---

see Glossary, page 12 – Sentences

Previous work

Book A
pages 24/25
pages 30/31
pages 34/35
pages 42/43

Book 1
pages 24/25
pages 28/29

Book 2
pages 44/45

Book 3
pages 12/13
pages 16/17
pages 30/31
pages 50/51
pages 52/53
pages 56/57

Pupil Book answers

Focus

1 direct speech
2 indirect speech
3 direct speech
4 indirect speech
5 indirect speech

Practice

A

1 A voice boomed over the loudspeaker asking all the passengers to go to platform 8.
2 Dad said that he liked porridge for breakfast.
3 One of the customers asked angrily/impatiently how long he had to wait to be served.
4 The actor said with a groan that he/she had forgotten his/her lines.

B

1 "My book is very dull,' said Chris.
2 "How far do we still have to go?" Owen asked.
3 "Have many people come to the show?" asked the singer.

4 "Tell me what has happened, Sandy," said Martha encouragingly.

Extension

A and B
Answers will be individual to the children.

Copymaster answers

"I've forgotten to bring my homework into school," I told my teacher. She wasn't very pleased.
"I got up late and I was in a rush to get to school," I explained.
"You should put your homework in your bag the night before," said the teacher.
"Yes, I should have done that. I'm very sorry," I replied.
"Being sorry isn't good enough. You will have to stay in at break time and do it again," she said.
"Could I go home and get it?" I asked.
"No, I cannot allow you to leave school. You will just have to learn your lesson the hard way," the teacher replied.

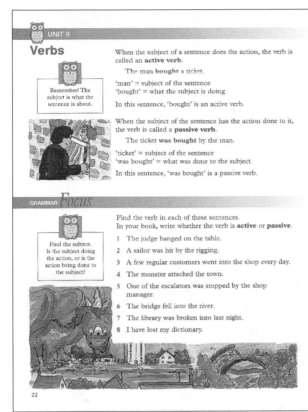

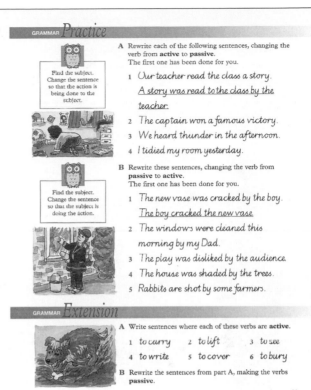

UNIT 9

Verbs

Remember! The subject is what the sentence is about.

When the subject of a sentence does the action, the verb is called an **active verb**.

The man **bought** a ticket.

'man' = subject of the sentence
'bought' = what the subject is doing

In this sentence, 'bought' is an active verb.

When the subject of the sentence has the action done to it, the verb is called a **passive verb**.

The ticket **was bought** by the man.

'ticket' = subject of the sentence
'was bought' = what was done to the subject

In this sentence, 'was bought' is a passive verb.

GRAMMAR *Focus*

Find the subject. Is the subject doing the action, or is the action being done to the subject?

Find the verb in each of these sentences.
In your book, write whether the verb is **active** or **passive**.

1 The judge banged on the table.
2 A sailor was hit by the rigging.
3 A few regular customers went into the shop every day.
4 The monster attacked the town.
5 One of the escalators was stopped by the shop manager.
6 The bridge fell into the river.
7 The library was broken into last night.
8 I have lost my dictionary.

22

GRAMMAR *Practice*

Find the subject. Change the sentence so that the action is being done to the subject.

A Rewrite each of the following sentences, changing the verb from **active** to **passive**.
The first one has been done for you.

1 Our teacher read the class a story.
A story was read to the class by the teacher.

2 The captain won a famous victory.
3 We heard thunder in the afternoon.
4 I tidied my room yesterday.

Find the subject. Change the sentence so that the subject is doing the action.

B Rewrite these sentences, changing the verb from **passive** to **active**.
The first one has been done for you.

1 The new vase was cracked by the boy.
The boy cracked the new vase.

2 The windows were cleaned this morning by my Dad.
3 The play was disliked by the audience.
4 The house was shaded by the trees.
5 Rabbits are shot by some farmers.

GRAMMAR *Extension*

A Write sentences where each of these verbs are **active**.

1 to carry   2 to lift   3 to see
4 to write   5 to cover   6 to bury

B Rewrite the sentences from part A, making the verbs **passive**.

23

---

see Glossary, page 14 – Verbs

Previous work

Workbook 1	Workbook 2
page 8	page 8
page 9	page 9
page 14	page 14
page 15	page 15
Book A	**Book 1**
pages 12/13	pages 26/27
pages 16/17	pages 30/31
pages 26/27	pages 38/39
pages 38/39	
Book 2	**Book 3**
pages 12/13	pages 26/27
pages 14/15	pages 32/33
pages 20/21	pages 34/35
pages 34/35	pages 54/55
pages 42/43	
Book 4	
pages 8/9	
pages 14/15	

Pupil Book answers

Focus

1 The judge **banged** on the table.	active
2 A sailor **was hit** by the rigging.	passive
3 A few regular customers **went** into the shop every day.	active
4 The monster **attacked** the town.	active
5 One of the escalators **was stopped** by the shop manager.	passive
6 The bridge **fell** into the river.	active
7 The library **was broken** into last night.	passive
8 I **have lost** my dictionary.	active

Practice

A
2 A famous victory was won by the captain.
3 Thunder was heard in the afternoon.
4 My room was tidied yesterday.
or Yesterday my room was tidied.

B
2 My Dad cleaned the windows this morning.
or This morning my Dad cleaned the windows.
3 The audience disliked the play.
4 The trees shaded the house.
5 Some farmers shoot rabbits.

Extension

A and **B**
Answers will be individual to the children.

Copymaster answers

A and **B**
Answers will be individual to the children.

 UNIT 10

Suffixes

A **suffix** is a word ending.
The suffix **ed** tells us that an action has happened in the past.

I smash**ed** the plate

The suffix **ing** is used with the verb 'to be' to tell us that an action is in the present tense or the past tense.

I **am** throw**ing** the ball.
I **was** throw**ing** the ball.

Comparative adverbs and comparative adjectives are used to compare things.

The suffix **er** makes a new word.
Lots of these new words are comparative adjectives, comparative adverbs or nouns.

One lady was calm**er** than the other one.

The vowels are a, e, i, o and u.

When we add **ed**, **ing** or **er** to words, we sometimes have to double the last letter.
We usually double the last letter if the one before it is a single vowel.

skip	skipped	skipping	skipper
fit	fitted	fitting	fitter

GRAMMAR *Focus*

Copy this table into your book and complete it.

Word	'ed' suffix	'ing' suffix	'er' suffix
warm	warmed	warming	warmer
jump			
fill			
wrap			
clean			
help			
count			

24

GRAMMAR *Practice*

Remember, you may need to double the last letter.

Add the **suffix** *ed*, *ing* or *er* to complete each sentence.

1 This ice cream is big___ than that one.
2 The pirates were look___ for the treasure.
3 We search___ and search___ but we could not find it.
4 The run___ who was first received the medal.
5 Cook___ is one of my hobbies.
6 The long___ you take to get ready, the less time we will have for fish___ .

GRAMMAR *Extension*

Find the verb ending in 'ed'. Use the verb 'to be' and an 'ing' word in its place.

A Use the **suffix** *ing* to change these sentences into the present tense.

1 The birds circled overhead.
2 A stranger moved into the village.
3 The garage door creaked in the wind.
4 I tried hard with my fractions.

Find the two words that make up the present tense verb. Use one word with 'ed' instead.

B Use the **suffix** *ed* to change these sentences into the past tense.

1 We are wondering if our decision was the right one.
2 I am posting a letter to my friend.
3 They are electing the team captain.
4 We are sailing into the harbour.

25

---

see Glossary, page 14 – Suffixes

Previous work

None

Pupil Book answers

Focus

WORD	'ED' SUFFIX	'ING' SUFFIX	'ER' SUFFIX
warm	warmed	warming	warmer
jump	**jumped**	**jumping**	**jumper**
fill	**filled**	**filling**	**filler**
wrap	**wrapped**	**wrapping**	**wrapper**
clean	**cleaned**	**cleaning**	**cleaner**
help	**helped**	**helping**	**helper**
count	**counted**	**counting**	**counter**

Practice

1 This ice cream is **bigger** than that one.
2 The pirates were **looking** for the treasure.
3 We **searched** and **searched** but we could not find it.
4 The **runner** who was first received the medal.
5 **Cooking** is one of my hobbies.
6 The **longer** you take to get ready, the less time we will have for **fishing**.

Extension

A
1 The birds **are circling** overhead.
2 A stranger **is moving** into the village.
3 The garage door **is creaking** in the wind.
4 I **am trying** hard with my fractions.

B
1 We **wondered** if our decision was the right one.
2 I **posted** a letter to my friend.
3 They **elected** the team captain.
4 We **sailed** into the harbour.

Copymaster answers

A

2	smaller	3	higher
4	frostier	5	sillier
6	fitter		

B

Answers will be individual to the children, but should include the following verbs:

	PRESENT TENSE	PAST TENSE
1	is laughing/are laughing	laughed
2	is worrying/are worrying	worried
3	is barking/are barking	barked
4	is living/are living	lived
5	is munching/are munching	munched

UNIT 11

Sentences

Clauses are small groups of words. They are similar to phrases, but clauses contain a proper verb.

The man was cold, so he wore his coat.

This sentence has two **verbs** and two **clauses**.

Clause 1 = The man was cold   **verb** = was
Clause 2 = so he wore his coat   **verb** = wore

In sentences with two clauses, one of the clauses is usually more important and is called the **main clause**.

The main clause in this sentence is 'The man was cold'. The main clause can usually be a sentence by itself.

The main clause does not have to come first.

After we had seen the elephants, we trudged back to our camp.

Main clause = we trudged back to our camp
Second clause = After we had seen the elephants

GRAMMAR

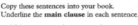

The clause that is not the main clause usually begins with a conjunction, such as **and, but, so, although, when, because, after** or **before**.

Copy these sentences into your book.
Underline the **main clause** in each sentence.

1 We were ready to go when it started to rain.
2 The procession came down the main street and went into the park.
3 Although we played very well, we didn't win the match.
4 When I do my sums, I don't use a calculator.
5 If I make a mess in my room, I have to tidy up.
6 The volcano erupted and lava poured down its sides.

26

GRAMMAR

Write out the **two clauses** in each sentence and underline the **main clause**.

1 The famous violinist was nervous but she played very well.
2 I am curious to know where you are going and how you will get there.
3 If you park on a double yellow line, you will get a parking ticket.
4 The builder finished his work and put away his tools.

GRAMMAR

Your second clause can begin with a conjunction.

A Add a **second clause** to each of these **main clauses**. You may be able to make more than one clause by using different conjunctions.

1 The apple was rotten _____.
2 I could see a town in the distance _____.
3 My brother and I quarrelled _____.
4 These feathers are similar _____.
5 The radiator was leaking _____.

B Add a **main clause** to each of these **second clauses**.

1 _____ and we enjoyed ourselves.
2 _____ when the race started.
3 Although I am a good swimmer _____.
4 _____ because he was very generous.
5 Before the bridge was built _____.

27

---

see Glossary, page 12 – Sentences

Previous work

Book A
pages 24/25
pages 30/31
pages 34/35
pages 42/43

Book 1
pages 24/25
pages 28/29

Book 2
pages 44/45

Book 3
pages 12/13
pages 16/17
pages 30/31
pages 50/51
pages 52/53
pages 56/57

Book 4
pages 20/21

Pupil Book answers

Focus

1 <u>We were ready to go</u> when it started to rain.
2 <u>The procession came down the main street</u> and went into the park.
3 Although we played very well, <u>we didn't win the match</u>.
4 When I do my sums, <u>I don't use a calculator</u>.
5 If I make a mess in my room, <u>I have to tidy up</u>.
6 <u>The volcano erupted</u> and lava poured down its sides.

Practice

The main clauses are underlined.
<u>The famous violinist was nervous</u> but she played very well.
<u>I am curious to know</u> where you are going and how you will get there.
If you park on a double yellow line, <u>you will get a parking ticket</u>.
<u>The builder finished his work</u> and put away his tools.

Extension

A and **B**
Answers will be individual to the children.

Copymaster answers

Answers will be individual to the children.

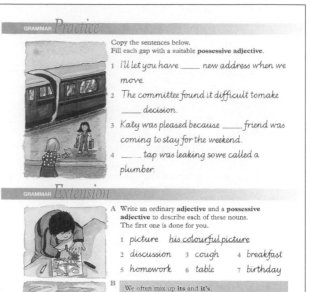

see Glossary, page 9 – Adjectives

Previous work

Workbook 1	Workbook 2
page 6 page 7 page 13	page 6 page 7 page 13
Book A	**Book 1**
pages 8/9 pages 10/11 pages 28/29 pages 44/45	pages 6/7 pages 22/23 pages 34/35 pages 42/43
Book 2	**Book 3**
pages 6/7 pages 22/23	pages 6/7 pages 24/25 pages 48/49
Book 4	
pages 4/5	

Pupil Book answers

Focus

1 The computer in <u>our</u> classroom is not working properly.

2 If you can remember that far back <u>your</u> memory is very good.

3 The castle was well preserved but <u>its</u> tower was in ruins.

4 The champion beat <u>his</u> opponent easily.

5 <u>Their</u> quarrel lasted for days.

Practice

1 I'll let you have **my/our** new address when we move.

2 The committee found it difficult to make **their** decision.

3 Katy was pleased because **her** friend was coming to stay for the weekend.

4 **Our** tap was leaking so we called a plumber.

Extension

A *Answers will be individual to the children, for example:*

  2 *our friendly discussion*
  3 *my irritating cough*
  4 *her cooked breakfast*
  5 *his untidy homework*
  6 *their wooden table*
  7 *my next birthday*

B

1 The dog slept in **its** kennel.

2 "**It's** a ghost!" screamed Jenny.

3 **It's** windier today than it was yesterday.

4 The kitten put out **its** sharp claws.

Copymaster answers

A

2 This is **your** book.

3 These are **her** shoes.

4 These are **our** tickets.

5 This is **their** dog.

B

1 The bird couldn't fly because **its** wing was broken.

2 I heard **his** radio so I knew he was in **his** room.

3 **My/His/Her/Our/Your/Their** bag is heavier than **your/his/her/my/our/their** bag.

4 We live in that street and **our** house is the last one on the left.

5 "**Your/His/Her/Their** work is very neat," said the teacher to Amit.

C

Answers will be individual to the children, for example:

1 *The cat washed **its** ears.*

2 ***It's** a lovely day today.*

UNIT 13

Adjectives

A clause has a verb, a phrase does not.

To make sentences more interesting, we can use **adjective phrases** and **adjective clauses**.

An adjective clause tells us more about a noun or pronoun in the main clause.

We went to the shop **that sold camping equipment**.

Main clause = We went to the shop

Adjective clause = that sold camping equipment.

The adjective clause tells us more about the **shop** in the main clause.

Adjective clauses do the same job as adjectives and adjective phrases.

They all describe nouns and pronouns.

Adjective clauses begin with these words:

who   which   that

We use **who** when we are writing about a person.

The nurse took care of the man **who had broken his arm**.

We use **which** or **that** when we are writing about an animal or a thing.

Can you find the key **which fits this lock**?

I saw the birds **that are nesting in our garage**

GRAMMAR *Focus*

Copy the following sentences into your book.

In each sentence, underline the **adjective clause** and put a ring around the **noun** or **pronoun** it tells us about.

1 I delivered the package which my mother had given to me.

2 Mark wrote to his friend who lives in Australia.

3 This is the badge which I bought at the zoo.

4 I want to find the boy who owns this bicycle.

30

GRAMMAR *Practice*

Copy the sentences below.

Use *who* or *which* to fill each gap.

1 They travelled by bus ____ took a long time.

2 I have thrown away the chair ____ had a broken arm.

3 Will you find someone ____ can take care of the dog?

4 There were several passengers ____ had lost their tickets.

5 Find the pencil ____ has a rubber on the end.

GRAMMAR *Extension*

Remember! Your adjective clause needs a proper verb.

Remember! Your main clause needs a proper verb. A main clause can be a sentence by itself.

A Add **adjective clauses** to these main clauses to complete the sentences.

1 I baked the bread _____.

2 The police went to the house _____.

3 They looked for the girl _____.

4 We visited the old lady _____.

B Add main clauses to the following **adjective clauses** to complete the sentences.

1 _____ who likes to play football.

2 _____ which grows in our garden.

3 _____ that I like best.

4 _____ which fell on our house.

31

---

see Glossary, page 9 – Adjectives

Previous work

Workbook 1	Workbook 2
page 6 page 7 page 13	page 6 page 7 page 13
Book A	**Book 1**
pages 8/9 pages 10/11 pages 28/29 pages 44/45	pages 6/7 pages 22/23 pages 34/35 pages 42/43
Book 2	**Book 3**
pages 6/7 pages 22/23	pages 6/7 pages 24/25 pages 48/49
Book 4	
pages 4/5 pages 28/29	

Pupil Book answers

Focus

The adjective clauses are in bold type, the nouns/pronouns are underlined.

1 I delivered the **package** <u>which my mother had given to me</u>.

2 Mark wrote to his **friend** <u>who lives in Australia</u>.

3 This is the **badge** <u>which I bought at the zoo</u>.

4 I want to find the **boy** <u>who owns this bicycle</u>.

Practice

1 I travelled by bus **which** took a long time.

2 I have thrown away the chair **which** had a broken arm.

3 Will you find someone **who** can take care of the dog?

4 There were several passengers **who** had lost their tickets.

5 Find the pencil **which** has a rubber on the end.

Extension

A

Answers will be individual to the children but should start as follows:

1 I baked the bread
   which/that ...

2 The police went to the house
   which/that ...

3 They looked for the girl **who** ...

4 We visited the old lady
   who ...

B

Answers will be individual to the children.

Copymaster answers

A

Answers will be individual to the children but should start as follows:

1 We drove along the road
   which/that ...

2 The teacher praised the girl **who** ...

3 I watched the young birds
   which/that ...

4 This chair **which/that** ... is very comfortable.

5 You will find the book **which/that** ... on the top shelf.

B

Answers will be individual to the children.

UNIT 14

Verbs

An auxiliary verb is a 'helper' verb.

Shall and will are part of the verb family 'to be'.

Sometimes we need more than one **verb** to make a sentence work properly.
We need to use an **auxiliary verb** to help the main verb.
The verb families '**to be**' and '**to have**' are often used as auxiliary verbs.

The wreckage is floating in the harbour.
The candle has burnt very low.

The words **can** and **may** are used as auxiliary verbs but they have special meanings.
Can means 'is able to'.
May means 'has permission to'.

He can answer that question.
You may leave the room.

Shall and **will** are often used as auxiliary verbs.
Shall comes after I and **we**.
Will comes after **you, they, he, she** and **it**.

I shall go out.
They will go out.

If we want to write a strong statement, we use them the other way around.

I will go out!
You shall go out!

GRAMMAR Focus

Copy the following sentences into your book.
Underline the **auxiliary verbs**.

1 The picture was hanging on that wall.
2 I have forgotten to do my homework.
3 I can jump over the fence.
4 We may buy some sweets.
5 The shield will keep you safe.

GRAMMAR Practice

A Copy the sentences below.
Use the **auxiliary verbs** *can* or *may* to fill each gap.

1 This book is quite difficult but I am sure you ____ read it.
2 You ____ go out to play when you have changed your clothes.
3 You ____ get to the top of that tree with a ladder.
4 You ____ not cross the road by yourself.

B Copy the sentences below.
Use the **auxiliary verbs** *shall* or *will* to fill each gap.

1 I ____ write very neatly today.
2 "You ____ eat all the carrots!" said Mum.
3 He ____ find these sums very difficult.
4 "We ____ not go to bed!" shouted the twins.

GRAMMAR Extension

Write sentences of your own using the following pairs of verbs.
Underline the **auxiliary verb** in each sentence.

1 has received   2 will recognise
3 can finish   4 may drop
5 is dodging   6 was carrying
7 shall obey   8 will do
9 may begin   10 can find

32   33

---

see Glossary, page 14 – Verbs

Previous work

Workbook 1	Workbook 2
page 8	page 8
page 9	page 9
page 14	page 14
page 15	page 15
Book A	**Book 1**
pages 12/13	pages 26/27
pages 16/17	pages 30/31
pages 26/27	pages 38/39
pages 38/39	
Book 2	**Book 3**
pages 12/13	pages 26/27
pages 14/15	pages 32/33
pages 20/21	pages 34/35
pages 34/35	pages 54/55
pages 42/43	
Book 4	
pages 8/9	
pages 14/15	
pages 22/23	

Pupil Book answers

Focus

1 The picture <u>was</u> hanging on that wall.
2 I <u>have</u> forgotten to do my homework.
3 I <u>can</u> jump over the fence.
4 We <u>may</u> buy some sweets.
5 The shield <u>will</u> keep you safe.

Practice

A

1 This book is quite difficult but I am sure you **can** read it.
2 You **may** go out to play when you have changed your clothes.
3 You **can** get to the top of that tree with a ladder.
4 You **may** not cross the road by yourself.

B

1 I **shall** write very neatly today.
2 "You **shall** eat all the carrots!" said Mum.
3 He **will** find these sums very difficult.
4 "We **will** not go to bed!" shouted the twins.

Extension

Sentences will be individual to the children. The auxiliary verbs are:

1 <u>has</u> received   2 <u>will</u> recognise
3 <u>can</u> finish   4 <u>may</u> drop
5 <u>is</u> dodging   6 <u>was</u> carrying
7 <u>shall</u> obey   8 <u>will</u> do
9 <u>may</u> begin   10 <u>can</u> find

Copymaster answers

A

1 able to   2 permission
3 permission   4 able to
5 permission

B

Answers will be individual to the children, for example:

1 ***has*** *managed*
   Tom has managed to open the jar.
2 ***will*** *happen*
   "I know what will happen next." said Ross.
3 ***have*** *eaten*
   You have eaten my lunch.
4 ***may*** *go*
   You may go out tonight.

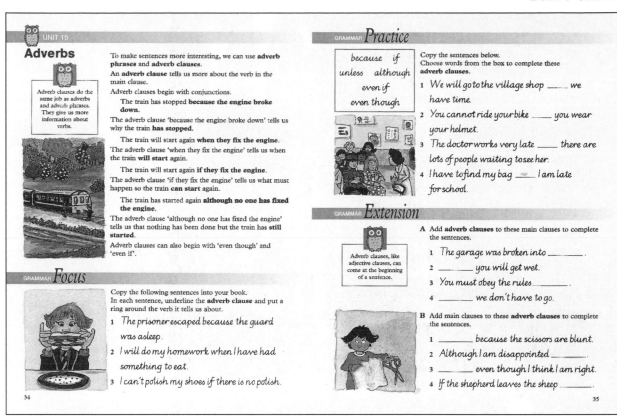

34
35

see Glossary, page 10 – Adverbs

Previous work

Book 2
pages 26/27
pages 40/41

Book 3
pages 42/43

Book 4
pages 16/17

Pupil Book answers

Focus

1 The prisoner **escaped** <u>because the guard was asleep</u>.
2 I **will do** my homework <u>when I have had something to eat</u>.
3 I **can't polish** my shoes <u>if there is no polish</u>.

Practice

1 We will go to the village shop **if** we have time.
2 You cannot ride your bike **unless** you wear your helmet.
3 The doctor works very late **because** there are lots of people waiting to see her.
4 I have to find my bag **although/even if/even though** I am late for school.

Extension

A and **B**
Answers will be individual to the children.

Copymaster answers

A and **B**
Answers will be individual to the children.

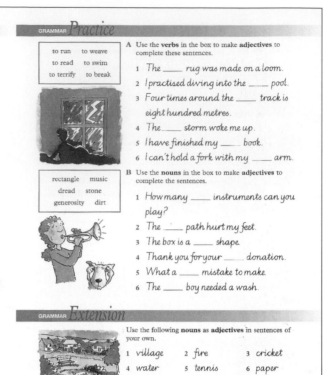

The above images reproduce the pupil book pages:

UNIT 16

Adjectives

Adjectives are describing words. We use them to make our writing more interesting and to give the reader a clear picture of what we are writing about.

Some **adjectives** are formed from verbs:

Verb	Adjective	Example
to bend	bent	a **bent** pin
to burn	burnt	the **burnt** toast
to groan	groaning	the **groaning** man

Some verbs are used as **adjectives**:

Verb	Use as an adjective
to rock	**rocking** chair
to skate	**skating** rink
to build	**building** block

Some **adjectives** are formed from nouns:

Noun	Adjective	Example
skill	skilful	a **skilful** player
child	childish	a **childish** joke
danger	dangerous	a **dangerous** situation

Some nouns are used as **adjectives**:

Noun	Use as an adjective
book	**book** cover
window	**window** sill
town	**town** hall

GRAMMAR *Focus*

Copy the following sentences into your book. Underline the **adjective** in each sentence and write whether it is formed from a **verb** or a **noun**.

1 The crying baby was in her pram.
2 The wooden hut was never used.
3 The dried flowers were thrown away.
4 The warlike warriors attacked at dawn.

36

GRAMMAR *Practice*

to run   to weave
to read   to swim
to terrify   to break

A Use the **verbs** in the box to make **adjectives** to complete these sentences.

1 The _____ rug was made on a loom.
2 I practised diving into the _____ pool.
3 Four times around the _____ track is eight hundred metres.
4 The _____ storm woke me up.
5 I have finished my _____ book.
6 I can't hold a fork with my _____ arm.

rectangle   music
dread   stone
generosity   dirt

B Use the **nouns** in the box to make **adjectives** to complete the sentences.

1 How many _____ instruments can you play?
2 The _____ path hurt my feet.
3 The box is a _____ shape.
4 Thank you for your _____ donation.
5 What a _____ mistake to make.
6 The _____ boy needed a wash.

GRAMMAR *Extension*

Use the following **nouns** as **adjectives** in sentences of your own.

1 village   2 fire   3 cricket
4 water   5 tennis   6 paper

37

---

see Glossary, page 9 – Adjectives

Previous work

Workbook 1	Workbook 2
page 6	page 6
page 7	page 7
page 13	page 13
Book A	**Book 1**
pages 8/9	pages 6/7
pages 10/11	pages 22/23
pages 28/29	pages 34/35
pages 44/45	pages 42/43
Book 2	**Book 3**
pages 6/7	pages 6/7
pages 22/23	pages 24/25
	pages 48/49
Book 4	
pages 4/5	
pages 28/29	
pages 30/31	

Pupil Book answers

Focus

1 The <u>crying</u> baby was in her pram. (verb)
2 The <u>wooden</u> hut was never used. (noun)
3 The <u>dried</u> flowers were thrown away. (verb)
4 The <u>warlike</u> warriors attacked at dawn. (noun)

Practice

A
1 The **woven** rug was made on a loom.
2 I practised diving into the **swimming** pool.
3 Four times around the **running** track is eight hundred metres.
4 The **terrifying** storm woke me up.
5 I have finished my **reading** book.
6 I can't hold a fork with my **broken** arm.

B
1 How many **musical** instruments can you play?
2 The **stony** path hurt my feet.
3 The box is a **rectangular** shape.
4 Thank you for your **generous** donation.
5 What a **dreadful** mistake to make.
6 The **dirty** boy needed a wash.

Extension

Answers will be individual to the children.

Copymaster answers

A

ADJECTIVES	For example:
1 spoken	spoken word
2 postage	postage stamp
3 broken	broken arm
4 drawn	drawn curtains

B

ADJECTIVES	For example:
1 horrible	horrible experience
2 boyish	boyish smile
3 microscopic	microscopic germ
4 charitable	charitable donation

C

Answers will be individual to the children, for example:

1 The **liquid** metal was poured into moulds.
2 The **gold** coins were in a chest.
3 We met in the **secret** cave.

Check-up 2
Sentences

A Write each of these sentences using **direct speech**.

1 David said that he had been on holiday.
2 Shehzad asked what the time was.
3 The policeman wanted to know who owned the canal boat.

B Write each of these sentences using **indirect speech**.

1 "Where are we going?" asked Mike.
2 "There are too many people on this bus!" shouted the driver.
3 "It's too early to go to bed," moaned Sally.

C Copy these sentences.
Underline the **main clause** in each.

1 It's necessary to water the plants although it has rained today.
2 Before the sun sets, we must find our way out of this wood.
3 A dictionary is very useful because it tells you the meaning of words.

D Join each pair of sentences, using *who* or *which* to make a **main clause** and an **adjective clause**.

1 I needed a new bag. I could take it to school.
2 We have two mice. They are white.
3 I visited a friend. He lives by the sea.

38

Adverbs

Add an **adverb clause** to each of these main clauses.

1 The gold ring slipped off my finger ____.
2 The secretary typed my letter _____.
3 _____ we discovered an old house.

Suffixes

Add the **suffixes** *ed, ing* or *er* to complete these sentences.

1 The clean__ swept the floor and polish__ the windows.
2 The teach__ was look__ for some chalk.
3 I have climb__ a high__ mountain than you have.

Verbs

A Find the **verb** in each of the sentences below.
Write whether the verb is **active** or **passive**.

1 The explosion was heard for miles around.
2 The buses crawled slowly along the road.
3 The packet was delivered by the courier.

B In the following sentences, fill each gap with *can* or *may*.

1 The children ____ have a dog if they look after it.
2 I ____ meet you at one o'clock.
3 You ____ write more neatly than that.

Adjectives

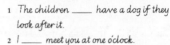

A Write the **adjectives** that are formed from the following nouns and verbs.

1 to fall   2 fright   3 to fry   4 rock

B Use these **possessive adjectives** in sentences of your own.

1 my   2 her   3 its   4 your

39

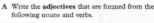

Sentences

A
1 "I have been on holiday," said David.
2 "What time is it?" Shehzad asked. *or* "What is the time?" asked Shehzad.
3 "Who owns the canal boat?" the policeman asked/enquired/demanded.

B
1 Mike asked where we were going.
2 The driver shouted that there were too many people on the bus.
3 Sally moaned that it was too early to go to bed.

C
1 It's necessary to water the plants although it has rained today.
2 Before the sun sets, we must find our way out of this wood.
3 A dictionary is very useful because it tells you the meaning of words.

D
1 I needed a new bag **which** I could take to school.
2 We have two mice **which** are white.
3 I visited a friend **who** lives by the sea.

Adverbs

Answers will be individual to the children.

Suffixes

1 The **cleaner** swept the floor and **polished** the windows.
2 The **teacher** was **looking** for some chalk.
3 I have **climbed** a **higher** mountain than you have.

Verbs

A
1 was heard   passive
2 crawled   active
3 was delivered   passive

B
1 The children **may** have a dog if they look after it.
2 I **can** meet you at one o'clock.
3 You **can** write more neatly than that.

Adjectives

A
1 fallen/falling
2 frightening/frightened
3 fried/frying
4 rocking

B
Answers will be individual to the children.

147

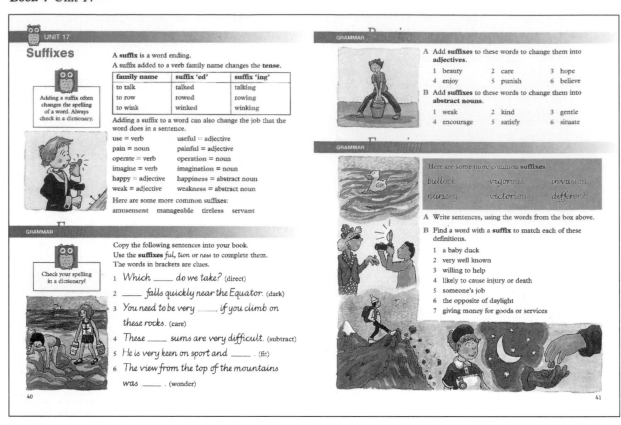

see Glossary, page 14 – Suffixes

Previous work

Book 4
pages 24/25

Pupil Book answers

Focus

1 Which **direction** do we take?
2 **Darkness** falls quickly near the Equator.
3 You need to be very **careful** if you climb on these rocks.
4 These **subtraction** sums are very difficult.
5 He is very keen on sport and **fitness**.
6 The view from the top of the mountains was **wonderful**.

Practice

A
1 beautiful
2 careful/careless/caring
3 hopeful/hopeless
4 enjoyable
5 punishing
6 believable

B
1 weakness
2 kindness
3 gentleness
4 encouragement
5 satisfaction
6 situation

Extension

A

Answers will be individual to the children.

B
1 duckling
2 famous
3 helpful
4 dangerous
5 occupation
6 darkness
7 payment/paying

Copymaster answers

A

Answers will be individual to the children, for example:
1 *happiness, kindness, sadness, fondness, gentleness, awkwardness*
2 *careless, thoughtless, merciless, remorseless, hopeless, aimless*
3 *dutiful, careful, sorrowful, pitiful, shameful, dreadful*
4 *situation, magnification, location, donation, imagination, reputation*

B
1 To win a victory is to be **victorious**.
2 To satisfy someone is to give them **satisfaction**.
3 If you believe what someone says it is **believable**.
4 If a country is invaded it has suffered an **invasion**.
5 The job you do to occupy your time is your **occupation**.
6 If you imagine something you are using your **imagination**.

UNIT 18
Sentences

All **sentences** begin with a capital letter.
All sentences end with:

a full stop	The dog was asleep.
a question mark	What time is it?
or an exclamation mark	The house is burning!

Commas are often used to help us understand the sense of a sentence.

We use commas between items in a list, or between groups of words.

My teacher told me to learn to spell alphabet, elephant, prophet and pheasant.

 We use and or or between the last two items in a list, instead of a comma.

We use commas to separate the actual words spoken in direct speech from the rest of the sentence.

"I came early to get a good seat," said Fiona.

We use commas between parts of a sentence to tell the reader where to make a short pause.

The hospital, which was built in the nineteenth century, will be closing down.
"No, I won't answer the telephone," cried Leah.
"That's a good photograph, isn't it?" cried Steve.

GRAMMAR *Focus*

Copy the following sentences into your book.
Add **commas** where they are needed.

1 I did maths English PE and music today.
2 Peter lost his pen his ruler his rubber and his pencil sharpener.
3 Thought bought sought nought and fought are rhyming words.
4 I have invited Ruth Eamon Shah and John.

42

GRAMMAR *Practice*

A The punctuation has been missed out after the spoken words in these direct speech sentences.
Copy each sentence and add a **comma, a question mark** or an **exclamation mark**

1 "The entrance is blocked" explained Tom.
2 "I'm going to be really late" cried Ben.
3 "Is it bedtime" asked Lena.

B Add commas to these sentences to show the reader where to make a short pause.

1 "Yes I would like to go to the cinema."
2 "He hurt his arm falling off his bike didn't he?"
3 "You will find that book won't you?"

GRAMMAR *Extension*

Commas often go around phrases and clauses in sentences.
The phrases and clauses give us extra information. If they were left out, the sentence would still make sense.
The clown, running around the ring, made everyone laugh.
The clown made everyone laugh.

Put **commas** around the phrases and clauses in the following sentences.

1 The customer angry and impatient shouted at the shop assistant.
2 My sister who is four years younger than me starts school next week.

43

---

see Glossary, page 12 – Sentences

Previous work

Book A	Book 1
pages 24/25	pages 24/25
pages 30/31	pages 28/29
pages 34/35	
pages 42/43	

Book 2	Book 3
pages 44/45	pages 12/13
	pages 16/17
	pages 30/31
	pages 50/51
	pages 52/53
	pages 56/57

Book 4	
pages 20/21	
pages 26/27	

Pupil Book answers

Focus

1 I did maths, English, PE and music today.
2 Peter lost his pen, his ruler, his rubber and his pencil sharpener
3 Thought, bought, sought, nought and fought are rhyming words.
4 I have invited Ruth, Eamon, Shah and John.

Practice

A
1 "The entrance is blocked," explained Tom.
2 "I'm going to be really late!" cried Bill.
3 "Is it bedtime?" asked Lena.

B
1 "Yes, I would like to go to the cinema."
2 "He hurt his arm falling of his bike, didn't he?"
3 "You will find that book, won't you?"

Extension

1 The customer, angry and impatient, shouted at the shop assistant.
2 My sister, who is four years younger than me, starts school next week.

Copymaster answers

A
1 I went to the shop to buy bread, kiwi fruit, sausages, rice and cheese.
2 At the restaurant you can have soup, melon, spaghetti, omelette, ice cream and apple pie.

B
1 The clouds, which were heavy with rain, came in from the west.
2 The mouse, small and timid, scuttles into the corner.
3 The grocer, who keeps the shop open until nine o'clock, has bought the shop next door.
4 The cat, hissing and spitting, leaped up the tree.
5 The curtains, which were old and dusty, needed cleaning.

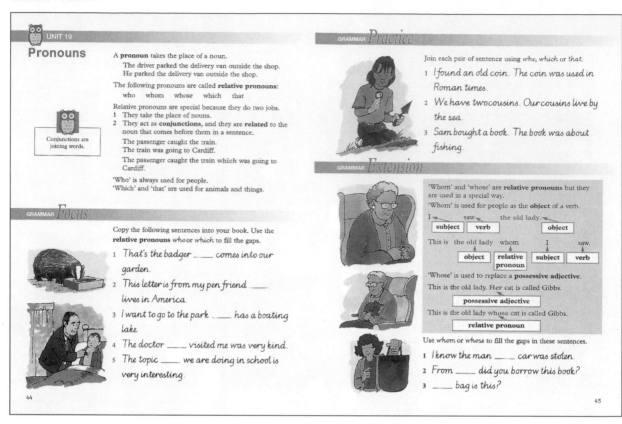

see Glossary, page 12 – Pronouns

Previous work

Book 1
pages 14/15 pages 40/41
Book 3
pages 14/15
Book 4
pages 10/11

Pupil Book answers

Focus

1 That's the badger **which** comes into our garden.
2 This letter is from my pen friend **who** lives in America.
3 I want to go to the park **which** has a boating lake.
4 The doctor **who** visited me was very kind.
5 The topic **which** we are doing in school is very interesting.

Practice

1 I found an old coin **which/that** was used in Roman times.
2 We have two cousins **who** live by the sea.
3 Sam bought a book **which/that** was about fishing.

Extension

1 I know the man **whose** car was stolen.
2 From **whom** did you borrow this book?
3 **Whose** bag is this?

Copymaster answers

A

1 We replaced one of the windows **which/that** was broken.
2 Jane borrowed a bicycle **which/that** belonged to the girl next door.
3 The car splashed water on the man **who** was standing beside the road.
4 I took my books back to the library **which/that** was in the middle of town.

B

1 **Whose** is this piece of work?
2 The woman **whose** horse was lame called the vet.
3 This is the footballer **whose** job it is to score goals.
4 **Whom** shall I say is calling?

UNIT 20

Sentences

Sentences contain **clauses**.
A **main clause** is a sentence in itself.

The girl washed her face.

It has a **subject** – 'the girl'.
It has a **predicate** – 'washed her face'.
It has a **proper verb** in the predicate – 'washed'.
An **adjective clause** tells us more about the **noun** in the main clause and has a proper verb.

I want to see the man who won the race.

The main clause is 'I want to see the man'.
The adjective clause is 'who won the race'.

An **adverb clause** tells us more about the **verb** in the main clause.

The man won the race because he ran so quickly.

The main clause is 'The man won the race'.
The adverb clause is 'because he ran so quickly'.

Adjective clauses begin with **who**, **which** or **that**.

Adverb clauses begin with a conjunction.

GRAMMAR *Focus*

Copy the following sentences into your book.
Underline the **main clauses**.

1 The creature slipped into the pool and swam away.
2 Before you go out you must have something to eat.
3 After the match the winners were presented with the cup.
4 I will practise my signature on that piece of paper.
5 I hit the ball and broke the window.

46

GRAMMAR *Practice*

Copy the sentences below.
Underline the **adjective clauses** in red and the **adverb clauses** in blue.

1 Although it is a warm day, you must take your coats.
2 I will wash the bicycle which is muddy.
3 The trip was cancelled because of the rain.
4 We will invite the twins who live on the farm.

GRAMMAR *Extension*

Remember!
Adjective clauses begin with who, which, that.
Adverb clauses begin with conjunctions.

A Complete these sentences by adding **adjective clauses** of your own.

1 This is the kitten _____.
2 Have you seen the rocket _____?
3 We saw the rider _____.
4 Can I speak to the teacher _____?

B Complete these sentences by adding **adverb clauses** of your own.

1 The little boy was naughty _____.
2 _____ will you let me know?
3 The zebra walked to the waterhole _____.
4 _____ you cannot watch that television programme.

47

---

see Glossary, page 12 – Sentences

Previous work

Book A	Book 1
pages 24/25 pages 30/31 pages 34/35 pages 42/43	pages 24/25 pages 28/29

Book 2	Book 3
pages 44/45	pages 12/13 pages 16/17 pages 30/31 pages 50/51 pages 52/53 pages 56/57

Book 4	
pages 20/21 pages 26/27 pages 42/43	

Pupil Book answers

Focus

1 <u>The creature slipped into the pool</u> and swam away.
2 Before you go out <u>you must have something to eat</u>.
3 After the match <u>the winners were presented with the cup</u>.
4 <u>I will practise my signature</u> on that piece of paper.
5 <u>I hit the ball</u> and broke the window.

Practice

The adjective clauses are in bold type, the adverb clauses are underlined:

1 <u>Although it is a warm day</u>, you must take your coats.
2 I will wash the bicycle **which is muddy**.
3 The trip was cancelled <u>because of the rain</u>.
4 We will invite the twins **who live on the farm**.

Extension

A and **B**
Answers will be individual to the children.

Copymaster answers

Answers will be individual to the children.

UNIT 21

Verbs

When we use **verbs** to tell us about something that has happened in the past, we use the **past tense**.

To make the past tense, we usually add **d** or **ed** to the verb family name.

The kittens **played**.   The man **signalled**.

When we want to write the past tense to show an action has gone on for some time or something else happens at the same time, we use a verb ending in **ing** with an **auxiliary verb**.

The children **were swimming** when it began to rain.

We can make the past tense in another way.
If two actions have happened in the past but one is 'further back' than the other one, we use 'had' and a past tense verb ending in **ed**.

I **had reached** the station before the train left.
The chef **had roasted** the chicken and then cooked the peas.
We found the shop but it **had closed**.

Auxiliary verbs are 'helper' verbs.

Some verbs do not make their past tense with **ed**. For example, write – wrote, keep – kept.

GRAMMAR *Focus*

Remember! Past tense verbs often have more than one word.

Copy the following sentences into your book.
Underline the **past tense verbs** in each sentence.

1 We were looking for our cat all day.
2 The comedian laughed and joked with the audience.
3 They had lived in a cottage before they moved to a new house.

48

GRAMMAR *Practice*

Complete this table, using the three ways you know of making the **past tense**.

Verb family name	past tense	past tense – 'to be' and 'ing'	past tense – 'had'
to talk	I talked	I was talking	I had talked
to find	we found	we were finding	we had found
to see	they ___		
to jump	you ___		
to sleep	we ___		
to throw	he ___		
to sing	she ___		

GRAMMAR *Extension*

Write a sentence in the **past tense** that includes each pair of actions below.
Action 1 happens first, before action 2.
The first one is done for you.

	Action 1	Action 2
1	watch a film	go to bed

I had watched a film before I went to bed.

2	walk	storm blows up
3	do homework	play tennis
4	eat breakfast	post arrives
5	write a story	go home

49

---

see Glossary, page 14 – Verbs

Previous work

Workbook 1	Workbook 2
page 8	page 8
page 9	page 9
page 14	page 14
page 15	page 15
Book A	**Book 1**
pages 12/13	pages 26/27
pages 16/17	pages 30/31
pages 26/27	pages 38/39
pages 38/39	
Book 2	**Book 3**
pages 12/13	pages 26/27
pages 14/15	pages 32/33
pages 20/21	pages 34/35
pages 34/35	pages 54/55
pages 42/43	
Book 4	
pages 8/9	
pages 14/15	
pages 22/23	
pages 32/33	

Pupil Book answers

Focus
1 We <u>were looking</u> for our cat all day.
2 The comedian <u>laughed</u> and <u>joked</u> with the audience.
3 They <u>had lived</u> in a cottage before they <u>moved</u> to a new house.

Practice

VERB FAMILY NAME	PAST TENSE	PAST TENSE – 'TO BE' AND 'ING'	PAST TENSE – 'HAD'
to talk	I talked	I was talking	I had talked
to find	we found	we were finding	we had found
to see	**they saw**	**they were seeing**	**they had seen**
to jump	**you jumped**	**you were jumping**	**you had jumped**
to sleep	**we slept**	**we were sleeping**	**we had slept**
to throw	**he threw**	**he was throwing**	**he had thrown**
to sing	**she sang**	**she was singing**	**she had sung**

Extension
Answers will be individual to the children.

Copymaster answers

A
Answers will be individual to the children, for example:
1 I **had reached** the shops before I realised I didn't have any money.
2 If you **had washed** properly, your hands wouldn't be dirty.
3 We **had planned** to go out before we knew you were coming.
4 I **had looked** in the cupboard so I am surprised you found it there.
5 Although you **had run** all they way, you were still late.

B
Answers will be individual to the children.

UNIT 22

Sentences

Direct speech is when we write the actual words that someone has spoken.

"Did you see the explosion?" asked Greg.
Greg asked, "Did you see the explosion?"

Sometimes we split the spoken words, so we have to be very careful with the punctuation.

"I saw the building was on fire," said Greg, "and I saw the explosion."

The sentence has been split by the words 'said Greg', so we use two sets of inverted commas and put a **comma** after 'said Greg'.

"I saw the building was on fire," said Greg. "I rushed over and heard the explosion."

This time, Greg said two sentences.
We still use two sets of inverted commas but we put a full stop after 'said Greg', before we begin the next sentence.

A sentence can end with a question mark or an exclamation mark, as well as a full stop.

GRAMMAR *Focus*

Copy the following sentences into your book.
Underline the **spoken words**.

1 "I won this medal," said Lesley, "for coming first in the high jump."
2 "Where did you find that fossil?" asked Pam.
3 "You can ring me at work," explained Nick, "if you need to get in touch with me."
4 The climber shouted, "Get away from the edge!"
5 "I'm not very musical," mumbled Grace. "I prefer art."

GRAMMAR *Practice*

Copy these sentences and put in the missing **punctuation** and **capital letters**.

1 that was a good goal shouted Sandy but we've got to score another one
2 go to the shop and buy some bread said Helen the money is in my purse
3 this photograph was taken last year said Rory we were on holiday at the seaside
4 we must be very quiet whispered Monica or we will wake the baby
5 i'm very tired moaned Chris i stayed up too late last night
6 can you find my blue shoes asked Mum and give them a polish

GRAMMAR *Extension*

The words in the box can all be used instead of 'said'.

cried	yelled	muttered	laughed
sobbed	shrieked	boasted	

Use each one in a **direct speech sentence** of your own.
Try to use some of them in between the spoken words.

50   51

---

see Glossary, page 12 – Sentences

Previous work

Book A	Book 1
pages 24/25	pages 24/25
pages 30/31	pages 28/29
pages 34/35	
pages 42/43	

Book 2	Book 3
pages 44/45	pages 12/13
	pages 16/17
	pages 30/31
	pages 50/51
	pages 52/53
	pages 56/57

Book 4	
pages 20/21	
pages 26/27	
pages 42/43	
pages 46/47	

Pupil Book answers

Focus

1 "I won this medal," said Lesley, "for coming first in the high jump."
2 "Where did you find that fossil?" asked Pam.
3 "You can ring me at work," explained Nick, "if you need to get in touch with me."
4 The climber shouted, "Get away from the edge!"
5 "I'm not very musical," mumbled Grace. "I prefer art."

Practice

1 "That was a good goal," shouted Sandy, "but we've got to score another one."
2 "Go to the shop and buy some bread," said Helen. "The money is in my purse."
3 "This photograph was taken last year," said Rory. "We were on holiday at the seaside."
4 "We must be very quiet," whispered Monica, "or we will wake the baby."
5 "I'm very tired," moaned Chris. "I stayed up too late last night."
6 "Can you find my blue shoes," asked Mum, "and give them a polish?"

Extension

Answers will be individual to the children.

Copymaster answers

Answers will be individual to the children.

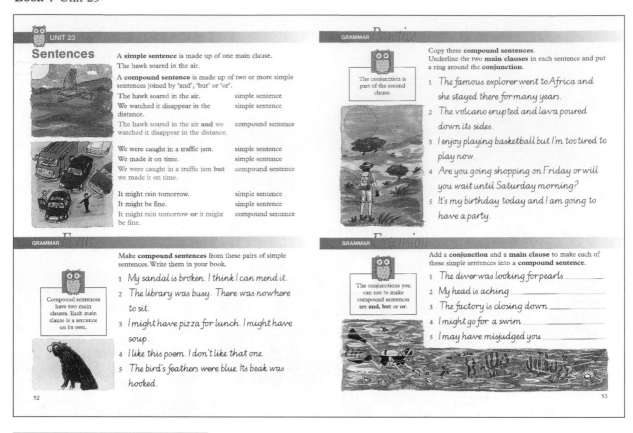

UNIT 23
Sentences

A **simple sentence** is made up of one main clause.
The hawk soared in the air.

A **compound sentence** is made up of two or more simple
sentences joined by 'and', 'but' or 'or'.

The hawk soared in the air.	simple sentence
We watched it disappear in the distance.	simple sentence
The hawk soared in the air **and** we watched it disappear in the distance.	compound sentence
We were caught in a traffic jam.	simple sentence
We made it on time.	simple sentence
We were caught in a traffic jam **but** we made it on time.	compound sentence
It might rain tomorrow.	simple sentence
It might be fine.	simple sentence
It might rain tomorrow **or** it might be fine.	compound sentence

GRAMMAR Focus

Compound sentences have two main clauses. Each main clause is a sentence on its own.

Make **compound sentences** from these pairs of simple
sentences. Write them in your book.

1 My sandal is broken. I think I can mend it.
2 The library was busy. There was nowhere to sit.
3 I might have pizza for lunch. I might have soup.
4 I like this poem. I don't like that one.
5 The bird's feathers were blue. Its beak was hooked.

52

GRAMMAR Practice

The conjunction is part of the second clause.

Copy these **compound sentences**.
Underline the two **main clauses** in each sentence and put
a ring around the **conjunction**.

1 The famous explorer went to Africa and she stayed there for many years.
2 The volcano erupted and lava poured down its sides.
3 I enjoy playing basketball but I'm too tired to play now.
4 Are you going shopping on Friday or will you wait until Saturday morning?
5 It's my birthday today and I am going to have a party.

GRAMMAR Extension

*The conjunctions you can use to make compound sentences are **and**, **but** or **or**.*

Add a **conjunction** and a **main clause** to make each of
these simple sentences into a **compound sentence**.

1 The diver was looking for pearls _____.
2 My head is aching _____.
3 The factory is closing down _____.
4 I might go for a swim _____.
5 I may have misjudged you _____.

53

---

see Glossary, page 12 – Sentences

Previous work

Book A	Book 1
pages 24/25 pages 30/31 pages 34/35 pages 42/43	pages 24/25 pages 28/29

Book 2	Book 3
pages 44/45	pages 12/13 pages 16/17 pages 30/31 pages 50/51 pages 52/53 pages 56/57

Book 4	
pages 20/21 pages 26/27 pages 42/43 pages 46/47 pages 50/51	

Pupil Book answers

Focus

1 My sandal is broken **but** I think I can mend it.
2 The library was busy **and** there was nowhere to sit.
3 I might have pizza for lunch **or** I might have soup.
4 I like this poem **but** I don't like that one.
5 The bird's feathers were blue **and** its beak was hooked.

Practice

1 <u>The famous explorer went to Africa</u> and <u>she stayed there for many years.</u>
2 <u>The volcano erupted</u> and <u>lava poured down its sides.</u>
3 <u>I enjoy playing basketball</u> but <u>I'm too tired to play now.</u>
4 <u>Are you going shopping on Friday</u> or <u>will you wait until Saturday morning?</u>
5 <u>It's my birthday today</u> and <u>I am going to have a party.</u>

Extension

Answers will be individual to the children.

Copymaster answers

Answers will be individual to the children.

UNIT 24

Sentences

A **simple sentence** is made up of one main clause.
The election was held on Thursday.

A **compound sentence** is made up of two or more simple sentences joined by 'and', 'but' or 'or'.
The election was held on Thursday and the result was announced on Friday.

A **complex sentence** is made up of two or more clauses which are not of equal importance.
There is one **main clause** in a complex sentence.
Other clauses are joined to it by these words:

The conjunctions **and, but** and **or** are used in compound sentences not in complex sentences.

Conjunctions			Pronouns
before	where	unless	who
until	because	so	which
although	while	as	when
wherever	even though	after	whose
if			

main clause → The house had been empty for many years before we bought it.

The clause 'before we bought it' is not a sentence on its own. It needs the main clause to make sense.

GRAMMAR *Focus*

Copy these **complex sentences** into your book.
Underline the **main clause** in each sentence.

1 The guitar was broken before I borrowed it.
2 We climbed the mountain although it was very steep.
3 My sister will come over when she has finished work.
4 The people next door have a noisy dog which barks all day.

54

GRAMMAR *Practice*

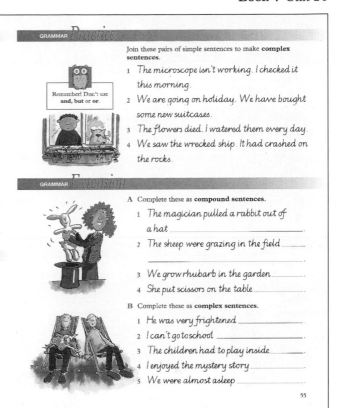

Join these pairs of simple sentences to make **complex sentences**.

Remember! Don't use **and, but** or **or**.

1 The microscope isn't working. I checked it this morning.
2 We are going on holiday. We have bought some new suitcases.
3 The flowers died. I watered them every day.
4 We saw the wrecked ship. It had crashed on the rocks.

GRAMMAR *Extension*

A Complete these as **compound sentences**.

1 The magician pulled a rabbit out of a hat _____
2 The sheep were grazing in the field _____
   _____
3 We grow rhubarb in the garden _____
4 She put scissors on the table _____

B Complete these as **complex sentences**.

1 He was very frightened _____
2 I can't go to school _____
3 The children had to play inside _____
4 I enjoyed the mystery story _____
5 We were almost asleep _____

55

---

see Glossary, page 12 – Sentences

Previous work

Book A	Book 1
pages 24/25 pages 30/31 pages 34/35 pages 42/43	pages 24/25 pages 28/29

Book 2	Book 3
pages 44/45	pages 12/13 pages 16/17 pages 30/31 pages 50/51 pages 52/53 pages 56/57

Book 4	
pages 20/21 pages 26/27 pages 42/43 pages 46/47 pages 50/51 pages 52/53	

Pupil Book answers

Focus

1 <u>The guitar was broken</u> before I borrowed it.
2 <u>We climbed the mountain</u> although it was very steep.
3 <u>My sister will come over</u> when she has finished work.
4 <u>The people next door have a noisy dog</u> which barks all day.

Practice

1 The microscope isn't working **although** I checked it this morning.
2 We are going on holiday **so** we have bought some new suitcases.
3 The flowers died **even though** I watered them every day.
4 We saw the wrecked ship **which** had crashed on the rocks.

Extension

A and **B**
Answers will be individual to the children.

Copymaster answers

A and **B**
Answers will be individual to the children.

UNIT 25

Sentences

We need to look very carefully at what we write to see if we can improve it.

We can improve our writing by **changing some of the words.**

I **got** a **nice** present for my birthday.

'Got' and 'nice' are words that are often used but there are better words.

I **received** a **wonderful** present for my birthday.

We can improve our writing by expanding it.
Adding **words**, **phrases** and **clauses** to make it more interesting.

The elephant drank the water.

The **large, grey** elephant **stretched out its long, flexible trunk to take a drink of refreshing** water **from the cool, shaded pool.**

Look at each sentence you write and ask yourself whether you could add more details to answer these questions:

What kind?	
How many?	adjectives, adjective phrases, adjective clauses
How much?	

When?	
How?	adverbs, adverb phrases, adverb clauses
Where?	
How often?	

GRAMMAR *Focus*

In your book, rewrite these sentences to **improve** them. Replace the green words with more interesting words.

1 Our nice hedge had grown a bit this spring.
2 "I've got a lot of work to do," said Harry.
3 I like cold weather because I've got a really warm coat.
4 "I like this topic a lot," said Nancy.

56

GRAMMAR *Practice*

Rewrite these sentences to give details which answer the questions in brackets.

1 The trees are growing. (What kind? Where?)
2 The children played football. (What kind? Where? How?)
3 The jockey won the race. (What kind? When? How?)
4 Can you see the butterfly? (What kind? Where?)
5 I walked into the valley. (How? What kind? Where?)

GRAMMAR *Extension*

Carefully look at each of the sentences below. Rewrite them:

A to include more **interesting words** than got, said, like, bit, nice, lot, big and little;
B to include words, phrases and clauses which give the reader **more detail.**

1 A little bird sat on the tree.
2 The bus got stuck.
3 "I've lost my ticket," said Linda.
4 Would you like an ice cream?
5 The wind was a bit strong.
6 I got a nice jacket.
7 You can get a lot in this bucket.
8 "Did you have a nice time?" said Dad.
9 "Did you see the big bull?" said Katy.
10 That meal was nice.

57

---

see Glossary, page 12 – Sentences

Previous work

Book A	Book 1
pages 24/25 pages 30/31 pages 34/35 pages 42/43	pages 24/25 pages 28/29

Book 2	Book 3
pages 44/45	pages 12/13 pages 16/17 pages 30/31 pages 50/51 pages 52/53 pages 56/57

Book 4	
pages 20/21 pages 26/27 pages 42/43 pages 46/47 pages 50/51 pages 52/53 pages 54/55	

Pupil Book answers

Focus

Answers will be individual to the children, for example:

1 Our **beautiful** hedge has grown **enormously** this spring.
2 "I've **a mountain** of work to do," **moaned** Harry.
3 I **enjoy** cold weather because I've **bought** a really warm coat.
4 "**I'm really interested in** this topic," said Nancy.

Practice

Answers will be individual to the children, for example:

1 The **oak** trees are growing **in the meadow**.
2 The **excited** children played football **noisily in the muddy field**.
3 **Last Saturday** the **champion** jockey won the last race **in a close finish**.
4 Can you see the **colourful** butterfly **on that orange flower**?
5 I walked **wearily** in to the **gloomy** valley **at then end of my journey**.

Extension

A and **B**
Answers will be individual to the children.

Copymaster answers

A and **B**
Answers will be individual to the children.

UNIT 26

Sentences

Moving in from the left-hand margin is called 'indenting'.

A **paragraph** is a group of sentences about one main idea. Dividing a long piece of writing into paragraphs makes it easier for the reader to follow.

We sometimes set out the paragraph so that the first line begins about 20 mm in from the left-hand margin.

Early morning on the farm was always a busy time. Cows to be milked, chickens to feed and a hundred and one other jobs to be done.

Anna climbed out of bed as soon as her alarm went off. She washed and dressed quickly as she had many things to do before breakfast.

When she arrived in the kitchen her mother was already busy, baking bread and getting things ready for the first meal of the day. Anna set the table and then went outside.

After an hour of hard work, Anna had only the chickens to feed before she could eat herself. She scattered the corn about the yard, washed her hands under the outside tap and went inside.

Each paragraph is about one main idea:
Paragraph 1: Introducing the reader to the farm
Paragraph 2: Introducing the reader to Anna
Paragraph 3: Moving the scene from Anna's bedroom to the kitchen
Paragraph 4: Moving the story on in time.

GRAMMAR

Use interesting words and give as much detail as possible.

Write the **first three paragraphs** of a story called 'The Dark Cave'.

Paragraph 1: Give a detailed description of the cave.
Paragraph 2: Introduce two characters who are exploring the cave.
Paragraph 3: Explain what happens to the two characters in the cave.

58

GRAMMAR

Read these **paragraphs** about animal environments and answer the questions.

Animals live in many different environments, such as hot, dry deserts, cold forbidding polar regions and high mountains.

In the desert, temperatures can reach over 50° C (120° F) during the day. There is not much water and animals have to keep cool without losing too much water by evaporation. They can shelter underground or in scarce shady areas. Animals that do spend time in the sun move in a special way so that as little of their bodies as possible touch the hot sand.

In the polar regions, the temperature can fall as low as –80° C (–112° F) in the winter. Here, animals have to keep warm and one way to do this is to stay under the snow in dens.

Living in the mountains, animals often experience low temperatures and harsh winds. They survive by sheltering in caves or on rock ledges, coming out during the day to look for food.

1 How many paragraphs has the writer used?

2 For each paragraph, write a sentence to explain the main idea.

GRAMMAR

A Find a short story you have enjoyed reading. Answer the following questions about the **first four paragraphs**.

1 What is the main idea in each paragraph?

2 Explain why the first paragraph is, or is not, a good opening to the story.

B Choose one of the following titles and write **one paragraph** of five to ten sentences about the topic. Underline one sentence in your paragraph to show what is the main idea.
A really bad day
Looking after a pet
My favourite sport

59

---

see Glossary, page 12 – Sentences

Previous work

Book A	Book 1
pages 24/25 pages 30/31 pages 34/35 pages 42/43	pages 24/25 pages 28/29

Book 2	Book 3
pages 44/45	pages 12/13 pages 16/17 pages 30/31 pages 50/51 pages 52/53 pages 56/57

Book 4	
pages 20/21 pages 26/27 pages 42/43 pages 46/47 pages 50/51 pages 52/53 pages 54/55 pages 56/57	

Pupil Book answers

Focus

Answers will be individual to the children.

Practice

1 Four paragraphs

2 *Answers will be individual to the children, for example:*
Paragraph 1: The different regions where animals live.
Paragraph 2: How animals survive in the desert.
Paragraph 3: How animals survive in polar regions.
Paragraph 4: How animals survive in the mountains.

Extension

A and **B**
Answers will be individual to the children.

Copymaster answers

Answers will be individual to the children.

Check-up 3

Adjectives

A Copy these sentences and underline the **adjective phrase** in each.

1 Eight large, hissing geese crossed the road.
2 The sea, calm and blue, sparkled in the sunlight.
3 The elephant with the longest tusks is the oldest.

B Copy the following sentences. Fill each gap with a suitable **possessive adjective**.

1 ____ boots were dirty so we had to clean them.
2 Sam and ____ friend went camping.
3 They packed ____ bags before breakfast.

C Add an **adjective clause** to complete each sentence.

1 This is the spaceship _____.
2 The children went to the park _____.
3 We saw the shopkeeper _____.

D Make **adjectives** from these nouns and verbs.

1 to colour   2 grass   3 to frighten
4 to scream   5 bravery   6 envy

Prefixes

Add a **prefix** to each word to make its opposite.

1 like   2 controllable   3 capable
4 literate   5 passable   6 climax

Verbs

A Copy the sentences below. Underline the **auxiliary verb** in each sentence.

1 We must find our key.
2 I would hate to swim in that dirty river.
3 If you go early, you might get a good seat.

B Copy these sentences. Use the **auxiliary verbs** can or may to fill each gap.

1 We ____ see the windmill from here.
2 You ____ have more potatoes when you finish those.
3 If you ____ tidy the bookcase I will be very pleased.

C Copy these sentences. Choose the **singular** or **plural verb** to complete each one.

1 The penguins was/were diving for fish.
2 The herd of cows need/needs to be milked.
3 £3 is/are the price of the tickets.

D Rewrite these sentences, changing the verb from **passive** to **active**.

1 The tree was blown down by the wind.
2 The topmost leaves were eaten by the giraffes.
3 The window was broken by a stone.

E Copy these sentences. Underline the **past tense verbs** in each one.

1 Our newspaper was delivered late today.
2 The gardener had cut the hedge before the birds built their nests.
3 I completed the quiz in ten minutes.

60   61

Adjectives

A
1 <u>Eight large, hissing</u> geese crossed the road.
2 The sea, <u>calm and blue</u>, sparkled in the sunlight.
3 The elephant <u>with the longest tusks</u> is the oldest.

B
1 **His/her/their/my/our** boots were dirty so we had to clean them.
2 Sam and **his** friend went camping.
3 They packed **their** bags before breakfast.

C *Answers will be individual to the children.*

D
1 colourful/colouring/coloured
2 grassy
3 frightening/frightful/frightened
4 screaming
5 brave/braver/bravest
6 envious/enviable

Prefixes
1 **dis**like
2 **un**controllable
3 **in**capable
4 **il**literate
5 **im**passable
6 **anti**climax

Verbs

A
1 We <u>must</u> find our key.
2 I <u>would</u> hate to swim in that dirty river.
3 If you go early, you <u>might</u> get a good seat.

B
1 We **can** see the windmill from here.
2 You **may** have more potatoes when you finish those.
3 If you **can** tidy the bookcase I will be very pleased.

C
1 The penguins **were** diving for fish.
2 The herd of cows **need** to be milked.
3 £3 **is** the price of the tickets.

D
1 The wind blew down the tree.
2 The giraffes ate the topmost leaves.
3 A stone broke the window.

E
1 Our newspaper <u>was delivered</u> late today.
2 The gardener <u>had cut</u> the hedge before the birds <u>built</u> their nests.
3 I <u>completed</u> the quiz in ten minutes.

Pronouns

A Use **possessive pronouns** to replace the blue words.

1 May I ride your bicycle. My bicycle has a puncture.
2 Their car is newer than our car.
3 You know that pen you found? Sally says it's her pen.

B Join each pair of sentences using a **relative pronoun**.

1 Fred watched a programme. It was about whales.
2 I have an uncle. He is a policeman.
3 Have you seen the kittens? They were born on the farm.

Nouns

Write a **noun** that is formed from each of these verbs.
1 to write   2 to imagine   3 to grow
4 to play   5 to injure   6 to live

Adverbs

A Copy these sentences.
Underline the **adverb phrases**.

1 Two days ago I visited my aunt.
2 The boy kicked the ball hard and straight.
3 The fox made its den in the middle of the wood.

B Write an **adverb clause** to complete each sentence.

1 The match was cancelled _____.
2 _____ you will get a sore throat.
3 I will go swimming again _____.

62

Suffixes

A Change these verb family names into the **present tense** using the **suffix** 'ing'.
1 to write   2 to live   3 to stop   4 to receive

B Change these verb family names into the **past tense** using the **suffix** 'ed'.
1 to paint   2 to dodge   3 to thread   4 to close

C Add a **suffix** to each of these words to change it into an **adjective**.
1 fever   2 saint   3 dust   4 danger

D Add a **suffix** to each of these words to change it into an **abstract noun**.
1 weary   2 dark   3 serve   4 child

Sentences

A Change these direct speech sentences into **indirect speech**.
1 "I am enjoying myself," said Len.
2 "This soup is cold!" complained Robert.
3 "Have you read the newspaper?" I asked Dad.

B Add capital letters and punctuation to these **direct speech** sentences.

1 can you get the bread said Helen and some butter
2 why does it always rain moaned Chris when I want to go out
3 one of the cedar trees fell down cried John and hit the car

C Copy these sentences and underline the **main clauses**.

1 I have to hurry because I am already late.
2 Although it snowed, I wasn't cold.
3 Brush your teeth before you go to bed.

63

Pronouns

A
1 May I ride your bicycle? **Mine** has a puncture.
2 Their car is newer than **ours**.
3 You know that pen you found? Sally says its **hers**.

B
1 Fred watched a programme **which/that** was about whales.
2 I have an uncle **who** is a policeman.
3 Have you seen the kittens **which/that** were born on the farm?

Nouns

1 writing/writer   2 imagination
3 growth   4 play
5 injury   6 life

Adverbs

A
1 <u>Two days ago</u> I visited my aunt.
2 The boy kicked the ball <u>hard and straight</u>.
3 The fox made its den <u>in the middle of the wood</u>.

B
Answers will be individual to the children.

Suffixes

A
1 writing   2 living
3 stopping   4 receiving

B
1 paint**ed**   2 dodg**ed**
3 thread**ed**   4 clos**ed**

C
1 fever**ish**   2 saint**ly**
3 dust**y**   4 danger**ous**

D
1 wear**iness**   2 dark**ness**
3 serv**ice**   4 weak**ness**

Sentences

A
1 Len said that he was enjoying himself.
2 Robert complained that the soup was cold.
3 I asked Dad if he had read the newspaper.

B
1 "Can you get the bread," said Helen, "and some butter?"
2 "Why does it always rain," moaned Chris, "when I want to go out?"
3 "One of the cedar trees fell down," cried John, "and hit the car."

C
1 <u>I have to hurry</u> because I am already late.
2 Although it snowed, <u>I wasn't cold</u>.
3 <u>Brush your teeth</u> before you go to bed.

D Copy these sentences.
Add **commas** where they are needed.

1 I would like some carrots turnips potatoes beans and sprouts.

2 He's wearing my sweater isn't he?

3 The gate unpainted and broken creaked in the wind.

E Join each pair of simple sentences to make a **compound sentence**.

1 I need to go to the doctor. I don't have time.

2 I'm sure I heard the phone. Was it the front doorbell?

3 The car's tyre was punctured. The bumper was bent.

F Complete these as **compound sentences**.

1 I wrote a long letter _____

2 She plays volleyball _____

3 We had a noisy celebration _____

G Improve these sentences by using more **interesting** words and more **detail**.

1 I got a bad mark in the test.

2 We had a nice day and did quite a lot.

3 "The cat got stuck up the tree," said Mandy.

H Write two **paragraphs** on one of the following subjects. Underline the sentence in each paragraph which contains the main idea.

A School Trip   Sports Day   A Lucky Escape

64

D

1 I would like some carrots, turnips, potatoes, beans and sprouts.

2 He's wearing my sweater, isn't he?

3 The gate, unpainted and broken, creaked in the wind.

E

1 I need to go to the doctor **but** I don't have time.

2 I'm sure I heard the phone **or** was it the front doorbell?

3 The car's tyre was punctured **and** the bumper was bent.

F, G and H
Answers will be individual to the children.

Improve Your Writing copymaster 1

Answers will be individual to the children.

Improve Your Writing copymaster 2

Answers will be individual to the children.

Improve Your Writing copymaster 3

Answers will be individual to the children.

Improve Your Writing copymaster 4

Answers will be individual to the children.

Improve Your Writing copymaster 5

A

Answers will be individual to the children, but might include:
1 *to depart, to rush, to leave, to hurry, to move, to travel, to walk, to run, to proceed.*

B

Answers will be individual to the children, but might include:
1 *to soar, to swoop, to glide*
2 *to see, to glance, to stare*
3 *to shriek, to yell, to bellow*
4 *to injure, to wound, to harm*
5 *to chat, to converse, to speak*
6 *to spring, to jump, to bound*

Improve Your Writing copymaster 6

Answers will be individual to the children, for example:
Although it was cold and dark, I got up early.
Creeping quietly so as not to wake anyone, I went downstairs.
Going to the back door, I turned the key quietly and went outside.
Even though I was wearing my dressing gown, I felt very cold.
Behind the big tree, I hid and waited for the hedgehogs to come out from under the shed.
Soon, I saw the first hedgehog to emerge.
As I watched, it ate some of the food I had left for it.

Improve Your Writing copymaster 7

"**If we are going to go to the cinema, we had better hurry up,**" shouted **Mum. It** was ten minutes to seven and **Tamsin** was still drying her hair. **The** film started at half past seven and it took at least half and hour to get from where they lived to the cinema.

"**I'm nearly ready,**" called **Tamsin.** "**I'll be down in a minute.**" **Andy** was already sitting in the car and **Dad** was just putting his coat on.

"**Are you two coming?**" he shouted to **Tamsin** and **Mum.**

"**We will be there in a minute,**" replied **Mum. Tamsin** came running down the stairs, grabbed her coat and got into the car. **Mum** locked the front door and climbed in just as **Dad** was starting the engine.

"**We'll just make it in time,**" he said as he drove out of the gate.

Improve Your Writing copymaster 8

Answers will be individual to the children.

Improve Your Writing copymaster 9

Answers will be individual to the children.